Jörg Rogge (ed.)
Recounting Deviance

MW01253658

Editorial

The **Mainzer Historische Kulturwissenschaften** [Mainz Historical Cultural Sciences] series publishes the results of research that develops methods and theories of cultural sciences in connection with empirical research. The central approach is a historical perspective on cultural sciences, whereby both epochs and regions can differ widely and be treated in an all-embracing manner from time to time. Amongst other, the series brings together research approaches in archaeology, art history, visual studies, literary studies, philosophy, and history, and is open for contributions on the history of knowledge, political culture, the history of perceptions, experiences and life-worlds, as well as other fields of research with a historical cultural scientific orientation.

The objective of the **Mainzer Historische Kulturwissenschaften** series is to become a platform for pioneering works and current discussions in the field of historical cultural sciences.

The series is edited by the Co-ordinating Committee of the Research Unit Historical Cultural Sciences (HKW) at the Johannes Gutenberg University Mainz.

JÖRG ROGGE (ED.)

Recounting Deviance

**Forms and practices of presenting divergent behaviour
in the Late Middle Ages and Early Modern Period.**

In collaboration with KRISTINA MÜLLER-BONGARD.

The print was sponsored by the Research Unit Historical Cultural Sciences (HKW).

Bibliographic information published by the Deutsche Nationalbibliothek
The Deutsche Nationalbibliothek lists this publication in the Deutsche Natio-
nalbibliografie; detailed bibliographic data are available in the Internet at
http://dnb.d-nb.de

© 2016 transcript Verlag, Bielefeld

Cover layout: Kordula Röckenhaus, Bielefeld
Proof-reading & typesetting: Kristina Müller-Bongard
Printed in Germany
Print-ISBN 978-3-8376-3588-1
PDF-ISBN 978-3-8394-3588-5

CONTENT

Preface

The Collection of articles based on papers provided and discussed at a workshop on forms and practices of presenting divergent behaviour in source material of the 15th to the 18th century. The workshop was hosted at the *Centro Tedesco di Studi Veneziani* 18-20 February 2015. The editor's gratitude is extended to the director of the Centro – Romedio Schmitz-Esser – for his generous hospitality.

The workshop was a result of the cooperation between the Research Unit *Historical Cultural Sciences* at the Johannes Gutenberg University in Mainz and the *Dipartimento Tempo, Spazio, Immagine, Società* of the University of Verona.

Mainz, March 2016   Jörg Rogge

Recounting Deviance

Forms and practices of presenting divergent behaviour in the Late Middle Ages and Early Modern Period – An Introduction

JÖRG ROGGE

In medieval and early modern societies norms[1] have been a popular means to judge behaviour and to decide whether it could be regarded as correct and in line with the perception of the majority of a given society. Norms transfer the nonspecific values of societies into specific rules of conduct or codes of behaviour and by doing so, they had been used to draw the line between accepted and divergent behaviour. In current research, there is a wide range of studies in the field of codes of behaviour: legal, social, ethnic – to name just a few.[2]

It is necessary to distinguish between behavioural expectations on one side and norms on the other. Norms have – in contrast to behavioural expectations – a more formalised claim of validity and acceptance because they are often the basis for law and lawgiving. In every society, professionals (priests, lawyers, judges, rulers) together with other staff (administration, police force) have been responsible to

---

1   JUSSEN, 2008, pp. 176-177.
2   BORNSCHIER, 2007; CLINARD/MEIER, 2001; FRANZESE, 2009; KÄSTNER/ SCHERHOFF, 2013.

protect the norms and to use them for the benefit of the society, the town, realm or the like.

The professionals have not only been in charge of the protection or production of norms, they have also applied and adapted them in specific contexts. Generally speaking, one can say that the more specific a norm the more likely it was to be broken.

Ordinary members of pre-modern societies had to deal with different norm systems. They had to behave properly according to the accustomed norms which had been in use in their social group: family, village, a town, gild or parish.

Norms are not static; they are subject to permanent change over space and time. Observing medieval and early modern societies, we can see how the efforts to stabilise a set of norms are related to the dynamic of change. The change takes place because people find themselves constricted by the way norms had been executed. They are discontent with a situation that forces them to be geared towards a norm that, for example, prohibits them to marry again or to articulate criticism against the political authorities. Another reason for deviant behaviour was the practice to use religious norms in order to force people into religious orthodoxy or a specific form of mundane living.

The articles in this volume deal with such persons who had – for one reason or another – been discontent with their situation. They tried to change this situation by using different means and activities. According to these means, their behaviour could have been judged as divergent in the light of the prevailing opinion or norms respectively.[3]

We have to consider that divergent behaviour was not necessarily regarded as criminal conduct; therefore, it is necessary to take into account the practise or the procedure, which we can observe in our material (sources) that had been used to mark behaviour as being divergent or criminal.

In recent research, one line of interpretation emphasises the connection between deviance and resistance in the early modern political culture. Acts of deviance and resistance are interpreted as a reaction

---

3 RODNEY/BAINBRIDGE, 1996, p. 5: "At the individual level: *Persons will conform to the norms to the extent that they are attached to others who accept the legitimacy of the norms.* Conversely, *people will deviate from the norms to the extent they lack attachment.* At the group level: *Deviance rates will be higher in groups having a lower mean level of attachments"*.

against structural processes such as juridification, social disciplining or state building.[4] There is a strong bias to underline the protest character of the people who had rebelled against their rulers or urban authorities. The reaction of the authorities to the social protest has been discussed in the relevant research literature as "social control". This is the term for a process of interaction and socialisation, which is characterised by formal and informal control, the development of positive and negative sanctions for behaviour as well as preventive and reactive measures.[5]

Criminal history is a second field of research I want to mention here. This approach claims to deal with the everyday deviance in contrast to the research on political and/or social protest which is regarded as deviant behaviour in conflicts and therefore in exceptional situations.[6] Here, we talk about delinquency, because the deviant person has transgressed penal and not just social norms.

Over the last 10 or 15 years it became quite apparent that the strict distinction between exceptional and mundane divergent behaviour is not fruitful. In both fields, deviance is not a factor or feature in an anthropological sense. It is, in fact, an attributed category. A category attributed by contemporaries judging the behaviour of people as being not in line with norms. In practice, people had been regarded as deviant with reference to religious, social or cultural norms – we can call this defamation. In cases where people were regarded as offending against law norms, we speak about criminalisation.[7] In other words: delinquency is a kind of deviance distinguished from other forms of deviance because delinquency is defined with reference to the norms of criminal law.[8]

In current research, two main methods are used in order to interpret sources, which allow us to obtain an impression of the various forms and practices of deviance. First, there is the quantification of deviance. The information given by the sources are transferred into numbers. This

---

4   WÜRGLER, 1999; HÄBERLEIN, 1999; GELTNER, 2012, p. 32 argues against the notion of a persecuting society and predicates, that the local authorities in medieval cities tried to include the deviants in the societies and to integrate stigmatized groups in the increasingly heterogeneous cities.
5   FÜSER, 2000, pp. 29-31.
6   WÜRGLER, 1999, p. 334.
7   IBID., p. 320.
8   PETERS, 1995, p. 154.

is a prerequisite to determine the representativeness of a divergent or criminal behaviour and for the comparison of this behaviour over the time or between different types of this behaviour in different societies. The main problem for the quantification is that, in most cases, we have no information about the exact numbers of cases and that we have to consider a high number of unreported cases or dark numbers. Consequently, we find a significant amount of close reading, case studies and micro history throughout our research. This is a reasonable method to take the experiences and motives of the people into account.[9] Another problem I like to mention concerns the categories of deviant behaviour or – more precisely – the problem to establish precise borders between categories of deviant behaviour. If, for example, we want to compare two towns referring to a specific type of this behaviour, it is necessary to work with precise categories. However, we have to bear in mind that it is not possible to collect all cases in one of the two towns in the categories established by the researcher. It is still a problem to decide whether we should count persons who have transgressed norms or the different practices of offences.

However, it is of course reasonable to organise the research on specific fields around such categories in order to characterise the practice of divergence and to identify definable social groups which had organised their social, political and economic behaviour with regard to relevant norms.

When we change the perspective – from the social groups to the source material, which has transferred the traces of divergent behaviour – it becomes apparent that all divergent behaviour is attributed, be it in the context of social, political, religious or criminal norms. We can analyse the different types of texts, which bear witness to the now long gone practices of attribution.

Before I turn to the texts, let me pay closer attention to the practice of attribution that in recent research has been successfully described and analysed by using the labelling approach to frame the perspective of the research. With the labelling approach[10] we can assume that deviant behaviour cannot be regarded without taking into account the social

---

9   SCHWERHOFF, 2011, pp. 58-59.
10 CLINARD/MEIER, 2001, pp. 131-139; KÄSTNER/SCHWERHOFF, 2013, pp. 27-34.

attribution. I quote the famous definition by Howard S. Becker: "The deviant is one to whom that label has been successfully applied; deviant behaviour is behaviour that people so label".[11]

This has been very important because it allowed a change of perspective for the sociological and historical research on deviant social as well as delinquent behaviour. The labelling approach takes into account the relevance of social norms and agencies of social control. That means the act of transgressing a social or law norm itself does not provide an own interpretation of this act.[12] This comes from the outside, namely from members of the family, priests, police or judges. The labelling approach is a very important contribution that helped to free research from the positivistic perpetrator-focused approach.

Nevertheless, the labelling approach has been criticised with two main arguments. The first criticism concerns the individual motives of the perpetrators – they seem to be neglected. The second argument is that the structural features, such as social inequality and governance or power structures, are not considered adequately.[13] The problem is that the main focus of this approach could be on the reactions rather than the norm violations. A person can be falsely accused of being deviant, yet still be labelled deviant by others who have the power to do so.[14]

Of course, a robber does not rob other people or a bank because he is called a robber. On the other hand, we can observe many activities in the sources which are not criminal in the strict sense of the word, but which are labelled divergent or delinquent. This fact justifies a more detailed examination of the discourse about divergence we find in our source material. I like to argue that in most sources we find narratives about deviant behaviour. These narratives of recounting deviant behaviour work with attributions or labels to support their argument. In a recounting manner, the writers of the texts are labelling the actions of people. Therefore, we cannot define deviance as reality *sui generis*; it is a phenomenon that was in the practice of the texts, designed or created in relation to the norms, which had been – as I have mentioned earlier – the product of a construction process. In our sources, we can observe

---

11 Quote in: FRANZESE, 2009, p. 72.
12 LAMNEK, 1997, pp. 45-49.
13 SCHWERHOFF, 2011, pp. 35-39.
14 INDERBITZIN et al., 2013, pp. 341-342.

the interaction processes or, to be more precise, interaction processes presented or recounted by writers. We can learn how the writers described situations in which norms had been negotiated, applied, rejected or enforced. The manner in which this is presented in the text or narrative is influenced by the power imbalance between the norm or lawgivers and their enforcement staff on one hand and those subjected to the social norm or law on the other.

It is necessary to take into account not only the institutions of authority and power, but also the fact that actors on every level within a society had contributed to the process of labelling behaviour, either in the role of deviant or delinquent. That is why the researcher had to struggle with different types of perception of deviance and the answer given to this behaviour. Ambivalence and contradictions concerning the manner in which people assessed behaviour as deviant are the prevailing characteristics in the sources.

If we bear in mind this complex situation, the labelling approach provides us with research tools to handle this situation. The various views of the persons involved in deviant behaviour can be considered important for the analysis as well as the question as to whether these views had any relation to the norm system. The views of persons in the analytical framework of the labelling approach are of relevance even if we have to question these views. Furthermore, we can see the interaction between the labelling institution/person and the labelled person/group.

Now, we can ask where this labelling is taking place. Obvious places are court and the legal proceedings.[15] The churches are another such place. During the service, priests used the opportunity to inculcate religious and moral norms from the pulpit.[16] In addition, there are mundane situations on the streets, market places, guildhalls etc. where we can observe various forms of defamation and stigmatisation, as well as forms of protest against political and social norms.

We can observe these different types of labelling deviant behaviour and the narratives of this behaviour in a variety of sources: chronicles,

---

15 See the articles of SCHÄFER, FROHNAPFEL-LEIS, VETTORE, MOROSINI in this volume.
16 FROHNAPFEL-LEIS refers to this aspect in particular.

sermons, moral, theological and political treaties, court records, travel accounts/travelogues and interrogation records.

The mutual basis of the articles collected in this volume is to pose the question as to how deviance is narrated or recounted in these sources. In particular, we can ask whether there is a relationship between the manner in which divergent behaviour is recounted and the type of source in which this behaviour is presented. Thus, we shift the perspective from the actors to the narratives of action. Looking at these narratives, we can compare the terms used in the specific text to label deviant or delinquent behaviour. By doing so, we obtain more information about the principal idea of deviance in the context of a given social group or society. Furthermore, we can see whether a society has used fixed vocabulary to label deviance, regardless of the precise situation (court, pulpit, office) in which a text has been produced. We may also see that the wording of deviance or delinquency is closely connected to the type of text in which we find the narrative.

In all cases, we have to consider a general problem, which I like to highlight by means of interrogation records. A clerk records the statements of the alleged prosecutor. In many cases, he translates the vernacular uttering of the interrogated person into Latin. Regardless whether or not this is the case, the clerk or any other writer will use terms he knows to describe and/or label the behaviour. So, what kind of narrative do we find in the text? Not the "original" narration of the interrogated person, but the narration produced by the clerk or writer, using his own ideas about deviance and the formal structure of a narrative that is required by the type of text he has to produce (in this case the interrogation record) by rephrasing the words of the interviewed person.

This is again an argument for the use of the labelling approach when we are dealing with narratives of deviance. Furthermore, it offers the chance to connect these narratives in the texts with political and cultural contexts in which they had been written. This is important, because recounting is not only a kind of recapitulation after the fact. It is, in fact, part of the process to shape a specific world view of people living in a specific culture.[17] My point here is: the writers did not write down a more or less accurate report of events about or around deviant behav-

---

17   ROGGE, 2015, pp. 15-27; KOSCHORKE, 2013, p. 22.

iour. The manner, in which they recounted this behaviour, is, in fact, a contribution to the process of world shaping. Listeners or readers could share their narrations about deviance. Narratives are the cement to provide the cohesion of societies. Narratives of deviant and delinquent behaviour offer orientations to behave properly or to avoid practices which are alleged to be a violation of social norms or law. This heuristic approach is very fruitful because it is no longer necessary to attempt writing a more or less objective reconstruction of a crime or offence against social and political norms. Instead, we can use this to analyse the dominant patterns of argumentation and the value systems of a given society.[18]

Another type of narratives informs us about the reactions of persons whose behaviour had been regarded or labelled deviant/delinquent. They have tried to defend themselves with words, witnesses or by using violence – to name just a few possibilities. It seems to have been a common practice to reply to their social or legal exclusion from the social group or society with verbal or/and physical violence.

I would like to draw your attention to the so-called European conflict culture ("Streitkultur"), which has a prominent status in current research about late medieval and early modern societies. According to this research, a ritualised escalation process marked the conflict culture. Starting with verbal confrontations and the use of a set of swearwords, including "thief" (for men) and "whore" (for women), the next step could have been the drawing of a knife. At this stage, it is possible to calm down or resolve the conflict by the intervention of a third party. Another possibility was the escalation of the conflict and the instigation of a fight in order for the opponents to defend or protect their honour.[19] This idea of a common logic of action in these conflicts about behaviour and honour – like other general concepts concerning late medieval and early modern societies – is the topic in a controversial debate about the use of violence as a rational instrument.

This concept of the ritualised use of violence is a reference point to compare the findings in our sources with this concept. In other words: Do we find narratives of deviant or delinquent behaviour that indicate

---

18 SCHWERHOFF, 2011, p. 49.
19 IBID., pp. 120-124.

such a conflict culture in the sources? Or will we contribute to the choir of critical voices concerning this culture?

The reader of the articles collected here find answers to this and other questions. The articles present examples of the recounting of deviance from 15th century England, 15th/16th Century Germany, 17th century Spain, 17th/18th century Venice and 17th/18th century Italy and France seen through the eyes of travellers from the British Isles. The authors or the articles have used Chronicles[20], travel accounts[21], court records,[22] the protocols of the Spanish inquisition[23] and the inquisition courts in Venice.[24]

In what follows, I would like to sketch the practices of labelling behaviour as deviant or delinquent in the mentioned source material, with which the contributors of this volume have worked. The general question is, whether the narrative patterns are the reflection of a social practice or whether they are more or less a consequence of the manner the source tell us about it?

Regina Schäfer stresses the point that in the records of the law court (Ingelheim) we only find traces of inappropriate behaviour that had the quality of criminal offences. She assumes that most of this behaviour, like disorderly conduct in public, was not brought before the court and is therefore not recorded. Recorded are many cases of attacks and defence of personal honour or the honour of the family, which had disturbed the public peace. The judges used the cases of insult to draw the line between inappropriate, deviant behaviour and delinquent, criminal behaviour that had to be prosecuted.

Judith Mengler analyses the narrations in the two continuations of the chronicles of the Croyland Abbey. The writers connect the deviances from religious forms and rules with the breaking of political norms and rules. In cases where people transgress rights and liberties of the Abby, the writers connect the wrongdoing in the legal sense with the breaking of norms in the moral sense. Mengler distinguishes between two levels in the narration: namely juristic religious, e.g. a story of sin and punishment. She concludes: "It shows the very central idea that the

---

20 MENGLER in this volume.
21 BECKER in this volume.
22 SCHÄFER in this volume.
23 FROHNAPFEL-LEIS in this volume.
24 VETTORE, MOROSINI, and BARBIERATO in this volume.

punishment of a crime should reflect the committed misdeeds as well as their underlying causes."[25]

Monika Frohnapfel-Leis uses material from the Spanish inquisition to show how deviant religious conduct was fabricated. In 17th century Spain, faithful people obtained knowledge of conformity and deviance by preachers from the pulpit. They learned how to behave properly and according to the religious norms by reading or listening to the 'Edict of faith'. While the contrary of the norm was communicated to the people, they had the words and categories at hand to label the actions of other people as deviant. Alongside the norms preached and taught by the church and inquisition, there was the everyday knowledge about good and faithful living and aberration from the social and religious norms. Frohnapfel-Leis shows how people used this knowledge to assess the behaviour of family members, neighbours and friends. If they considered this behaviour to be forbidden practice (sorcery, false saintliness, performing prophecies), they sometimes prepared a denunciation.

Three articles are concerned with different aspects of deviance and delinquency in early modern Venice. In his article, Luca Vettore explains that blasphemy was a manner of speaking on one hand, but was regarded a sin and/or crime in specific circumstances on the other. However, blasphemy could be used as a means to express deviant beliefs or views. Vettore sees two prevailing patterns of talking about blasphemy before the inquisition. People referred to their emotional state to explain why they had offended God or used blasphemy to impress other people and become famous in a quarter, a street or parish. Giulia Morosini analyses love magic often performed by prostitutes (to secure their living) and enquires about the connection between witchcraft accusation and deviant love concerning prostitutes. She finds narrative patterns used by contemporaries to label the relation of a (former) prostitute and a 'normal' man as illicit. "Unforeseen" and "against nature" were adjectives to describe the love and marriage of a prostitute. A second recount pattern is revenge. It is used to explain why women/prostitutes turned to witches if they had been rejected by a man, who had promised to marry them. The women were alleged to have used witchcraft to harm the man, who had broken a marriage promises. In the accounts, the difference between a woman and a witch is marked

---

25 MENGLER, 2016, p. 70.

by conduct or behaviour. In narratives, a witch is a person who exhibits exuberant conduct (loud voice, unfitted gesture etc.) They demonstrated their sin to an extent that the members of the society were forced to react. Open deviant behaviour was not tolerated.

Federico Barbierato uses Venetian inquisitorial material to discuss whether they present women as libertine and disbelieving persons. He asks whether this type of women had been part of the female representation of the Inquisitors and of the male culture in Modern times. It seems that the judges have not regarded manifestations of female dissent as a threat, because they did not take the divergent arguments and speeches of women seriously. In most cases, they considered feminine divergence as the result of being taught by men not to believe in catholic doctrines. Barbierato shows that women themselves had been able to develop deviant ideas and practices. He stresses that sexual behaviour was some sort of common ground "where, with the same authority, men and women could manifest their own distance from dogma, on which they could practically rely on divergent behaviour and conception of religious faith as a mere convention".[26] Experience was the reason why one considered religion and religious norms as a fraud. Both men and women had taken this starting point to develop thoughts of heterodoxy and for deviant practices of their conduct of life.

Travel accounts of two British travellers – Sachaverell Stevens and Bishop Gilbert Burnet – to France and Italy are the basis for Sebastian Becker's examination of deviant behaviour. In his article, he focuses on the narrative patterns the travellers have used to describe confessional differences. Both were Protestants with a strong antipapist attitude and used this as an initial point to label the behaviour of people in the catholic regions of continental Europe they had observed. In their narratives, the travellers mark the difference between book knowledge and experiential knowledge (things you know because someone told you about in contrast to things you have seen with your own eyes). They use their experience and stylistic abilities to attribute deviance through the narrative of difference. It is important to them to distinguish between 'difference' in a neutral and 'deviance' in a negative moral sense. Therefore, they use the stylistic device of derisive remarks about persons, countries

---

26 BARBIERATO, 2016, p. 172.

and social groups. Bishop Burnt, for example, labels the entire Venetian society as being deviant toward its own religious values and norms.

I would like to conclude with a few general observations. Deviant behaviour becomes apparent when the behaviour of a person is considered a threat to the peaceful cohabitation of people in a house, street or parish. The examples from Venice and Ingelheim show that a family or a neighbourhood willingly tolerated forms of illicit behaviour. However, in case this triggered the attention of the authorities, people tended to label the tolerated behaviour as deviant or even delinquent. Deviant behaviour seems to have been a specific label for bad or incorrect conduct, which had to be sanctioned in public and/or by authorities responsible to officially sanction behaviour.

If a person was accused of deviant behaviour before of a court of justice or the inquisition, he or she tried to refer to a temporary bad state of mind due to alcohol, love sickness or other emotionally exceptional circumstances in order to explain their behaviour. This behaviour could be sanctioned on different levels and by different social and/or juridical agents. The reaction of family, kin and friends could result in the exclusion of the person from his/her social environment. In cases where the malefactor infringed a law as well, he/she was brought before the courts of law – usually after a denunciation, as it seems.

A third observation concerns the norm a person transgressed or breached. Our sample does not contain serious political deviance, e.g. against the authorities in a village, town or kingdom. Therefore, the problem of how the breach of political norms was labelled did not occur here, although this is a general issue and well analysed in the current research.[27] In most cases presented here, we find narratives of transgressed social and religious norms. Only in the continuations of the Croyland Chronicles, we find the conjunction of moral and religious misbehaviour and the transgression of political boundaries.

With regard to the patterns of narrating deviant behaviour, we have to keep in mind the sources in which this behaviour is recorded. The examples from the inquisition trials in Spain and Venice presented here show that persons who felt offended by another person narrated deviance in form of a revenge story. The accused persons used a kind of excuse narrative to explain their behaviour and demonstrate their will-

---

27 KINTZINGER et al., 2015; BORNSCHIER, 2007; WÜRGLER, 1999.

ingness to live in general according to the rules. A third pattern is built around the self-concept/identity of a person. It was used by Venetian women and men, and by the British travellers on the continent to express their decision to deliberately live outside the rules established by religious authorities. We can call them identity patterns of deviance narratives. The monks in Croyland Abbey described the behaviour of their competitors as deviant to defend their rights, positions and liberties. Therefore, we can denote this specific writing a defence pattern.

However, readers of the following articles shall see that these four types of narrative patterns to recount deviance occur intermingled in the cases discussed.

Literature

BARBIERATO, FEDERICO, Representations of Deviance: Inquisitorial Practices and feminine divergence in Venice between the Sixteen and Seventeen Hundreds, in: Recounting Deviance. Forms and practices of presenting divergent behaviour in the late middle Ages and Early Modern period (Mainzer Historische Kulturwissenschaften), ed. by JÖRG ROGGE, Bielefeld 2016, pp. 163-178.

BECKER, SEBASTIAN, "Miscellaneous remarks". Recounting deviance in Early Modern travel-accounts, in: Recounting Deviance. Forms and practices of presenting divergent behaviour in the late middle Ages and Early Modern period (Mainzer Historische Kulturwissenschaften), ed. by JÖRG ROGGE, Bielefeld 2016, pp. 179-205.

BORNSCHIER, VOLKER, Konflikt, Gewalt, Kriminalität und abweichendes Verhalten. Ursachen, Zeit- und Gesellschaftsvergleiche, Berlin 2007.

CLINARD, MARSHALL B./MEIER, ROBERT F., Sociology of deviant behaviour, 11th ed., Fort Worth 2001.

FRANZESE, ROBERT J., The sociology of Deviance. Differences, Tradition, and Stigma, Springfield 2009.

FROHNAPFEL-LEIS, MONIKA, An enchantress, a saint and a prophetess. How religious deviance is described in Spanish Inquisition's trials, in: Recounting Deviance. Forms and practices of presenting divergent behaviour in the late middle Ages and Early Modern period

21

(Mainzer Historische Kulturwissenschaften), ed. by JÖRG ROGGE, Bielefeld 2016, pp. 77-95.

FÜSER, THOMAS, Mönche im Konflikt, Münster 2000.

GELTNER, GUY, Social Deviance. A medieval approach, in: Why the Middle Ages matter. Medieval light on modern injustice, ed. by CELIA CHAZELLE et al., London, New York 2012, pp. 29-40.

HÄBERLEIN, MARK, Einleitung, in: Devianz, Widerstand und Herrschaftspraxis in der Vormoderne, ed. by MARK HÄBRLEIN, Konstanz 1999, pp. 9-32.

INDERBITZIN, MICHELLE et al. (Eds.), Deviance and Social Control. A Sociological Perspective, Los Angeles 2013.

JUSSEN, BERNHARD, Normen, in: Enzyklopädie des Mittelalters 1, Darmstadt 2008, pp. 176-177.

KÄSTNER, ALEXANDER/SCHWERHOFF, GERD, Religiöse Devianz in alteuropäischen Stadtgesellschaften. Eine Einführung in systematischer Absicht, in: Göttlicher Zorn und menschliches Maß, ed. by ID., Konstanz 2013, pp. 9-43.

KINTZINGER, MARTIN et al. (Eds.), Gewalt und Widerstand in der politischen Kultur des späten Mittelalters (Vorträge und Forschungen 80), Ostfildern 2015.

KOSCHORKE, ALBRECHT, Wahrheit und Erfindung. Grundzüge einer Allgemeinen Erzähltheorie. 3rd ed., Frankfurt am Main 2013.

LAMNEK, SIEGFRIED, Neue Theorien abweichenden Verhaltens, 2nd ed., Paderborn 1997.

MENGLER, JUDITH, The Presentation of Deviant Behaviour in the Crowland Chronicle Continuations, in: Recounting Deviance. Forms and practices of presenting divergent behaviour in the late middle Ages and Early Modern period (Mainzer Historische Kulturwissenschaften), ed. by JÖRG ROGGE, Bielefeld 2016, pp. 57-75.

MOROSINI, GIULIA, "... Fossimo presi per incantamento". Witchcraft and love deviances in the trials of Venice's Santo Uffizio in the XVII century, in: Recounting Deviance. Forms and practices of presenting divergent behaviour in the late middle Ages and Early Modern period (Mainzer Historische Kulturwissenschaften), ed. by JÖRG ROGGE, Bielefeld 2016, pp. 131-162.

PETERS, HELGE, Devianz und soziale Kontrolle. Eine Einführung in die Soziologie abweichenden Verhaltens, 5th ed., Weinheim et al. 1995.

ROGGE, JÖRG, Narratologie interdisziplinär. Überlegungen zur Methode und Heuristik des historischen Erzählens, in: Musikpädagogik der Musikgeschichte, ed. by MELANIE UNSELD/LARS OBERHAUS, Münster/New York 2016, pp. 15-27.

SCHÄFER, REGINA, Talking about deviance? Insult and humiliation in the Ingelheim court records, in: Recounting Deviance. Forms and practices of presenting divergent behaviour in the late middle Ages and Early Modern period (Mainzer Historische Kulturwissenschaften), ed. by JÖRG ROGGE, Bielefeld 2016, pp. 25-56.

SCHWERHOFF, GERD, Historische Kriminalitätsforschung, Frankfurt am Main 2011.

STARK, RODNEY/BAINBRIDGE, WILLIAM SIMS, Religion, Deviance and Social Control, New York 1996.

VETTORE, LUCA, Blasphemy on Trial: splinters of deviant recounts from 17th century Venice, in: Recounting Deviance. Forms and practices of presenting divergent behaviour in the late middle Ages and Early Modern period (Mainzer Historische Kulturwissenschaften), ed. by JÖRG ROGGE, Bielefeld 2016, pp. 97-129.

WÜRGLER, ANDREAS, Diffamierung und Kriminalisierung von „Devianz" in frühneuzeitlichen Konflikten. Für einen Dialog zwischen Protestforschung und Kriminalgeschichte, in: Devianz, Widerstand und Herrschaftspraxis in der Vormoderne, ed. by MARK HÄBRLEIN, Konstanz 1999, pp. 317-347.

Talking about deviance?

Insult and humiliation in the Ingelheim court records

REGINA SCHÄFER

> *"hait ers mit dem maull*
> *dar gethan sals auch do*
> *mit widder hene weg thun"*[1]

In the year 1476, Enders von Schwabenheim takes proceedings against Henne Bußer von Hilbersheim. He complains Henne Bußer von Hilbersheim insulted him in front of Pedergin Gocz by using words which could damage reputation. January 1477, the court judges that Enders has not yet proved that these words were damaging. So, it would be sufficient if Henne Bußer swore he had only spoken these words because he wanted to be paid.[2] We will never find out the cause for their argument. In July 1477, the court finally decides that each party has to name two friends and those four shall act as a court of arbitration. If necessary, they can choose a fifth person as a chairman.[3] So ends a quite typical case of the Ingelheim court.

---

1 Nieder-Ingelheim 2 fol. 66v-67.
2 "Did he insult him with words, he should undo with words"; Ober-Ingelheim 1 fol. 10v.
3 Ober-Ingelheim 1 fol. 36v.

1. The Ingelheim court

In the Late Middle Ages, Ingelheim was a joint community of the villages Ober-Ingelheim, Nieder-Ingelheim, Großwinternheim and six smaller settlements. Together with the close-by village of Nierstein, it was part of the Emperor's properties that had remained at his direct disposal. In 1379, Ingelheim and Nierstein were impawned by Karl IV to Count Palatine in order to secure his vote for the election of Karl's son Wenzel. Nevertheless, Ingelheim and Nierstein continued to regard themselves as imperial villages.

Fortunately, a unique and extraordinary set of records of the Ingelheim court has been preserved – at least in parts. The *Ingelheimer Reichsgericht* served as a consultation court for villages and individuals in a 50 km radius. Here, most of the records, the so-called *Oberhofprotokolle* or high court records, are lost. The court also dealt with local issues, concerning the nine mentioned villages, which formed an administrative unit called the *Ingelheimer Grund*.

The records commence at around the time of the impawning and continue with only small gaps until 1534. The convolute comprises 19 volumes, each containing between 100 and 300 pages and several thousand entries. Unfortunately only the court records themselves have been preserved, whereas the rest of the sources are lost.[4] The Ingelheim court records are of exceptional size and coverage, but they are typical for courts in wealthy villages and small cities of the region.[5] They provide a comprehensive view of routines and procedures of a local court which handled any kind of civil and penal proceedings that were of relevance to the community, from unpaid wages to illegal hunting, from property transfer to unnatural death. They reveal a wealthy community of significant size with an excellent infrastructure: a market, fortifications, a hospital and a school, and at times a public bath and a dancing hall. Society was stratified in Ingelheim: noblemen and day-labourer, mayor and maid appeared before the court as plaintiff,

---

4   OPITZ, 2010, pp. 29-41; BLATTMANN, 2008, pp. 55-57. Ober-Ingelheim 1;
     Nieder-Ingelheim 1; Nieder-Ingelheim 2; Ober-Ingelheim 2.
5   RIEDEL/SCHMITT, 1999; SCHÄFER 2012a, pp. 65-85.

prosecutor or defendant. Such a community had ceased to be plain rural, but could not yet be considered fully urban.[6] The court consisted of 14 lay judges, most of which were members of the nobility, and was presided by the sheriff or mayor, who also acted as judge. Further, there was the clerk, who took the records, two bailiffs and four so-called *Fürsprecher* or supporters, who acted as semi-professional advocates. Regular sessions of the court were held by a committee of rarely more than two lay judges and convened up to six times a week in the three main villages Ober-Ingelheim, Nieder-Ingelheim and Großwinternheim. Plenary sessions were held about once in three months. The noble lay judges were fiefs of Count Palatine or the archbishop of Mainz, their families owned fortresses and small villages nearby; some of them lived in Ingelheim, others in the Rheingau. They had a basic education; some knew how to read Latin and most had experience in administrative tasks.[7]

In Germany, the research of court records was intensified at the beginning of the 21th century. Researchers were especially interested in the investigation of delinquency,[8] control of power in societies, the legitimation of dominion[9] and the specific conditions of literacy in an oral society[10] and the relation between customary law and written legal norms.[11]

In Germany, historical research concentrated on criminal records of bigger cities.[12] The Ingelheim court is different. The court records mention cases subjected to severe punishment, even death penalties. But those are rare. About 95% of the records deal with unpaid debts, and many legal proceedings resemble dunning procedures, where debtors are reminded to settle bills and overdue payments. Such cases were typically settled by acknowledgement of the debt, payment by

---

6 SCHÄFER, 2012b; SCHÄFER 2012c.
7 SCHÄFER, 2014.
8 SCHWERHOFF, 2000, pp. 23-25; SCHWERHOFF, 2006; BURGHARTZ, 1990; SCHWERHOFF, 1991; SCHUSTER, 1995; SCHUSTER, 2000; SCHUSTER, 2008; HENSELMEYER, 2002; BEHRISCH, 2009.
9 BAUMGÄRTNER, 2006.
10 TEUSCHER, 2012; WETZSTEIN, 2008; BLATTMANN, 2008; BLATTMANN, 2007.
11 PILCH, 2010; WEITZEL, 1985; KALB, 2014; DILCHER, 1992; WEITZEL, 1992; LÜCK, 1992; TEUSCHER, 2012.
12 SCHWERHOFF, 1991, pp. 444-446; KRUG-RICHTER, 2010, pp. 342-347.

instalments, extension of payment, conversion of debt or seizure. Only a minor part of the records is connected to issues such as inheritance battles, criminal assault and insult.

Moreover, verdicts are rare in the court records; this differs from the high court records, were the same court acted in another function.[13] Thus, the rarity of decisions in the *Haderbücher* needs an explanation. I assume that the main target of the Ingelheim court was to restore peace in the community. Mediation was preferred over giving judgements which would most likely deepen conflicts. Therefore, the court tried to postpone decisions, delegate them to arbitration courts and forced the opposing parties to swear peace until the next session. In some cases, the court explicitly declared that the dispute should not be brought before the court again.[14] The main target of the court was therefore not the enforcement of law, but to keep peace and secure the independence of Ingelheim and its special status within the *Pfalzgrafschaft*.[15]

Most of the entities within the *Haderbücher* are quite short and standardised. The book contains mostly reminders and acknowledgments of debt, but one can also find real proceedings, transcripts of documents and testimonials of witnesses. The court clerk took notes during sessions and wrote the minutes afterwards. Even when the court records suggest direct speech, the interaction in front of the court is seen through the eyes of the court clerk. The role of the court clerk cannot be underestimated. He was permanently employed in Ingelheim. Usually, the court chose professionals who had previously worked as town clerks or public notaries. The court clerk not only wrote the *Haderbücher,* but also the court records of the high court and the *Ufgiftbuch*, which documented changes in ownership of estates.[16]

---

13 ERLER, 1952-1963.
14 Ober-Ingelheim 1 fol. 36v, 61r-v, 172, 182, 4, 4v
15 SCHÄFER 2014.
16 SCHÄFER, 2012c, p. 66; SCHÄFER, 2014, p. 161.

2. Inappropriate Behaviour – Divergent Behaviour – Deviant Behaviour

Although the court clerk did not record the discussions at court verbatim, the sources provide an insight in the labelling of divergent behaviour within a rural town. Deviant behaviour could be reported by complaint or via denunciation.[17] The *Ingelheimer Hadergericht* was not a denunciation-court,[18] cases were brought before court by one of the parties.

However, divergent behaviour was not only a cause for seeking libel; the testimonials of witnesses or the argumentation of the parties could also hint to deviant behaviour. The sources also reveal traces of codes of legal and social behaviour, but, strangely, no religious codes. The term *Recht* is used abundantly by all parties; *Recht* could mean justice, but it could also mean special law, written law as well as traditional customary law – court rules, *Landrecht* and common law. The court argues in accordance with the court rules and does not render any explanation for its decisions. The parties and the witnesses constantly mention common law.[19] Most parties argue according to commonly accepted legal norms, e.g. one cannot disinherit one's children, one needs witnesses to give legality to any selling, etc. However, we also find hints of political statements: water and pasture are free,[20] the prince is expected to keep his promises and should maintain the rights and liberties of the people of Ingelheim.[21] Obviously there are also uncodified but omnipresent social norms: Children should

17 SCHWERHOFF, 1991, pp. 85-94, 444-446.
18 There is a denunciation court as well but it only deals with trespasses on farmland; Ober-Ingelheim 2 fol. 270. This seems to be different in other German countries where denunciations are more common, see KRISCHER, 2002, pp. 333-369.
19 "Daz nuw Antz yne nit lest zu sine(m) deil kome(n) nach lands recht vnd gewonheit ..."; Nieder-Ingelheim 1 fol. 271; see SCHÄFER, 2014.
20 "Da sagt Wilhelm: Obe ma(n) ey(n) arme(n) man also schrecken wolle. Und finde er eyne(n) hasen ader etwas so hofft er doch nach dem waßer und weide frij sihi ungefreffelt dar an zu hain. ... Wilhelm geantwort: Das rehe sij verkaufft(en) obe ma(n) eyne(n) armen man(n) also schreck(e)n wolle. Dan(n) er hoffte, fynge er noch morne ey(n) rehe er solt eß macht hain.": Ober-Ingelheim 1 fol. 90.
21 "bij altem h(er)ko(m)me(n) und fryheit"; Ober-Ingelheim 1 fol. 90v.

take care of their parents, neighbours should act neighbourly,[22] promises are to be kept, if you see a brawl you should separate the fighters, you cannot attack arbitrators,[23] gambling debts must be paid, and so on.[24] Those are not norms for which one could sue, but they were of great relevance in common live and we find a lot of arguments between neighbours: a man takes a shortcut by crossing the neighbours ground, a downspout between two houses must be repaired, and so on.[25] We find unkindness and social hardship. Although this is inappropriate behaviour, it is usually not in the focus of the court.

I assume that the mayor was well informed about what was going on in the small town of Ingelheim. I have come across three different cases in which the mayor took action after he obtained knowledge of deviant behaviour. In the first case, an apprentice who lived alone had not been paid his wages and the mayor intervened and effected the payment.[26] There is also the case of a violent and probably epileptic husband. His wife was overburdened and unable to cope with his disease. The mayor and the town council contracted a caretaker to assist the wife at the expense of the husband.[27] In a third case, four men from Ingelheim are accused of poaching deer. In their defence they stated that the deer stumbled to death across the thread they had laid out to catch hares. On hearing about this, the mayor sends one of his bailiffs to the leader of the group with a proposal to surrender the deer to him, so he can give it to Count Palatine's bailiff as a gift. He was trying to cover the deed or at least mitigate its consequences. Only after the four men declined his proposal and even entered into provocations, the mayor was left with no choice but to denunciate them to Count palatine's bailiff.[28]

Nevertheless, the court records usually only report divergent behaviour if it was brought before court; therefore, we know mostly about the criminalised part of divergent behaviour. To find out more

22　Nieder-Ingelheim 2 fol. 29 r-v; Nieder-Ingelheim 2 fol. 61; Nieder-Ingelheim 1 fol. 123.
23　Ober-Ingelheim 1 fol. 107 r-v; Ober-Ingelheim 1 fol. 127.
24　Nieder-Ingelheim 2 fol. 66r-v; Ober-Ingelheim 1 fol. 122. Nieder-Ingelheim 1 fol. 145r-v.
25　Nieder-Ingelheim 1 fol. 255.
26　Ober-Ingelheim 1 fol. 74.
27　Ober-Ingelheim 1 fol. 38v-39.
28　Ober-Ingelheim 1 fol. 89v-92v; SCHÄFER 2014.

about ordinary deviance and the relation between deviant and criminalised behaviour, I chose to take a closer look at the aspect of insult and humiliation. German research emphasised that honour was a main category for social life in medieval and early modern societies. Any harm to the reputation was considered a threat to the social status of both men and women.[29] The conclusions to this thesis were ambivalent. Some researchers argued that cases of libel were on a regular basis brought before court;[30] others emphasise the importance of non-jurisdictional structures which dealt with breaches of social norms.[31] An opinion recurrent in literature is that seeking legal action against libel, the degradation of somebody's honour, was the rule and not the exception. Both meanings are based on the assumption that honour and good repute were invaluable assets in premodern societies. Let's have a look at insult and humiliation in the village of Ingelheim in the 15th and 16th century.

3. Insult in Ober- and Nieder-Ingelheim

I worked through four volumes, two from Ober-Ingelheim and two from Nieder-Ingelheim, covering the years from 1468 to 1485 and from 1518 to 1535. These four volumes contain about 1000 pages and thousands of complaints. In these records, only 60 cases related to insult and humiliation were found, less than one case per year on average. This seems not to be in line with the common opinion that insult and humiliation were brought before court on a regular basis. It may make us think of the people of Ingelheim as particularly peaceful and polite – however, we know they were not. In addition to lawsuits and trials, the records mention cases where penal fees had to be paid for inappropriate behaviour in court and disorderly conduct in the public – the so called *"frevel"*.[32] The number of cases varies from about 20 to 80 per volume. We do not know if the records are complete with respect to such cases,

---

29   SCHREINER/SCHWERHOFF, 1995, pp. 1-28; DINGES, 1995, pp. 29-62.
30   WALZ, 1992.
31   SCHUSTER, 2008; DINGES, 1995, pp. 49f.
32   Nieder-Ingelheim 1 fol. 10v

but of those recorded we know that most were settled by the payment of a fee and not subject to further legal proceedings.

3.1 The legal disputes about insults

Obviously, many cases of insult and humiliation were not brought before court. If so, what caused insult and humiliation to become a matter of legal dispute? Taking a closer look, we see that more often than not they were not the cause of legal proceedings but were brought forward by the accused as a means of defence. The following typical cases show this in more clarity.

A maid named Katherin, working in a public bath, is hit with a sabre by a man named Contz im Schöffenhaus and part of her dress and her belt are torn to pieces. She issues a lawsuit against Contz, however not for assault or humiliation. Instead, she claims that a money bag has vanished that had been tied to the belt. Contz in turn states that the maid very well deserved the beating for having insulted him in the first place.[33] In Kathrin's vague narrative, she was sitting in the tavern when Contz entered and she said to him "if he wanted to know who he was, she could tell him". Most probably, Kathrin said nothing along such lines. Both make remarkable effort to avoid repeating any of the insults literally.

Not just the parties of a case, but witnesses as well turned hesitant and close-lipped when it came to insults.[34] This is very well illustrated by another case which also shows that insult and humiliation were not an exclusive phenomenon of the lower classes. Here, the mayor and the wealthiest of the noble lay judges had engaged in a controversy and one day, probably after a plenary session of the court – the town council was present as well – they had a drink and started an argument. The mayor called the lay judge an impostor and blatherer.[35] In the further course of the case, the noblemen among the lay judges were simply absent or declined to make a statement because they were related to one

---

33 Ober-Ingelheim 1 fol. 153. Similar in the early modern town Heiden; FRANK, 2005, p. 320.
34 Nieder-Ingelheim 2 fol. 1v, 2, 14, 19.
35 Ober-Ingelheim 1 fol. 63v.

of the parties. The other present witnesses refused to make a statement based on the grounds that they were sworn to secrecy and that the specific legal status of the house required them to remain silent.[36]

A final verdict has not been recorded in both cases and they were probably settled out of court. This is not only common in cases of insult and humiliation – it appears to be a general rule rather than an exception.

Generally, bringing an insult before court had three objectives: First, the plaintiff wanted to state that the insult was not based on facts and therefore not just,[37] second, that the insult should be recanted at the place where it was made,[38] namely in front of the court[39] or in front of the whole community[40] and third, that the accused party be punished.[41]

Lawsuits could be settled quickly given the parties were willing to end the dispute and the defendant was reasonable and understanding. In such cases, the defendant would state that a misunderstanding had occurred and that he or she had nothing but good things to tell about the other party, and the plaintiff would accept.[42]

Defendants confessing to a wrongdoing often used standard phrases along the lines of "I was in error and have nothing to tell about the plaintiff but good things, and I apologise for what I have done"[43] or more personal and honest: "I was beside myself with anger and what I said was not meant that way."[44] Even being a member of the weaker sex was put forward as an excuse.[45] Not always were plaintiffs satisfied with such excuses and, instead, insisted on carrying on with the legal proceedings. Defendants showed defiance in the face of the accusation,

---

36 Ober-Ingelheim 1 fol. 66.
37 Nieder-Ingelheim 2 fol. 13, 29v, 49v, 52v, 71, 194v; Ober-Ingelheim 2 fol. 40, 93, 202v, 270r-v,274.
38 Nieder-Ingelheim 2 fol. 29v, 194v-195; Ober-Ingelheim 2 fol. 40r-v, 93, 202v, 270r-v, 274.
39 Nieder-Ingelheim 2 fol. 66-67, 71; Ober-Ingelheim 2 fol. 270r-v.
40 Nieder-Ingelheim 2 fol. 46v.
41 Nieder-Ingelheim 2 fol. 29v; Ober-Ingelheim 2 fol. 202v, 270v.
42 Ober-Ingelheim 2 fol. 33.
43 Nieder-Ingelheim 2 fol. 61; Ober-Ingelheim 2 fol. 214v.
44 Ober-Ingelheim 1 fol. 168v; Nieder-Ingelheim 2 fol. 66v, Ober-Ingelheim 2 fol. 161r-v.
45 Ober-Ingelheim 2 fol. 161v: "bitt Theißenn als ein blode weip ir solichs zuverzeigen".

tried to delay the proceedings by bringing in evidence and witnesses, claimed that formalities had not been properly observed[46] or resorted to simple excuses, such as having been under the influence of alcohol and failing to remember anything – an excuse the court did not accept.[47]

Getting a verdict was not very easy. Apart from a general preference to settle cases out of court, verdicts could only be decided on in plenary sessions which took place once in about three months. Moreover, the court sometimes argued a party had not yet proved the accusation did in fact do any damage – as in the previously mentioned case of Enders of Schwabenheim and Pedergin Gocz against Henne Bußer. Quite meaningful is the argument between Peter Bender and Henne Winß. Henne Winß told Peter Bender that he does not pay any attention to his age. Obviously, there is another meaning behind these words. Henne Winß charges him and demands that he must speak aloud what he meant with these words; they both knew the meaning behind them. Peter declares that the words themselves were not insulting and he could not be forced to declare what he thought. The court decides Henne Winß was right and did not need not answer to the claim.[48]

Verdicts often fell short of the plaintiff's expectations, for example when the court declined a plaintiff's request to sentence the defendant to publicly recant an insult, but declared that doing so in court would be satisfactory.[49] Obviously, the court preferred to close cases as soon as possible and public recants not only delayed this, but had to be witnessed and recorded and may have resulted in uproar.[50]

The expenses of legal proceedings had to be covered by the defendant, if found guilty. Parties were obliged to recognise verdicts and behave accordingly, and often had to swear to it explicitly. From the court's perspective, a case was then considered settled and the peace of the community restored.

Sometimes, plaintiffs claimed that "the insult touched heart and soul", meaning they had also suffered physically, and sometimes

---

46 Nieder-Ingelheim 2 fol. 52v. The case against Else Schnad was mentioned more than ten times before court; Ober-Ingelheim 2 fol. 93, 96, 102, 109, 110v, 130v, 145, 149v-150, 161r-v, 173.
47 Nieder-Ingelheim 2 fol. 61r-v, 65v, 71r-v.
48 Ober-Ingelheim 1 fol. 148v-149 "er schone sein Alter nicht".
49 Ober-Ingelheim 2 fol. 173; Ober-Ingelheim 2 fol. 238.
50 See for another example in Köln KRISCHER, 2011, p. 145.

converted the damage or injury into an amount of money.[51] A man named Hans Knod was taken to court by a group of wine porters in two separate and one joint lawsuit. The wine porters argued they rather suffered a loss of 200, 400 or even 1000 guilders than bear the insults of Hans Knod.[52]

The amounts mentioned did not represent specific claims for compensation but served to illustrate the severity of the insult taken. Amounts of 10, 100 or 1000 guilders appear as typical measures in many lawsuits, also in those unrelated to insult or humiliation. The sum of 1000 guilders seems to demarcate the maximum damage. This sum appears in some cases of insult[53] but also when a cask of wine was stolen from a wine cellar. We know that many cases were settled out of court and the mentioned sums were never paid. This becomes evident in the records of follow-up lawsuits where the principal dispute relating to the insult is described as settled by mutual agreement, but secondary claims have not yet been satisfied, such as the costs of medical treatment.

3.2 Categories of insult and humiliation

It is evident that only particular cases of insult and humiliation were taken to court. What made these cases special? I would like to take a closer look at insult and humiliation by place, form and context.

3.2.1 Places

Classifying places of divergent behaviour in the examined sources resulted in the following seven categories:

---

51 Ober-Ingelheim 2 fol. 40; Ober-Ingelheim 2 fol. 202v, 270; Nieder-Ingelheim 2 fol. 194v.
52 Ober-Ingelheim 2 fol. 202-203; Nieder-Ingelheim 2 fol. 13.
53 Ober-Ingelheim 1 fol. 168r-v; Nieder-Ingelheim 2 fol. 29r-v; Nieder-Ingelheim 2 fol. 226; Nieder-Ingelheim 1 fol. 23v; Nieder-Ingelheim 1 fol. 40; Nieder-Ingelheim 1 fol. 254v.

1. The court itself[54]
2. Public places where specific rules of behaviour were in effect, such as the market[55] or the house of the lay judges.[56]
3. the tavern[57] or the kermis[58]
4. at work[59] or on the road, often at the threshold[60]
5. at home[61]
6. on the conclusion of a contract. Contracts were either trade contracts – called *Weinkauf*, when agreed upon and signed in a tavern – or marriage contracts, arranged in private houses, and then called Hinlich.
7. the community as a virtual entity. The parties refer to the general gossip *"eyn gemein gerucht".*[62] The gossip could be quite specific, e.g. the priest heard the brides man was already married to another woman who was still alive.[63] Once, a witness tells us how such a gossip, the fama, comes to live: He went along a street with his fellows and then he incidentally heard something; he thought, it was "flying words" he heard.[64] These flying words formed the

54 Ober-Ingelheim 1 fol. 168r-v; Nieder-Ingelheim 1 fol. 254v; MEYER, 2011, pp. 87-145.
55 Nieder-Ingelheim 1 fol. 130; Ober-Ingelheim 1 fol.140r, 234r; Ober-Ingelheim 2 fol. 274.
56 Ober-Ingelheim 1 fol. 65-66, 153. The house of the lay judges had many functions and it served as a dancing hall as well; CORDES, 1993; SCHWERHOFF, 2011; RAU, 2011; RAU/SCHWERHOFF, 2004; KRISCHER, 2004.
57 Ober-Ingelheim fol. 31v-32v, 126, 239r-v.; Nieder-Ingelheim 1 fol 1r-10, 32v-33, 36, 46v, 49r-v, 66r-v, 72v, 87, 186r-v, 221v-222, 276v; Ober-Ingelheim 2 fol. 40, 129. KÜMIN, 2011; RAU, 2011, pp. 56-59; RAU/SCHWERHOFF, 2004, pp. 40-44; DÜRR/SCHWERHOFF, 2005; SCHWERHOFF, 2006; HÜRLIMANN, 2010, pp. 237-259.
58 Nieder-Ingelheim 2 fol. 27, 81v, 117, 127r-v, 124r-v; Ober-Ingelheim 2 fol. 62v.
59 Nieder-Ingelheim 2 fol. 45v, 46v; Ober-Ingelheim 2 fol. 93.
60 Ober-Ingelheim 1 fol. 166; Nieder-Ingelheim 2 fol. 117, 194-195; Ober-Ingelheim 2 fol. 40; Nieder-Ingelheim 1 fol. 16v-17, 40, 142v-143, 264.
61 Ober-Ingelheim 2 fol. 201v, 278v-279; Nieder-Ingelheim 1 fol. 123.
62 Ober-Ingelheim 2 fol. 181."daß diße artickel alles jres jnhalts ware sin vnd do von zu obern jngelnheijm eijn gemeijne sage und leumat vnther dem volck"; Ober-Ingelheim 2 fol. 40v.
63 Ober-Ingelheim 2 fol. 181.
64 Nieder-Ingelheim 2 fo. 14v "vor swebende und fliegend wort geacht".

reputation, which affected his businesses[65] but also his function within the community, so he could be rejected as a witness because he was known as flippant.[66]

We learn that the tavern was a place where insults were uttered on a regular basis, but rarely became a cause for seeking legal action.[67] Instead, they were used as a means of defence in cases of criminal assault.

At court, parties were subject to specific rules of behaviour to ensure an orderly and peaceful course of events. The sources reveal nothing about insult and humiliation under those circumstances. We know about this only because a penal fee had to be paid when the peace of the court was broken.[68] Insults in business negotiations rarely made it into the records.[69] Also insults in private homes are rarely taken to court. The sources refer to one case of a maiden taking offence at reports about her brought to her master by two brothers, and another of a husband overhearing an insult to his wife made by a neighbour.[70] Again, the presence of witnesses is the reason why this incident is brought before court.

As can be expected, remarks about deviant behaviour were considered particularly insulting when they were made in public places or threatened to degrade someone's good reputation. Degradation of good repute was regarded as a substantial threat and always came into play when a doubt was raised about somebody's honour or integrity. However, this is rarely rendered explicit before court. One example involves the aforementioned Hans Knod, who worked as a wine porter, transporting casks and barrels. Knod, obviously a novice to the trade or maybe an apprentice, is being instructed by Johann von Duphusen. Knod states that Duphusen "is not good enough to teach me". Upon these words being expressed in front of the other wine porters, Johann

---

65 Nieder-Ingelheim 2 fol. 14v.
66 Nieder-Ingelheim 2 fol. 4v "angesehn sinen lichtfertigen standt".
67 HÜRLIMANN, 2010, p. 109f.
68 Ober-Ingelheim 1 fol. 143.
69 Ober-Ingelheim 2 fol. 198v "uff eynem he(n)lich … die fruntschafft abgerett".
70 Ober-Ingelheim 2 fol. 201v; Ober-Ingelheim 2 fol. 278v-279.

von Duphusen takes offence and sees his honour and good repute endangered, and takes the case to court.[71]

3.2.2 Forms

Looking at forms, we see that physical harm, which was rarely brought before court,[72] was not considered humiliation.[73] Humiliating behaviour without physical harm, such as exposing someone to public ridicule, triggers legal action in a few cases, but later on disappears from the court records. The sources mention cases of mockery by imitating the way people dance or act[74] and cases where manure or dung was thrown at people in expression of somebody's contempt;[75] also spitting on someone is mentioned in the court records.[76] Obviously, most of those cases are settled out of court, and not much can be learned about them.

This leaves verbal degradation as the prevailing form of insult and humiliation. I have categorised the contents of verbal degradations into five groups; some of them overlap[77]:

1. The allegation of dishonesty which, if not rebutted, could cause severe damage to any business. This type of verbal degradation includes libel and slander, that is, stating a lie as if it was a fact. Calling somebody a betrayer, a thief or a swearer of false oath and a rogue (*Schelm*) all fall into this category. These accusations were quite common in medieval as well as in modern villages.[78] Also the

---

71 Ober-Ingelheim 2 fol. 203.
72 With a similar result HÜRLIMANN, 2000, pp. 116-122. This contrasts with the example of the early modern village Heiden, where violence is often topic of an accusation; FRANK, 1995, p. 334.
73 One argues, paying the frevel was enough punishment (Ober-Ingelheim 1 fol. 88v), others mention fighting as something, which just happened, "verschiener zijth mit eijnander geslagen"; Nieder-Ingelheim 2 fol. 4v. See also SCHWERHOFF, 2006.
74 Ober-Ingelheim 2 fol. 171.
75 Nieder-Ingelheim 1 fol. 181v.
76 Nieder-Ingelheim 1 fol. 143.
77 See also FRANK, 1995, p. 325; HÜRLIMANN, 2000, pp. 110-116.
78 Nieder-Ingelheim 2 fol. 29, 45v, 46v; Ober-Ingelheim 1 fol. 44,65v, 126; Ober-Ingelheim 2 fol. 40, 129, 139v-140, 203; Nieder-Ingelheim 1 fol. 16v,

allegation of incapability and incompetence might fall into this category: broken promises of judges[79] or the accusation of an official to be unfair and unjust,[80] and the allegation of a doctor killing a patient instead of healing her.[81]

2. name-calling and the usage of degrading allegories, such as "meagre, leprous and stinking hag"[82], "whore",[83] "wimp from Frankfurt",[84] "blood hound" (*Bluthund*)[85] and "rogue" (*Schalck*)[86], "you should have been drowned 10 years ago".[87] Very common is also "villain" (*Bösewicht*).[88]

3. threats[89]

4. Insults against the family: Your mother is a liar,[90] your wife is a thief,[91] your father – the surgeon – killed my mother,[92] and you and your son are sodomites.[93]

5. The general reproach of deviance against religious norms. Deviations against religious and sexual norms were rare in Ingelheim, whereas they were quite common in early modern towns and vil-

---

23v, 40, 186v, 189, 198. See also TOCH, 1993, pp. 316f.; FRANK, 1995, p. 327. Wrong accusations: Ober-Ingelheim 2 fol. 270.

79 Ober-Ingelheim 1 fol. 65v.

80 Ober-Ingelheim 1 fol. 228; Nieder-Ingelheim 2 fol. 46v; Nieder-Ingelheim 1 fol. 143.

81 Nieder-Ingelheim 2 fol. 5v; "daß Pauels Hen zu Joistenhen gesagt, wie daß Joistenhen vatter hab jme Pauels Hen sin frau zu doijt geheijlt, vnd solich geld daß er Joisten hab gebenn, hab er jme geben, als het jß jme Joijst vß dem buttel genomen".

82 Ober-Ingelheim 2 fol. 93.

83 Nieder-Ingelheim 2 fol. 45v.

84 Ober-Ingelheim 2 fol. 202v.

85 Ober-Ingelheim 2 fol. 203.

86 Nieder-Ingelheim 1 fol. 5, 16v, 40, 123, 143; Nieder-Ingelheim 2 fol. 81v.

87 Ober-Ingelheim 2 fol. 93.

88 Nieder-Ingelheim 1 fol. 40, 123, 186v, 189; Ober-Ingelheim 1 fol. 168r-v; Nieder-Ingelheim 2 fol. 46; Ober-Ingelheim 2 fol. 18v: "verreterßen boßewicht"; fol. 19: "verreterßen fleijsch boße [wicht]"; Nieder-Ingelheim 1 fol. 143 "grunt bosewicht".

89 Death-threats: Ober-Ingelheim 1 fol. 140r-v. Threatening someone with whipping: Nieder-Ingelheim 2 fol. 5v, 6, 46v, 137; Nieder-Ingelheim 1 fol. 96r-v, 99-100, 254v.

90 Ober-Ingelheim 1 fol. 44.

91 Nieder-Ingelheim 2 fol. 45v.

92 Nieder-Ingelheim 2 fol 4v, 5v, 6v.

93 Nieder-Ingelheim 2 fol. 194v.

lages.[94] I was able to find only one case where someone is accused of cursing a fellow, which he denies.[95] However, we find "sucker" (*Lecker*),[96] calling somebody's wife or mother "priest's darling" or "priest's son" and "priest's daughter"[97] and the allegation against somebody of being a sodomite,[98] which was threatened with the death penalty, as the victims lawyer explicitly voices.[99] Only two cases are known from Ingelheim, whereas they appear more frequently in the 150 years younger court records of the near-by Nierstein together with cases of adultery, swapping wives, bigamy and witchcraft.[100] Interestingly, the Ingelheim court records do not mention any of these types of offence or crime but one unproven case of bigamy.[101] Also, cases of superstition[102] and blasphemy[103] do not seem to be recorded.

3.2.3 Context

Let us take a look at the contexts in which insult and humiliation take place. Unfortunately, not every case in the records reveals something about its context. But one thing is obvious: many of the verbal injuries and cases of criminal assault occurred under the influence of alcohol, often in the tavern.[104] The guests of the taverns formed groups – for example journeymen would drink together (with or without their master) and most Ingelheimers were part of different and changing

---

94 See FRANK, 1995, p. 327.
95 Nieder-Ingelheim 1 fol. 143r-v.
96 Ober-Ingelheim 1 fol. 44, 166, "grunt-lecker", fol. 234v. "soppen lecker"; Nieder-Ingelheim 1 fol. 16v, 143, 198; Nieder-Ingelheim 2 fol. 81v; Ober-Ingelheim 2 fol. 40.
97 Ober-Ingelheim 2 fol. 203, 274. Ober-Ingelheim 2 fol. 201v "das sie von eynem phaffenn mehe dan sie ie jr lebenn lang genutzt sy worde(n)".
98 Nieder-Ingelheim 2 fol. 49v, 194-195.
99 Nieder-Ingelheim 2 fol. 226 "diße hoch schme und jniurien die jme nit alleyn seyn eher sonder auch seyn leben berorn".
100 RIEDEL/SCHMITT 1999; WALZ, 1996; SCHWERHOFF 1991, pp. 407-409, 424-441; FRANK, 1995, pp. 325-328.
101 Ober-Ingelheim 2 fol. 180v-181v.
102 Different in the early modern village Heiden; FRANK, 1995, pp. 328-331.
103 SCHWERHOFF, 1995.
104 Ober-Ingelheim 1 fol. 31v-32v; see also FRANK, 1995, pp. 334f.

fellowships. The exclusion of a fellowship could be a reason for insult and violence.[105] The examined cases involve persons that were familiar with each other and linked through acquaintance, such as neighbours and co-workers. Cases involving foreigners or strangers rarely appear in the records. This is true for both, cases of insult and criminal assault.[106]

In some cases, we see weeks or months pass after the deed before it is taken to court. Again, the infamous Hans Knod stands as an example. Several cases against him, all brought before court by wine porters, appear in the records in consecutive order, but the misdeeds of which he is accused happened at unconnected arbitrary points in time. Obviously, Knod was a notorious drunkard and foul-mouther, and the wine porters decided they could no longer put up with his behaviour and took collective action. Hen Thomas and Christgen Schneider were neighbours who seemed to be incapable of getting along with each other. Over a period of six years their quarrels kept the court busy. But notorious troublemakers were rare. Apparently, the internal affairs of a household, including those of the staff, were not in the court's sphere of interest. Men and women alike did not hesitate to call each other names and to utter vulgarities, and it did not matter if the target of their profanities was of the same or the opposite sex. In total, insults of men against men happened most frequently.[107] Nevertheless there are differences: The Ingelheim court records contain two cases of a man physically harming a woman and none of a woman harming a man. In those cases, the men regularly justify their doing by declaring the woman had insulted them first. Also, alcohol is not mentioned as causing women to misbehave.[108] Moreover it must be taken into account, that the legal standing of women changed during the period in question. In a case from 1528, the defendant manages to prevent a woman from being interrogated as a witness.[109] The court affirms the

---

105 Ober-Ingelheim 2 fol. 129; Nieder-Ingelheim 2 fol. 9, 68, 72v; Ober-Ingelheim 1 fol. 32. SCHWERHOFF, 2005b; KRISCHER, 2011.

106 KRUG-RICHTER, 2010.

107 A woman against a man: Ober-Ingelheim 1 fol. 153, Ober-Ingelheim 2 fol. 17-19v. A man against a woman: Nieder-Ingelheim 2 fol. 45v. A woman against a woman: Ober-Ingelheim 2 fol. 91v; Ober-Ingelheim 2 fol. 93, 96, sqq. See also WALZ, 1996, p. 179.

108 WALZ, 1992, pp. 189-191.

109 Nieder-Ingelheim 2 fol. 269v.

defendant's argument that a woman cannot appear as a witness in a criminal case, which had not presented a problem in the past. The new attitude to exclude women may be due to the adaption of the Carolina penal code.

4. Public space

An opinion recurrent in literature is that seeking legal action against libel, the degradation of somebody's honour, was the rule and not the exception. This is based on the assumption that honour and good repute were invaluable assets in a time when asserting one's legal right was difficult.[110] The Ingelheim court records show, quite to the contrary, that insult and humiliation, even in extreme cases, rarely caused people to seek the assistance of the court. Instead, sweeping insults under the carpet, avoiding mentioning and talking about them seemed to be the preferred alternative. Most insults occurred in the tavern and were met with tolerance as long as they did not lead to fights and injuries. The individual person subjected to insult beyond the sufferable often resorted to escape in order to avoid escalation.[111]

As a rule, insults occurring in the tavern are of no concern to the court, but are brought forward by the accused as legitimate motives for their deeds, reverting the blame to the plaintiffs for provoking the incriminating deed by insulting beyond measure or leaving him no way but to defend himself.[112] The court does not weigh one against the other. This is left to the arbitration tribunals whose actions, unfortunately, were rarely documented in writing. However, there is reason to assume that lay judges were involved. Arbitration tribunals were an option to move quarrels from the public into a semi-public space, such as *Winkauf/Hinlich*. Arbitration tribunals dealt with the full range of offences and crimes, including cut-off thumbs, stabbing and attempted

---

110 WECHSLER, 1991, pp. 374-420.
111 Hans von Isenach asked one of his fellows to pay his wine and tried to leave the tavern as fast as possible; Ober-Ingelheim 1 fol. 32. Similar Nieder-Ingelheim 2 fol. 1v-2.
112 Ober-Ingelheim 1 fol. 31v-32v,

manslaughter.[113] As mentioned before, every party sent two "friends" and both parties chose a fifth as chairman. The decisions of the arbitration court were binding. It is obvious that in most cases insults were only a manifestation of a deeper conflict between the parties – often an inheritance dispute or conflicts between neighbours or journeymen and their master[114] or the tragic case of a woman who died six months after a medical treatment and the family thought it was the fault of the Scherer.[115] The arbitration court tried to reconcile the parties. Physical harm was usually compensated with money.[116] We do not know if insults were compensated with money, too. The victims always claimed that an attack was unprovoked and that they had expected nothing but good things from the opponent.[117] This may be an indication that provocation reduced the punishment. We have at least one note that there was an agreement between parties as to what insults were considered tolerable. Obviously, the repertoire of tolerable profanities depended on the location and the parties' social standing.[118] In one case, a witness is cited as saying that a woman uttered "profanities so bad that even a hangman could not be expected to bear them".[119]

The publicity of the place and the audience are of great importance as well. Recent research discussed whether the distinction between a public and a non-public or private sphere is more an invention of early modern times, whereas the Middle Ages know only the distinction between public and clandestine. This may be true for the public opinion.[120] In the small village of Ingelheim we find different grades of publicity, public places but not public spaces.[121] *Weinkauf* and *Hinlich*

---

113 Manslaughter: Nieder-Ingelheim 2 fol. 1-10; Ober-Ingelheim 1 fol. 31v-32v. See KRUG-RICHTER, 2010, p. 341.
114 Ober-Ingelheim 1 fol. 234r-v; vgl. Nieder-Ingelheim 2 fol. 29, 30.
115 Nieder-Ingelheim 2 fol. 1-10, 13-15.
116 Nieder-Ingelheim 2 fol. 7v; Nieder-Ingelheim 1 fol. 279.
117 Ober-Ingelheim 1 fol. 235r-v "one alle ursache und wort"; Nieder-Ingelheim 2 fol. 33; Ober-Ingelheim 2 fol. 18v.
118 LORENZEN-SCHMIDT, 1978, p. 17; different FRANK, 1995, pp. 331f.
119 Ober-Ingelheim 2 fol. 19 "den selbigen Jacoben also vbel gescholten [...] eijn nachrichter kum lijden soltt".
120 KINTZINGER/SCHNEIDMÜLLER, 2011; KRISCHER, 2011 pp. 129f.; SCHWERHOFF, 2011, pp. 5-7; VON MOOS, 2004; EMMELIUS, 2004; MELVILLE/VON MOOS, 1998; WECHSLER, 1991, pp. 213-227; BAUER, 1981.
121 MONNET, 2011, pp. 337-347.

were contracts which were private but not clandestine. They took place in taverns and the witnesses could be asked to give testimonials to every detail they heard.[122] Taverns were in between private and public places. They were not just places to articulate hidden transcript and the wrath about the neighbour.[123] Men had to follow different rules in a tavern than at the market or in the town hall.[124]

5. Conclusion

I would like to conclude by bringing forward a number of theses: Only the presence of witnesses makes an insult insulting. Insults at the market were considered to be intentional; the market was the place with a maximum of publicity. Honour was not a category which existed without publicity, as Martin Dinges points out.[125] All of the examined cases of insult and humiliation were taken to court by one of the involved parties. There is no example of a case started by way of denunciation as is frequently documented in modern times. This is a strong indicator that the court had little interest in checking the validity of insults; it was mainly interested in the social effects. Insult is considered deviant behaviour. At the same time, insults provide an occasion to discuss deviant behaviour and to draw the lines. Insults provided occasions for marking deviant behaviour which was deviant but not criminal. Honour is an important factor in the Ingelheim society but it is rarely mentioned explicitly. Every man has to answer for his reputation, as Joist Scherer states.[126] It is not acceptable for an honest man (*Biedermann*) to suffer from insults[127] or invectives,[128] this is not just.[129] Moreover, those

---

122 MIERAU, 2011, pp. 278-280; RAU, 2004, p. 51.
123 TLUSTY, 2004; KRUG-RICHTER, 2004; KÜMIN, 2011, p. 679; SCHWERHOFF, 2006, pp. 374-376.
124 Nieder-Ingelheim 2 fol. 13, 15; different: SCHWERHOFF, 2011, pp. 11-18; RAU/SCHWERHOFF, 2004b, pp. 27-33.
125 DINGES, 1989, p. 423; see also SCHWERHOFF, 2011; FRANK, 1995; HÜRLIMANN, 200, pp. 100f.
126 Nieder-Ingelheim 2 fol. 13 "daß diß clage jnen Joisten jn sin eijgen person selbst beroren, vnd er vnd eijn jglicher frommer man, sin eere schuldig zu verantwortenn".
127 Nieder-Ingelheim 2 fol. 52v, 83.
128 Nieder-Ingelheim 2 fol. 6v, 13, 13v, 151v, 194r-v; Ober-Ingelheim 2 fol. 40

wrongly uttered words endanger social reputation and businesses. Once spoken, the effects were hard to contain.[130] One could act against slander, defamation and wrong accusations[131] but not against gossip and words voiced behind the back.[132] Insulted parties were forced to act immediately. Keth, the wife of Hen Graben overheard a rumour she had stolen flour. Hen Graben asked the court to discuss the case immediately because Keth "could miss her honour no longer than it takes a swallow to cross a street".[133]

There is still the question about the connection between insults and violence. Are there specific codes which required violence as an answer to insults – especially insults against father or mother? Is the premodern society of Ingelheim more violent than in modern times?[134] Rainer Walz has emphasised that latent violence was omnipresent in early modern villages. He explains this violence as an expression of a special male, agonal culture, which was typical for these villages.[135] In Ingelheim, this is no surprise, violence mostly occurred in the tavern and we find some escalation of conflict in certain cases – after a verbal exchange, the men fought with fists and knives. We find all kinds of injuries, attacks against the head,[136] throwing of mugs,[137] retching and pulling hair.[138] Often, hands were hurt which indicates defensive wounds;[139] also mediators and hosts were injured.[140] All kinds of weapons were

---

129 Nieder-Ingelheim 2 fol. 13, 13v.
130 Ober-Ingelheim 1 fol. 234v. "an ernn leumat vnd kintheit zuschmehen vnderstanden"; Nieder-Ingelheim 2 fol. 194v; ähnlich Ober-Ingelheim 2 fol. 40; Ober-Ingelheim 2 fol. 202v.
131 Nieder-Ingelheim 2 fol. 15.
132 Nieder-Ingelheim 2 fol. 13 "ane sin eere zu rucke geredt", 14v "smelich zu rucke jniurert vnd nachgeredt". See also HÜRLIMANN, 2000, pp. 282-278.
133 "dann disse clegerinn kann ir ernn nit enbernn als lang eynn swalb moecht vber ein weg gefligenn"; Ober-Ingelheim 2 fol. 140. The court refused the suggestion; Ober-Ingelheim 2 fol. 144, 147v, 158.
134 TEUSCHER, 2011, pp. 80-82.
135 WALZ, 1992; HÜRLIMANN 2000, pp. 116-122.
136 Nieder-Ingelheim 2 fol. 2, 27, 36, 39, 87v, 124r-v.
137 Nieder-Ingelheim 2 fol. 5v, 66v, 103, 109; Nieder-Ingelheim 1 fol. 145, 276v.
138 Nieder-Ingelheim 1 fol. 16v-17, 221v-222, 223v.
139 Nieder-Ingelheim 2 fol. 9, 87r-v.
140 Ober-Ingelheim 2 fol. 38v-39; Nieder-Ingelheim 1 fol. 223v; Nieder-Ingelheim 2 fol. 76r-v, 77; Nieder-Ingelheim 2 fol 127v. The landlord's narration contrasts vividly with the one of the witnesses, who argue it was

employed: knives,[141] epees,[142] swords,[143] sticks (*Stoczler/Stöcke*),[144] spears,[145] axes,[146] and a halberd which needed to be fetched from home before it could be used to threaten the opponent. Outside the house or the village, the opponents also used stones[147] und tools – axes[148] a pale from a vineyard[149] or a pork skewer.[150] The brawl, which started in the tavern, sometimes continued outside. Some fights were perfidious, men waylaid others or two fought against one and would not stop.[151] There is only one known case of manslaughter in Ingelheim during these years. One man, who was involved, was sentenced to death, another died as a consequence of his injuries.[152] Five or six victims of other fights are known to have been seriously injured, they were at least partially paralysed, one was incapacitated and another lost his thumb.[153] Nevertheless, violent offenses were rare in the *Ingelheimer Haderbücher*; in 80 years I was able to count twenty cases. Of course, one explanation is that not every delict was mentioned before court. But it is likely that we find a least a trace of every offense in the *frevel*. Violation of the public order – insults voiced in front of the court as well as drawing knifes, and so on – was punished by a *frevel*, which had

---

the landlord himself, who offended his guests; Nieder-Ingelheim 2 fol. 143v-145. See Tlusty, 2004.
141 Ober-Ingelheim 1 fol. 32v, 239r-v; Nieder-Ingelheim 2 fol. 2, 8v-9, 66v, 72v, 76r-v, 117, 127r-v, 143v; Nieder-Ingelheim 1 fol. 40.
142 Ober-Ingelheim 1 fol. 32v, 140r-v, 239v.
143 Nieder-Ingelheim 1 fol. 145r-v.
144 Ober-Ingelheim 1 fol. 140r-v, 143, 276v.
145 Ober-Ingelheim 2 fol. 129; Nieder-Ingelheim 1 fol. 16v-17.
146 Nieder-Ingelheim 2 fol. 87v, 94; Nieder-Ingelheim 1 fol. 189.
147 Nieder-Ingelheim 2 fol. 30, 46; Nieder-Ingelheim 1 fol. 40, 143r-v, 145r-v, 181v.
148 Nieder-Ingelheim 2 fol. 83, 91.
149 Nieder-Ingelheim 1 fol. 145v.
150 Nieder-Ingelheim 2 fol. 46.
151 Nieder-Ingelheim 2 fol. 8v, 30, 124r-v; Nieder-Ingelheim 1 fol. 145r-v.
152 Nieder-Ingelheim 2 fol. 10 "Nach dem sin mitkund Michel von Griffensteijnn lijplich gestraijfft zum dote"; Nieder-Ingelheim 2 fol. 5v; "so sij nu g(e)n(ann)ter Balthasar sinth dem nehsten gericht mit doijt verscheiden vnd agbangen dem Got gnade".
153 Ober-Ingelheim 2 fol. 103r-v; Nieder-Ingelheim 2 fol. 87r-v, 117, 124r-v; Ober-Ingelheim 2 fol. 84; Ober-Ingelheim 2 fol. 160, 171.

to be paid to the mayor.[154] Thus, the mayor was quite interested in pursuing every misdeed. I counted 140 mentioned *frevel*, 70 in Nieder-Ingelheim during the years between 1521 and 1530, which means 7 deeds per year. It is not clear if the court records mention every *frevel* or just those which needed to be claimed before the court because the malefactors needed to be coerced into payment. The latter is more probable, since we find wrongdoers who argued why they had not paid – it was not a real fight, just fun,[155] nobody was harmed and the dispute was stopped before it could escalate.[156] Therefore: We cannot tell how many acts of violence happened in Ingelheim during the 15th and 16th century. Moreover, there is no mention of domestic violence in the records. But even if we cannot tell whether violence was omnipresent in Ingelheim, it is quite certain that this was not a culture of violence. The offenders mostly claimed they had used violence only to defend themselves.[157] I could find only three cases where the use of force was legitimated by the insults – two cases of men using violence against women and one of a man injuring another man. The offenders argued that they had been insulted beyond measure. The victims rejected this argumentation, voicing explicitly that nobody should be allowed to use violence.[158] In all other cases, the insulted was tempted by the verbal attacks, but refrained from violence.[159] This argumentation may be part of a strategy to demonstrate innocence and a peace-loving character. Nevertheless, these argumentations show that violence was not accepted in Ingelheim and could not be justified – violence is injustice and forbidden.[160] Violence in Ingelheim lacked the often described ritualism.[161] There is only one case of a provoked and ritualised escalation which

---

154 Nieder-Ingelheim 1 fol. 150v; Nieder-Ingelheim 1 fol. 181v; Nieder-Ingelheim 2 fol. 12, 100, 101v, 102v-103, 104, 109, 113.
155 Nieder-Ingelheim 1 fol. 188v.
156 Nieder-Ingelheim 1 fol. 12, 188v.
157 POHL 1999.
158 Nieder-Ingelheim 2 fol. 197r-v; "daß idoch keynes wegks gepurt, dan gewalt eynem iglichen verbotten"; Nieder-Ingelheim 1 fol. 12; Ober-Ingelheim 1 fol. 153.
159 Nieder-Ingelheim 2 fol. 6v "welch smehlich wort Joijstenhen hochlich bewegt, aber nichts angefangen, sunder der zijt hijnweg gangen".
160 Nieder-Ingelheim 2 fol. 197v; Ober-Ingelheim 2 fol. 84.
161 See also WALZ, 1996, p. 190; different: DINGES, 1995, pp. 51sq.; FRANK, 1995, pp. 335f.

happened on at market between Henne Scherer and Peter Stortzkopp. Peter Stortzkopp threatened the servant of Henne by pointing the epee to his chin.[162]

Rainer Walz argued that in premodern suburban society people were not able to respond to aggressions adequately so that conflicts regularly turned violent.[163] In Ingelheim, this picture can be modified. There is spontaneous violence and insults caused by too much alcohol, but more often we find insults as a manifestation of a conflict between families and neighbours.[164] The spontaneous incidents seemed to happen without warning[165] or reason.[166] In the other cases, violence was in the air and conflicts could not be resolved – not even by arbitration courts. This is true for the tragic case of Jost Scherer against Hen Pauel. Hen Pauel lost his wife and claimed this to be the fault of the surgeon Jost, who did not treat her correctly. This conflict resulted in tragedy for both families. In the end, Hen Pauel was paralysed and the brother of Jost Scherer was dead.[167] But mostly an escalation could be avoided and the arbitration court found a compromise. This may be a result of the prudent policy of the court. Part of this strategy was to ignore divergent behaviour. I would therefore like to conclude that deviant behaviour was ignored as far as possible and insofar not publicly marked as deviant. Insult and humiliation had no consequences if they happened in certain places and if nobody was physically harmed. However, insults had to be prevented from happening at the market and the town hall, as they brought deviant behaviour not only to the attention of a wider public. If public order was threatened, the court intervened. The court's primary objective was to preserve public order and peace in Ingelheim and its status as a quasi-autonomous community. For this to happen, it seems that the court as well as the commoners of Ingelheim preferred discounting deviance over recounting it.

---

162 Ober-Ingelheim 1 fol. 140r-v. See for ritualized conflicts HÜRLIMANN, 2000.

163 WALZ, 1992, p. 226; FRANK, 1995, pp. 332f.

164 See also HÜRLIMANN, 2000, pp. 102-108.

165 Nieder-Ingelheim 2 fol. 124; Ober-Ingelheim 2 fol. 62v, 84, 88.

166 Nieder-Ingelheim 2 fol. 194r-v.

167 Nieder-Ingelheim 2 fol. 1-19, 36v-39, 41, 55r-v.

Literature

Sources

ERLER, ADALBERT (ed.), Die älteren Urteile des Ingelheimer Oberhofes (Vol. 1-4), Frankfurt a.m. 1952-1963.

Nieder-Ingelheim 1: MARZI, WERNER (ed.), Das Niederingelheimer Haderbuch 1468-1485 (Die Ingelheimer Haderbücher 2), Alzey 2012.

Ober-Ingelheim 1: MARZI, WERNER (ed.), Das Oberingelheimer Haderbuch 1476-1485 (Die Ingelheimer Haderbücher 1), Alzey 2011.

Nieder-Ingelheim 2: MARZI, WERNER (ed.), Das Niederingelheimer Haderbuch 1521-1530 (Die Ingelheimer Haderbücher 3), Alzey 2014.

Ober-Ingelheim 2, Stadtarchiv der Stadt Ingelheim.

RIEDEL, KERSTIN/SCHMITT, SIGRID (eds.), Das Protokollbuch des Niersteiner Rittergerichts (1654-1661) (Quellen und Forschungen zur hessischen Geschichte 122), Darmstadt/Marburg 1999.

Secondary Literature

BAUER, MARTIN, Die „Gemain Sag" im späteren Mittelalter. Studien zu einem Faktor mittelalterlicher Öffentlichkeit und seinem historischen Auskunftswert, Diss. Erlangen-Nürnberg 1981.

BAUMGÄRTNER, INGRID, Gerichtspraxis und Stadtgesellschaft. Zu Zielsetzung und Inhalt, in: Praxis der Gerichtsbarkeit in europäischen Städten des Spätmittelalters (Rechtsprechung. Materialien und Studien 23), ed. by FRANZ-JOSEF ARLINGHAUS et al., Frankfurt a.M. 2006, pp. 1-18.

BEHRISCH, LARS, Gerichtsnutzung ohne Herrschaftskonsens. Kriminalität in Görlitz im 15. und 16. Jahrhundert, in: Verbrechen im Blick. Perspektiven der neuzeitlichen Kriminalitätsgeschichte, ed. by REBEKKA HABERMAS/GERD SCHWERHOFF, Frankfurt-New York 2009, pp. 219-248.

BLATTMANN, MARITA, Beobachtungen zum Schrifteinsatz an einem deutschen Niedergericht um 1400: die Ingelheimer Haderbücher, in:

Als die Welt in die Akten kam. Prozeßschriftgut im europäischen Mittelalter (Rechtsprechung. Materialien und Studien 27), ed. by SUSANNE LEPSIUS/THOMAS WETZSTEIN, Frankfurt a.M. 2008, pp. 51-91.

BLATTMANN, MARITA, Protokollführung in römisch-kanonischen und deutschrechtlichen Gerichtsverfahren im 13. und 14. Jahrhundert, in: Rechtsverständnis und Konfliktbewältigung. Gerichtliche und außergerichtliche Strategien im Mittelalter, ed. by STEFAN. ESDERS, Köln e. a. 2007, pp. 141-164.

BURGHARTZ, SUSANNA, Leib, Ehre und Gut. Delinquenz in Zürich Ende des 14. Jahrhunderts, Zürich 1990.

CORDES, ALBRECHT, Stuben und Stubengesellschaften. Zur dörflichen und kleinstädtischen Verfassungsgeschichte am Oberrhein und in der Nordschweiz, Stuttgart 1993.

DILCHER, GERHARD, Zu Rechtsgewohnheiten und Oralität, Normen und Ritual, Ordnungen und Gewalt, in: Zeitschrift für historische Forschung 38 (2011), pp. 65-80.

DINGES, MARTIN, Die Ehre als Thema der historischen Anthropologie. Bemerkungen zur Wissenschaftsgeschichte und zur Konzeptualisierung, in: Verletzte Ehre. Ehrkonflikte in Gesellschaften des Mittelalters und der Frühen Neuzeit (Norm und Struktur 5), ed. by KLAUS SCHREINER/GERD SCHWERHOFF, Köln et al. 1995, pp. 29-62.

ID., Die Ehre als Thema der Stadtgeschichte. Eine Semantik am Übergang von Ancien Régime zur Moderne, in: Zeitschrift für Historische Forschung 16 (1989), pp. 409-440.

DÜRR, RENATE/SCHWERHOFF, GERD (eds.), Kirchen, Märkte und Tavernen. Erfahrungs- und Handlungsräume in der Frühen Neuzeit, Frankfurt a.M. 2005.

EMMELIUS, CAROLINE (ed.), Offen und verborgen. Vorstellungen und Praktiken des Öffentlichen und Privaten in Mittelalter und Früher Neuzeit, Göttingen 2004.

FRANK, MICHAEL, Ehre und Gewalt im Dorf der Frühen Neuzeit. Das Beispiel Heiden (Grafschaft Lippe) im 17. und 18. Jahrhundert, in: Verletzte Ehre? Ehrkonflikte in Gesellschaften des Mittelalters und der Frühen Neuzeit (Norm und Struktur 5), ed. by KLAUS SCHREINER/GERD SCHWERHOFF, Köln et al. 1995, pp. 320-338.

HENSELMEYER, ULRICH, Ratsherren und andere Delinquenten. Die Rechtsprechungspraxis bei geringfügigen Delikten im spätmittelalterlichen Nürnberg (Konflikt und Kultur. Historische Perspektiven 6), Konstanz 2002.

HÜRLIMANN, KATJA, Soziale Beziehungen im Dorf. Aspekte dörflicher Soziabilität in der Landvogtei Greifensee und Kyrburg um 1500, Zürich 2000.

KALB, HERBERT, Rechtswissenschaften, Rechtsgeschichte und der Gesetzesbegriff im Mittelalter, in: Das Gesetz - The Law - La Loi (Miscellanea mediaevalia. Veröffentlichungen des Thomas-Instituts an der Universität Köln 38), ed. by ANDREAS SPEER/GUY GULDEN-TOPS, Berlin et al. 2014, pp. 3-18.

KINTZINGER, MARTIN/SCHNEIDMÜLLER, BERND (eds.), Politische Öffentlichkeit im Spätmittelalter (Vorträge und Forschungen 75), Ostfildern 2011.

KRISCHER, ANDRÉ, Im Dienst der Gemeinde. Zur Funktion des spätmittelalterlichen Landgerichts, in: Archiv für hessische Geschichte und Altertumskunde NF 60 (2002), pp. 333-369.

ID., Rituale und politische Öffentlichkeit in der Alten Stadt, in: Stadt und Öffentlichkeit in der Frühen Neuzeit (Städteforschung A 83), ed. by GERD SCHWERHOFF, Köln u.a. 2011, pp. 125-157.

KRUG-RICHTER, BARBARA, Streitkulturen. Perspektiven der Volkskunde/Europäischen Ethnologie, in: Die Kunst des Streitens. Inszenierung, Formen und Funktionen öffentlichen Streits in historischer Perspektive (Super alta perennis 10), ed. by MARC LAUREYS/ROSWITHA SIMONS, Bonn 2010, pp. 331-351.

ID., Das Privathaus als Wirtshaus. Zur Öffentlichkeit des Hauses in Regionen mit Reihebraurecht, in: Zwischen Gotteshaus und Taverne. Öffentliche Räume in Spätmittelalter und Früher Neuzeit (Norm und Struktur 21), ed. by SUSANNE RAU/GERD SCHWERHOFF Köln et al. 2004, pp. 99-117.

KÜMIN, BEAT, In Vino res publica? Politische Soziabilität im Wirtshaus der Frühen Neuzeit, in: Stadt und Öffentlichkeit in der frühen Neuzeit – Perspektiven der Forschung (Städteforschung A 83), ed. by GERD SCHWERHOFF, Köln et al. 2011, pp. 65-79.

LORENZEN-SCHMIDT, KLAUS-J., Beleidigungen in schleswig-holsteinischen Städten im 16. Jahrhundert. Soziale Norm und soziale

Kontrolle in Städtegesellschaften, in: Kieler Blätter zur Volkskunde 10 (1978), pp. 5-29.

LÜCK, HEINER, Nach Herkommen und Gewohnheit. Beobachtungen zum Gewohnheitsrecht in der spätmittelalterlichen Gerichtsverfassung Kursachsens, in: Gewohnheitsrecht und Rechtsgewohnheiten im Mittelalter (Schriften zur Europäischen Rechts- und Verfassungsgeschichte 6), Berlin 1992, pp. 149-160.

MELVILLE, GERT/VON MOOS, PETER (eds.), Das Öffentliche und Private in der Vormoderne (Norm und Struktur 10), Köln et al. 1998.

MEYER, CHRISTOPH H.F., Das Publicum als Instrument spätmittelalterlicher Justiz, in: Politische Öffentlichkeit im Spätmittelalter (Vorträge und Forschungen 75), ed. by MARTIN KINTZINGER/BERND SCHNEIDMÜLLER, Ostfildern 2011, pp. 87-145.

VON MOOS, PETER, „Öffentlich" und „privat" im Mittelalter. Zu einem Problem historischer Begriffsbildung, Heidelberg 2004.

MIERAU, HEIKE JOHANNA, Fama als Mittel zur Herstellung von Öffentlichkeit und Gemeinwohl in der Zeit des Konziliarismus, in: Politische Öffentlichkeit im Spätmittelalter (Vorträge und Forschungen 75), ed. by MARTIN KINTZINGER/BERND SCHNEIDMÜLLER, Ostfildern 2011, pp. 237-286.

MONNET, PIERRE, Die Stadt, ein Ort der politischen Öffentlichkeit im Spätmittelalter? Ein Thesenpapier, in: Politische Öffentlichkeit im Spätmittelalter (Vorträge und Forschungen 75), ed. by MARTIN KINTZINGER/BERND SCHNEIDMÜLLER, Ostfildern 2011, pp. p. 329-359.

PILCH, MARTIN, Rechtsgewohnheiten aus rechtshistorischer und rechtstheoretischer Perspektive, in: Rechtsgeschichte. Zeitschrift des Max-Planck-Instituts für europäische Rechtsgeschichte 17 (2010), pp. 17-39.

POHL, SUSANNE, Ehrlicher Totschlag. Rache, Notwehr. Zwischen männlichem Ehrencode und dem Primat des Stadtfriedens (Zürich 1376-1600), in: Kulturelle Reformation. Sinnformationen im Umbruch 1400-1600, ed. by BERNHARD JUSSEN. Göttingen 1999, pp. 239-283.

RAU, SUSANNE, Orte – Akteure – Netzwerke. Zur Konstitution öffentlicher Räume in einer frühneuzeitlichen Fernhandelsstadt, in: Zwischen Gotteshaus und Taverne. Öffentliche Räume in Spätmittelalter und Früher Neuzeit (Norm und Struktur 21), ed. by SUSANNE RAU/GERD SCHWERHOFF, Köln et al. 2004, pp. 39-63.

RAU, SUSANNE/SCHWERHOFF, GERD: Öffentliche Räume in der Frühen Neuzeit. Überlegungen zu Leitbegriffen und Themen eines Forschungsfeldes, in: Zwischen Gotteshaus und Taverne. Öffentliche Räume in Spätmittelalter und Früher Neuzeit (Norm und Struktur 21), ed. by SUSANNE RAU/GERD SCHWERHOFF, Köln et al. 2004, pp. 11-52.

SCHÄFER, REGINA, Rechtsprechung ohne Gesetz? Die Rechtsentscheidungen der Schöffen von Niedergerichten, in: Das Gesetz – The Law – La Loi (Miscellanea mediaevalia. Veröffentlichungen des Thomas-Instituts an der Universität Köln 38), ed. by ANDREAS SPEER/GUY GULDENTOPS, Berlin 2014, pp. 152-178.

SCHÄFER, REGINA 2012a, Friede durch Recht. Zur Funktion des Dorfgerichts in der Gemeinde. In: Dorf und Gemeinde. Grundstrukturen der ländlichen Gesellschaft in Spätmittelalter und Frühneuzeit (Kraichtaler Kolloquien 8), ed. by KURT ANDERMANN/OLIVER AUGE, Epfendorf 2012, pp. 65-85.

SCHÄFER, REGINA, 2012b, Ingelheim im Spätmittelalter – eine Gemeinde zwischen Dorf und Stadt, in: Alltag, Herrschaft, Gesellschaft und Gericht im Spiegel der spätmittelalterlichen Ingelheimer Haderbücher. Ein Begleitband zum Editionsprojekt „Ingelheimer Haderbücher" (Beiträge zur Ingelheimer Geschichte 50), ed. by WERNER MARZI/REGINA SCHÄFER, Alzey 2012, pp. 47-63.

SCHÄFER, REGINA 2012c, Das soziale Gefüge im Ort Ober-Ingelheim, in: Alltag, Herrschaft, Gesellschaft und Gericht im Spiegel der spätmittelalterlichen Ingelheimer Haderbücher. Ein Begleitband zum Editionsprojekt „Ingelheimer Haderbücher" (Beiträge zur Ingelheimer Geschichte 50), ed. by WERNER MARZI/REGINA SCHÄFER, Alzey 2012, pp. 65-80.

SCHREINER, KLAUS/SCHWERHOFF, GERD, Verletzte Ehre? Überlegungen zu einem Forschungskonzept, in: Verletzte Ehre. Ehrkonflikte in Gesellschaften des Mittelalters und der Frühen Neuzeit (Norm und Struktur 5), ed. by KLAUS SCHREINER/GERD SCHWERHOFF, Köln et al. 1995, pp. 1-28.

SCHULZE, REINER „Gewohnheitsrecht" und „Rechtsgewohnheiten" im Mittelalter – eine Einführung, in: Gewohnheitsrecht und

Rechtsgewohnheiten im Mittelalter (Schriften zur Europäischen Rechts- und Verfassungsgeschichte 6), ed. by GERHARD DILCHER et al., Berlin 1992, pp. 9-20.

SCHUSTER, PETER, Der gelobte Frieden. Täter, Opfer und Herrschaft im spätmittelalterlichen Konstanz, Konstanz 1995.

ID., Eine Stadt vor Gericht. Recht und Alltag im spätmittelalterlichen Konstanz, Paderborn et al. 2000.

ID., Verbrechen und Strafe in der spätmittelalterlichen Nürnberger und Augsburger Chronistik, in: Recht und Verhalten in vormodernen Gesellschaften. Festschrift für Neithard Bulst, ed. by ANDREA BENDLAGE et al., Bielefeld 2008, pp. 51-65.

SCHWERHOFF, GERD, Gewaltkriminalität im Wandel (14.-18. Jahrhundert). Ergebnisse und Perspektiven der Forschung, in: Kriminalisieren, Entkriminalisieren, Normalisieren (Schweizerische Gesellschaft für Wirtschafts- und Sozialgeschichte 21), ed. CLAUDIA OPITZ et al., Zürich 2006, pp. 55-72.

ID., Köln im Kreuzverhör. Kriminalität, Herrschaft und Gesellschaft in einer frühneuzeitlichen Stadt, Bonn 1991.

ID., Das Gelage. Institutionelle Ordnungsarrangements und Machtkämpfe im frühneuzeitlichen Wirtshaus, in: Das Sichtbare und das Unsichtbare der Macht. Institutionelle Prozesse in Antike, Mittelalter und Neuzeit, ed. by GERT MELVILLE, Köln 2005, pp. 159-176.

ID. (ed.), Stadt und Öffentlichkeit in der frühen Neuzeit – Perspektiven der Forschung. In: Stadt und Öffentlichkeit in der frühen Neuzeit (Städteforschung A 83), Köln et al. 2011, pp. 1-28.

ID., Blasphmare, dehonestare et maledicere Deum. Über die Verletzung der göttlichen Ehre im Spätmittelalter, in: Verletzte Ehre. Ehrkonflikte in Gesellschaften des Mittelalters und der Frühen Neuzeit (Norm und Struktur 5), ed. by KLAUS SCHREINER/GERD SCHWERHOFF, Köln et al. 1995, pp. 252-278.

ID., Die Policey im Wirtshaus. Obrigkeitliche und gesellschaftliche Normen im öffentlichen Raum der Frühen Neuzeit. Das Beispiel der Reichsstadt Köln, in: Machträume der frühneuzeitlichen Stadt, ed. by CHRISTIAN HOCHMUTH/SUSANNE RAU, Konstanz 2006, pp. 355-376.

ID., Gewaltkriminalität im Wandel (14.-18. Jahrhundert). Ergebnisse und Perspektiven der Forschung, in: Kriminalisieren – Entkriminalisieren – Normalisieren (Schweizerische Gesellschaft für Wirtschafts- und Sozialgeschichte 21), ed. by CLAUDIA OPITZ et al., Zürich 2006, pp. 55-72.

TEUSCHER, SIMON, Erzähltes Recht. Lokale Herrschaft, Verschriftlichung und Traditionsbildung im Spätmittelalter, Frankfurt a.M. 2007 = Lord's Rights and Peasant Stories: Writing and the Formation of Tradition in the Later Middle Ages, Philadelphia 2012.

ID., Devianz, Gewalt, Soziabilität und Verwandtschaft am Übergang vom Mittelalter zur Neuzeit, in: Traverse 18 (2011), pp. 77-103.

TLUSTY, B. ANN, ‚Privat‘ oder ‚öffentlich‘? Das Wirtshaus in der deutschen Stadt des 16. Und 17. Jahrhunderts, in: Zwischen Gotteshaus und Taverne. Öffentliche Räume in Spätmittelalter und Früher Neuzeit (Norm und Struktur 21), ed. by SUSANNE RAU/GERD SCHWERHOFF, Köln et al. 2004, pp. 53-73.

TOCH, MICHAEL, Schimpfwörter im Dorf des Spätmittelalters, in: Mitteilungen des Österreichischen Instituts für Geschichtswissenschaft 101 (1993), pp. 311-327.

WALZ, RAINER, Schimpfende Weiber. Frauen in lippischen Beleidigungsprozessen des 17. Jahrhunderts, in: Weiber, Menschen, Frauenzimmer. Frauen in der ländlichen Gesellschaft, ed. by HEIDE WUNDER/CHRISTINA VANJA, Göttingen 1996, pp. 175-198.

ID., Agonale Kommunikation im Dorf der Frühen Neuzeit, in: Westfälische Forschungen 42 (1992), pp. 215-251.

WECHSLER, ELISABETH, Ehre und Politik. Ein Beitrag zur Erfassung politischer Verhaltensweisen in der Eidgenossenschaft (1440-1500) unter historisch-anthropologischen Aspekten, Zürich 1991.

WEITZEL, JÜRGEN, Dinggenossenschaft und Recht. Untersuchungen zum Rechtsverständnis im fränkisch-deutschen Mittelalter (Quellen und Forschungen zur höchsten Gerichtsbarkeit im alten Reich 15), Köln et al. 1985.

ID., Gewohnheitsrecht und fränkisch-deutsches Gerichtsverfahren, in: in: Gewohnheitsrecht und Rechtsgewohnheiten im Mittelalter (Schriften zur Europäischen Rechts- und Verfassungsgeschichte 6), ed. by GERHARD DILCHER et al., Berlin 1992, pp. 67-86.

WETZSTEIN, THOMAS, Prozeßschriftgut im Mittelalter – einführende Überlegungen, in: Als die Welt in die Akten kam. Prozeßschriftgut im europäischen Mittelalter (Rechtsprechung. Materialien und Studien 27), ed. by SUSANNE LEPSIUS/THOMAS WETZSTEIN, Frankfurt a.M. 2008, pp. 1-27.

The Presentation of Deviant Behaviour in the Crowland Chronicle Continuations

JUDITH MENGLER

Crowland is situated in the county Lincolnshire. The Crowland abbey was a Benedictine monastery and founded in 714 by Ethelbald, King of Mercia, in memory of St. Guthlac, a saint who was believed to have settled down in Crowland in 699. Up to the 12th century, the monastery had an eventful history and was destroyed several times: In 866 or 870 it was not only vandalised by the Danes, but the entire community of monks had been slaughtered as well. After the reestablishment of the abbey in 966, it was again destroyed by fire in 1091 and a second time in 1170.[1] Shortly after this second fire disaster, it was rebuilt and, according to the official webpage, "From this time the history of Crowland was one of growing and almost unbroken prosperity down to the time of the Dissolution."[2]

This sounds like a happy end to a fairy tale and, according to Pronay and Cox, the editors of the Second Continuation of the Crowland chronicle, it is indeed a fairy tale or at least not the whole truth. From the outset, the geographical situation proved to be a blessing and a curse at the same time. The monastery was hidden away in the marches of the fen land, which meant, it was also hidden from the appetites of foreign enemies, the depredations caused by passing armies and the dangers of

---

1   PRONAY/COX, 1986, pp.1-2.; see also the webpage: http://www.crowland abbey.org.uk/history/ (19.8.2015).
2   http://www.crowlandabbey.org.uk/history/ (19.8.2015).

disturbances such as riots or rebellions. However, the monastery was also far away from the liveliness and the markets of the cities and important trade routes. Initially, the abbey had access to an area of rich soils, but as times went by, the growing abbey of Peterborough, built between the Crowland abbey and the area in question, stopped the potential flow of money like a cork in a bottle of wine. In addition to that, agriculture work in the fens was quite difficult and the small area of solid land on which the abbey was built left restricted scope for additional buildings. Much work had been done and much money had been spent to build a drainage system, the maintenance of which was very costly.[3] The other famous landmark of the town of Crowland, the Trinity Bridge, built in the 14th century, may be a symbol for the original landscape and also a lifestyle dominated by water. Until the 19th century, it was common to use waterways and canals in the fens and the Trinity Bridge spans the point, where the River Welland divided into two streams, both used as waterways; one led past the abbey, the other one northwards towards the village Spalding.[4]

The Crowland Abbey and its neighbours

The rather unfavourable geographical location led, hardly surprising, to an increasing struggle for resources; especially the rise of the abbey of Peterborough, which had considerably better conditions, was watched suspiciously by the community of Crowland. The abbey of Peterborough was surrounded by rather rich soil and was located directly on the old Roman road connecting London and York. Therefore, this abbey accumulated noteworthy wealth, which enabled it to improve its status and reputation and this, in an upwards spiral, increased its wealth. At the time of the English reformation and the dissolution of the monasteries, Peterborough was almost twice as rich as Crowland. The competitive situation, in which Crowland was clearly disadvantaged, lead to envy and jealousy and, finally, to hostility. The abbeys accompanied their struggle with protracted and expensive lawsuits, for example,

3   PRONAY/COX, 1986, pp. 1-2.
4   http://www.transportheritage.com/find-heritage-locations.html?sobi2Task =sobi2Details&sobi2Id=238 (19.8.2015).

about the belonging of the church of Bringhurst and the marsh of Alder-land.[5] The following sentences concerning the mentioned dispute about the marsh of Alderland may provide an impression of the aversion and bitterness the monks of Crowland felt.

> "But all this kind of disturbance is slight in comparison [...] which William Ramsey, abbot of Peterborough, then our over-close (would that I could say good!) neighbour created concerning the marsh of Alderland and other lands and rights which belonged, without doubt, to this monastery. In these affairs, which were long in dispute, you might have seen the lamb arguing with the wolf, the mouse with the cat. However, since all this litigation was finally brought to an end by the arbitration and award of Lord Thomas Rotherham, recently bishop of Lincoln, ordinary of this place and subse-quently Archbishop of York, (as is fully recorded in certain letters of attes-tation then drawn up, where it is quite plain which side's interest and hon-our more fully concerned him), we have decided to conclude the whole tragic story at the time of the death of this father, Abbot Richard."[6]

But what was the other disturbance the author wrote about? The abbey of Crowland not only had disagreements with the abbey of Peterbor-ough, it had problems with the villages in the vicinity, too. The author tells us about conflicts with the men of Deeping[7], the tenants and pa-rishioners of Whaplode[8], and with the inhabitants of Moulton and Wes-ton[9]. The conflicts were about claims of land, payment of duties, most frequently about the expenses and work performance to maintain the drainage, and a bulk of other things. In some instances, the mere desire for revenge seems to have played the strongest role. The disputes re-sulted in never-ending and countless lawsuits as well as, occasionally, in acts of violence against the monks of Crowland.

---

5   PRONAY/COX, 1986, pp. 167-169; 189; pp. 199-201.
6   IBID., pp.167-169.
7   IBID., p.167.
8   IBID.
9   IBID., p.187; RILEY, 1854, pp. 394-396.

The Continuations of the Crowland Chronicle

But why are these things important for the understanding of the continuations of the Crowland Chronicle? The continuations of the chronicle of the monastery were both written in the 15th century. The First Continuation was written by an unnamed prior of the abbey and is therefore called "Prior's Continuation". The author starts his report with the reign of King Stephen and concludes with the death of Abbot John in January 1470. The anonymous Second Continuation of the chronicle covers the period from October 1459 until 1486.[10] Both continuations are regarded as an important source for the disturbances and uprisings in England in the late 15th century, which subsequently became known as "The Wars of the Roses". The Second Continuation is famous as "the best of the rather scanty narratives of the Yorkist era"[11] and especially for its critical assessment of King Richard III.[12] The parts of the continuations in which the high politics of England, the exciting events on the battlefields or the ingeniously planned intrigues at court are given, deemed to be the mostly read texts by historians concerned with the Wars of the Roses. In consequence, one could deplore the non-observance of the parts of the chronicle concerning the history of the abbey of Crowland, which were not infrequently underestimated as "irrelevant details about interim events of concern only to the monks of Crowland Abbey."[13] It must be borne in mind that the chronicle was not intended to be "A short history of the Wars of the Roses" and that using only fragments of it will limit our understanding and impede knowledge about the narrative structure of the text.[14] But it was also not intended to be a nice collection of stories about pious monks. In his concluding sentences, the prior explains his reasons for writing his continuation.

---

10 WILLIAMS, 1987, p. 371; HICKS, 2005, p. 350.
11 HICKS, 2007, p. 349.
12 "*The Continuations of the Crowland Chronicle* will not be the favourite reading of most members of the Richard III Society." as Hanham puts it with a wink. HANHAM, 2008, p. 1.
13 IBID.
14 WILLIAMS, 1987, p. 380.

"It was our design, in conformity with the introductory remarks at the beginning of this volume in due order, although in different style, to hand down to posterity the agreements made between the kings of England and the abbots of this monastery, together with a multitude of incidents which bore reference to the state of the kingdom or of this place."[15]

In other words, his part of the chronicle is, first and foremost, a history of the rights and contracts of the monastery and only secondarily a report of events in which we are interested today. The "incidents which bore reference to the state of the kingdom" are the broader frameworks in which "the incidents of this place" are inserted. As we shall see, these incidents of the monastery are mostly stories about the evil and malicious neighbours and serve as illustration of the unlawfulness of their claims against Crowland. The primary purpose is to prove and justify the rights and claims of the abbey; the aim is "to enhance for legal purposes the authenticity of the abbey's lands, rights, jurisdictions or claims to them, by using history as a vehicle of chronology and memory for ancient and previous grants – fictitious or otherwise."[16] This intention is artfully hidden behind or linked with the mentioned "vehicle", the history of the kingdom.[17] In his introductory remarks, the author of the Second Continuation also provides some hints of the planned content.

"[...] there now follows a continuation of relevant events in the English state as well as elsewhere, and of affairs in the monastery of Crowland, in particular."[18]

Obviously, he doesn't explicitly mention any agreements or contracts. In the next sentences the general orientation of his work becomes clearer. The author explains, why, in his opinion, the overlapping of the reporting period of the two continuations is necessary.

---

15 RILEY, 1854, p. 450.
16 WILLIAMS, 1987, p. 373.
17 IBID.
18 PRONAY/COX, 1986, p. 109.

"[...] some things should be noted which were omitted from the foregoing account by the said prior-chronicler – either because of his commitment to holy religion which usually ignores worldly matters or for the sake of brevity, as he expressly declares – so that it might be clear from the beginning how the kingdom of England was agitated by many warlike incursions [...]"[19]

This means, that the author describes especially the history of England until his report reaches January 1470, because his predecessor was more orientated on religious matters. Therefore, he left out events, which the second continuator considered as quite important. In his point of view, these are the "worldly matters". The descriptions in the Prior's Continuation of the struggle with and law-suits against the neighbours are, in our perspective, clearly "worldly", but in the author's perspective, everything belonging to the history of the abbey seems to be religious.[20] After the given date, the author of the Second Continuation refers to the history of the kingdom as well as to the history of the monastery. The continuator strictly separates the history of England from that of the abbey of Crowland by following a strict narrative structure. He gives the events relating to the kingdom and always stops at the date of the abbot's death. Then he tells something about the merits of the abbot and the incidents, which took place during his lifetime. He gives a short introduction of the next abbot, a very brief prospect about his deeds and the date of his death and ends up with the promise of providing more details when this date is reached. Then the history of England is continued.[21]

For the sake of completeness, it should be mentioned now, that the Second Continuation was repeatedly the subject of discussions. One could say without exaggeration that multitudes of articles have been written about the intention, the dating and especially the authorship of the Second Continuation of the Crowland Chronicle.[22] This paper is not

---

19 IBID.
20 HICKS, 2005, p. 185.
21 PRONAY/COX, 1986, pp. 69-70.
22 See HICKS, 2005, p. 173, footnote 6 for a list of publications concerning the continuation and its authorship. The candidates suggested up to now are Piers Curteys, Dr John Gunthorpe, Dr Richard Lavender, Bishop John

designed to be an independent chapter in "the long-running whodunit produced by those scholars who have attempted to solve the mystery of Crowland's anonymous Historian."[23] Without new evidence, the question of authorship has to remain unresolved and the proposal of new (or old) candidates will be highly speculative and guesswork, however educated it may be. The subject of the analysis in this paper is the narration and assessment of deviant behaviour in the continuations of the Crowland Chronicle. According to the reasons and explanations about the authors' purpose for writing their texts as well as their specific orientation, differences in both concerning this subject are expectable. To be more concrete, the expectations are as follows:

- The prior is especially concerned with religious matters and will therefore be extremely sensitive to deviances from religious norms and rules.
- The second continuator is more concerned with the politics of the kingdom and will therefore be extremely sensitive to breaking political norms and rules.
- Both authors have to deal with the struggles of the monastery with its neighbours, so we can expect that both accuse them of breaking rules and norms. In this case, maybe the prior may stress the religious sphere whereas the second continuator concentrates on the worldly.

The analysis: The Case of Richard III and Elizabeth of York

I shall begin with quite well known personalities, Richard III and Elizabeth of York. Without doubt, one could comment on many issues concerning Richard III and the assessment of deviancy in the chronicles as well as the Second Continuation of the Crowland Chronicle.[24] This

---

Russell, Dr Henry Sharp, and Richard Langport. HICKS, 2005, p. 174, footnote 7.

23 HANHAM, 2008, p. 2.

24 See for example: PRONAY/COX, 1986, p. 156 (capture of King Edward's relatives), p. 159 (execution of Lord Hastings), p. 161 (executions of Earl Rivers and Richard Grey), p. 165 (death of Thomas St. Leger).

question alone could provide enough material for another paper, but, for the sake of brevity and in accordance with the purpose to present rather unfamiliar parts of the chronicle, I chose this story and will leave it at that.

For the year 1484, after deploring the high taxes and the waste of money, a complaint popular at all times, the author reports an event, which should appear to be a huge scandal.

> "There are many other things besides, which are not written in this book and of which it is grievous to speak; nevertheless it should not be left unsaid that during this Christmas feast too much attention was paid to singing and dancing and to vain exchanges of clothing between Queen Anne and Lady Elizabeth, eldest daughter of the dead king, who were alike in complexion and figure. The people spoke against this and the magnates and prelates were greatly astonished and it was said by many that the king was applying his mind in every way to contracting a marriage with Elizabeth either after the death of the queen, or by means of a divorce for which he believed he had sufficient grounds. He saw no other way of confirming his crown and dispelling the hopes of his rival. A few days later the queen began to be seriously ill and her sickness was then believed to have got worse and worse because the king himself was completely spurning his consort's bed. Therefore he judged it right to consult with doctors. What more is there to be said? About the middle of the following March, on the day when a great eclipse of the sun took place, Queen Anne died and was buried at Westminster with honours no less than befitted the burial of a queen."[25]

Firstly, the author criticises the luxury and exuberance, here the singing and dancing and vain exchange of clothing at Christmas. This criticism is directly associated with the aforesaid complaint about the tax situation and is also linked with the problem of the relationship between King Richard, Queen Anne, and Lady Elizabeth. The interchangeability of the clothes could be read as a symbol for the interchangeability of the two women intended by King Richard. It is said that Richard planned to marry Elizabeth in order to confirm his power and that he would even take into account a divorce. A few days later, the queen took ill. The mention of the eclipse of the sun could be a hint that, in the author's

25 PRONAY/COX, 1986, p. 175.

opinion, not everything was above board with the death of Queen Anne. And the author was not alone in this opinion; although he does not clearly express it in this part of the text, there naturally were rumours about the possibility that the queen had been poisoned by her husband. He continues with the report about a meeting in London on 30th March 1485[26] and only now he provides details of the suspicion of murder and the true scandal. According to the continuator, Richard III was compelled to deny in public that he ever intended to marry Elizabeth, otherwise

"[...] the northeners, in whom he placed the greatest trust, would all rise against him, charging him with causing the death of the queen, the daughter and one of the heirs of the earl of Warwick and through whom he had obtained his first honour in order to complete his incestuous association with his near kinswoman, to the offence of God."[27]

Here, he let the cat out of the bag. Not only were the dubious circumstances of the death of Queen Anne subject of discussions, but also the degree of kinship between Richard and Elizabeth. Lady Elizabeth was not only the "eldest daughter of the dead king", as it is stated in the text; she was, of course, King Richard's niece. Therefore, the planned marriage was "incestuous" and "to the offence of God". To confirm this assessment, more than a dozen doctors of theology were present "who asserted that the Pope had no power of dispensation over that degree of consanguinity".[28] One could easily claim that this is quite a lot of effort to prove a fact that is presented as being self-evident. In fact, there was a contemporary theological and legal discourse on such questions, as Kelly lines out in detail in his paper and concludes "If Richard had seriously desired to marry his niece, he would have been well advised to request a dispensation" and "his request might very well have met

---

26   The content of the rumours and the public denial is also given in the Acts of Court of the Mercers' Company: "[...] that the quene as by concent & will of the Kyng was poysoned for & to thentent that he might then marry and haue to wyfe lady Elizabeth, eldest doughter of his broder [...]". LY-ELL/WATNEY, 1936, p. 173.

27   PRONAY/COX, 1986, p. 175.

28   IBID., p. 177.

with success".[29] Besides the Pope's power of dispensation, the question of the correct reading of Leviticus 18 was frequently discussed.

The point I would like to make is that there were enough possibilities for the continuator to insert biblical references or religious remarks, according to his own opinion for or against. But the statement that the whole affair was to the offence of God, which could be read as an assessment, is only given at the very end of the story; in addition to that it is somehow softened by it being imbedded in the political framework. It is not stated as a matter of plain fact, but is said in council by two squires of the body that the Northerners, the political pillar of the reign of Richard III, could bring such a charge besides others. Obviously, the religious aspect of the problem is clearly subordinate to the political.

Other parts of the Second Continuation confirm this impression. In 1477, the author witnessed the trial against Stacey and Burden, both, among other things, accused of attempted murder by the means of necromancy and black magic. They were arrested and sentenced to death, even though they declared their innocence.[30] The author provides the information about the trial as part of the developments which led to the execution of the Duke of Clarence.[31] Consequently, he does not linger on the malpractice of black arts. But, unlike in the foregoing example, he uses a biblical reference[32], namely the case of Susanna.[33] Already under the gallows, Burdet "with great spirit and many words as though, like Susanna, in the end he was saying 'Behold I die, though I have done none of these things'".[34] With the mention of Susanna, the author makes it implicitly clear that the declaration of innocence rendered by Burdet is trustworthy. Susanna was wrongly accused and sentenced to death. To mention her name here creates an association between her innocence and that of Burdet. This declaration of innocence, one has to add, was read out at the instigation of the Duke of Clarence in the council one day after the execution. It was this incident, the author claims, which led to the arrest of the duke and finally his execution. The func-

29 KELLY, 1967, p. 307.
30 PRONAY/COX, 1986, p. 145.
31 IBID., p. 147.
32 See HANHAM, 2008, pp. 9-10 for more examples of biblical references in the Second Continuation.
33 DANIEL 13, 1-64.
34 PRONAY/COX, 1986, p. 145, see also HICKS, 2005, p. 183.

tion of the biblical reference is therefore quite political: The continuator sharply criticises the killing of the Duke of Clarence.

Again, although it was a good opportunity for religious remarks, especially about the detestable practice of black magic and devil worship, the author is more interested in the political impact. The possible objection that he would omit such remarks for the sake of brevity can be refuted by looking at some further examples in which the author proves his eye for detail.

In his quite short report about the entry of King Edward after his victories at Barnet and Tewkesbury into London, he provides such a detail: The king had ordered to unfurl his banner and carries it before him.[35] The entire procedure of the entry, and one could imagine it was remarkable, is not really described. However, this special detail is given, as well as the reaction of the spectators – they "were shocked and surprised at this, knowing that there was no enemy left"[36] – and an attempt of an explanation, here the following punishment of the Kentish rebels. Naturally, the spectators were shocked, because the unfurled banner is a sign which belongs on a battlefield and signals open conflict and war. It is not just unusual in this context; it is clearly breaking the rules of political communication and an explanation of this unheard-of event is therefore needed and given. Here, the author does not miss the opportunity to make additional remarks about the deviation from political rules.

The struggles of the Abbey

The author is possibly more concerned with religious matters when he writes about the history of a religious place that is Crowland. Because of the struggle with their neighbours, the monks of Crowland witnessed many disturbances of their pious calm. In 1483, the people of Whaplode attacked "brother Lambert Fossedyke, seneschal of the place, with unheard-of violence",[37] because he had forbidden them to uproot trees in the cemetery. He was attacked so fiercely that, according to the

---

35 PRONAY/COX, 1986, p. 129.
36 IBID.
37 IBID., p. 167.

chronicle, he was in fear for his life. Fortunately, he could escape and locked himself into the sacristy of the church.[38] Again, the story could have been a nice opportunity to mention the holiness of places such as churches and graveyards and again the author decided to remain silent. A more serious attack was committed by the people of Deeping, who came with 300 men into the lands of the abbey, more exactly to the marsh of Coggyslound, and the village of Crowland. They took away the reeds collected by the tenants as well as grain and victuals and levied distraints along the water-way. The tenants offering resistance were not treated very gently.[39] Both incidents took place within a short period of time because, in the author's opinion, the enemies were encouraged to rise against the abbey by the fact that the abbot showed a "simple innocence and innocent simplicity".[40] Here, pious devotion seems to be a handicap. The people of Deeping are, consequently, not stigmatised as bad Christians. Instead, their loathsomeness is illustrated by the description of a senseless act of violence, the transfixion with arrows of the cellarer's guard-dog. Brutality and unwarranted or "unheard-of violence" are considered negatively, not the unchristian behaviour.

The Case Witham

In the Prior's Continuation, the lack of good character traits of the opponents is described by other means. For the year 1450, the following story is reported: A certain John Witham, Esquire, held some rights in the village of Baston, whereas the abbey of Crowland held the principal manor in the village. Therefore, it was the position of the abbot, that John Witham owed him an annual rent of two pounds of incense, as it was paid in former times, and that Witham should stop usurping liberties which belonged to the abbot as the principal lord. Witham denied the accusations and the case became an activity field for the lawyers.[41] In the matter of plain facts, the story is as simple as this. But the prior wants to convince his readers that Witham was not only wrong in a

---

38 IBID.
39 IBID.
40 IBID.
41 RILEY, 1854, pp. 414-415.

legal but also in a moral sense. Before he informs us about possible proceedings of the law courts, he tells us about a chapel upon the land in question, which had been consecrated a long time ago. Witham didn't only claim this land to be his, but initially held court in the originally holy place and then

> "[...] for the purpose of profaning the place, with sacrilegious lips ordered a stable to be made therein, for his horses; and then, besides, a thing more incident still, encouraging the others who were with him to do the same, he irreverently made water against the walls thereof; and thus did he, so far as in him lay, disgrace to the house of the Lord."[42]

It was this behaviour, the prior continues, which prompted the abbot to prosecute Witham with the utmost eagerness before the courts of the kingdom and the church. The multiple and lengthy lawsuits finally ruined Witham; he was no longer able to support his household and had to frequent the houses of his neighbours. At the end of this development, he had to beg for his daily subsistence. Only then, in his greatest disgrace, he acknowledged his mistakes and asked the abbot to forgive him. A deed was drawn up and sealed, in which he confessed himself guilty and declared, neither he nor his heirs would make any such claims in the future and he would always be willing to pay the owed rent. The provisions of the deed are given precise and in length.[43]

Obviously, the prior uses two different levels in his narration. The first level is the juristic one. As already said, a summary of the story in which only the legal side is regarded could be very short and simple: Witham claimed rights which belonged to the abbot of Crowland, and because he could not afford the costs for the lawyers any longer, he finally had to surrender. For the purpose of the chronicle, the justification and proving of the rights of the abbey, it would be helpful to insert and name precisely the rights and liberties as well as the lands in question. Furthermore, the settlement of the dispute to the advantage of the abbey should be carefully preserved for posterity. The prior did both in his report, in accordance with his duties. The second is a religious level and the story rendered is a story of crime (or sin) and punishment. It

---

42 IBID.
43 IBID.

shows the very central idea that the punishment of a crime should reflect the committed misdeeds and also their underlying causes. Witham's wrongdoing is the disgracing of the chapel, but this sin expanded and became increasingly detestable in a number of evolution stages. At the beginning, he profaned the place by holding court there. In a second step, the chapel was further degraded by turning it into a stable for horses. The third step is the maximum of disgracing a holy place; Witham not only urinates against the walls, but also requests others to do the same. In the same manner the punishments Witham had to face for his crimes evolved. At the beginning, he was not able to support a household adequate to his rank any longer which means he was threatened by social decline. But he had not lost his rank yet, because, in a second step, he was compelled but also able to frequent his neighbours. The reliance on the neighbours, meaning to Whitham's peers, showed them his needy position and had the potential to degrade him in their eyes. Finally, he was so impoverished that he had to worry about his daily subsistence and became a laughing stock. He was not only degraded, he was totally disgraced just as he had degraded and disgraced the chapel. Moreover, one could suggest that the problems he had to face securing his daily subsistence are the direct consequence of his most disrespectful action: Godlessness shown by output could cause huge problems to the deserved input. Salvation from his pitiful condition presupposed Witham's confession and the absolution by a priest. This was achieved by his submission to the abbot of Crowland and the sealing of the mentioned document in which he gave up his rights.

Interestingly, after the conclusion of the story concerning Witham, the prior inserted the history of the second protagonist, the history of the consecration of the chapel.[44] This passage also culminates in a deed, this time a letter testimonial about the consecration of the chapel and it's belonging to Crowland. Thus, the first part of the story ends with the reconciliation with Witham, the second part ends with the, at least verbal, re-consecration or reassuring of the consecration. In a more pragmatic point of view, the prior managed to recount two deeds in just one story. In summary, it is a story about the origins of juristically relevant documents where the opponent is illustrated as a despicable person by the means of showing his unchristian behaviour.

44 IBID., pp. 415-417.

70

With regard to the political sphere, I am inclined to agree with the second continuator. The prior chronicler omitted many events, which makes it difficult to assess. For example, the years 1453 to summer 1459, which are the years of the outbreak of the Wars of the Roses, are all together mentioned in less than two pages.[45] Usually, only events with an effect or a connection to the abbey of Crowland are described in detail, for example the visit of King Henry to the abbey.[46] The prior was either not particularly well informed or not interested in the politics of England.

The Case John Wayle

The assumption that the prior was obviously most interested in religious issues is confirmed by the longest story in his part of the chronicle. The story is exceptional in two aspects: Firstly, it is exceptionally long and detailed. It took the prior no less than six pages to describe the events which took place in 1463.[47] Apparently, he was aware of the quite unusual length of his explanations and therefore gave a foreword in which he excuses his prolixity. Secondly, the story does not really fit into the categories we have already classified. It is clearly not a story about politics or the history of the kingdom. It is a part of the history of Crowland, but one would seek in vain any deeds, agreements or documents. Nor are there narrations of wrongdoings of neighbours or other enemies of the abbey. But what is the story about? It is about the worst and strongest enemy not only of the abbey, but of mankind – the devil and his evil spirits.

In 1463, the day labourer John Wayle committed a particular crime. Because the day of the Lord's Resurrection was near, he went to Holy Confession like all the other inhabitants of Crowland. There, he brought to light several sins but remained silent about this particular crime. Although he had not eased his conscience, he took part in the Holy

---

45 Number of pages refers to the edition of the text: RILEY, 1854, pp. 418-419.

46 RILEY, 1854, pp. 420-421.

47 Number of pages refers to the edition of the text: RILEY, 1854, pp. 433-439.

Communion at Easter. Three days later he was seized by the devil and fell into a state of uncontrollable madness. He ripped his clothes, inflicted violence onto himself and was not able to tolerate his wife or his children in his presence. Soon, his neighbours became aware of his strange behaviour, seized him forcibly and bound him with irons and heavy stocks. Not surprisingly, the incident quickly became known to and was discussed by all villagers and the rumour finally reached the abbey. The monks came to Wayle and tried to cure his obsession. They sprinkled him with holy water and read aloud the Gospel of St. John. Their efforts were accompanied by fierce actions of Wayle: He let out bloodcurdling yells, gnashed his teeth, grinned like a wild beast, tried to bite at everything and was shaken by trembles. After the monks had finished reading the Gospel, they showed him an image of the crucified Lord and dropped holy water on Wayle's bare head. At this point Wayle displayed his utmost aggressiveness and, with his feet, lifted up the stocks in which he was enclosed. According to the prior, the stocks could hardly have been moved by four men. After this, it was decided to bring him to church on the next day. There, Wayle was fixed to a pillar before an image of the holy mother and placed under constant guard. The monks visited him every day, but Wayle, already hoarse and exhausted, was not able to speak coherent words or to make his confession. After a few days, he made clear to the monks that he was willing but not able to do so. He was untied from the pillar, led to a bench and several attempts were made to reach the deserved result, but all in vain. The monks recognised that it was the evil spirits who silenced Wayle's voice and changed their strategy. Fortunately, Crowland was the burial place of St. Guthlac, a specialist for the expulsion of such spirits.[48] Wayle – although he, or more likely the spirits, resisted in every possible way – was forced before the shrine of St. Guthlac where several prayers were spoken. This procedure was repeated every day; Wayle was untied from his pillar, pushed to the shrine and afterwards tied to the pillar again, with a cross in his hands. The decisive breakthrough was achieved by the idea of a single monk. He offered Wayle the possibility to make his confession to another priest from outside of the community of Crowland. Wayle agreed, the priest was fetched and heard the confession. After that, Wayle went home, unattended and by him-

---

48 BLAKE/SAUER, 1999, col. 1803.

self and was totally cured after seven days. Although the tranquillity of his soul was restored, he felt greatly ashamed and feared the reaction of his neighbours. Because of this, he finally decided to leave the village of Crowland.[49]

Obviously, the prior was deeply impressed by the above mentioned events to which he most likely was an eyewitness. But above all, in his religious point of view it makes sense to describe the most severe threat to a Christian, the possession by evil spirits, in utmost detail. The difference between the "Case Witham" and the "Case Wayle" is clear. Witham's actions were wilful and deliberate. By disgracing the chapel, he showed the godlessness which lay in himself. Wayle was forced to his actions by an evil spirit, which took possession of his mind. He was not able to do things which had previously been easy for him, for example to speak words. And he was able to do things beyond human ability, for example to lift the very heavy stocks with his feet. Other symptoms of his obsession are a mixture of illnesses, for example the trembling and bestiality, the biting and grinning.

As well as their difference, the cases also have something in common: Both men had to face social problems as a consequence of their deviant behaviour. Wayle is only willing to confess when a priest from outside of the community was fetched. The committed crime, one could only assume, was a crime which would cause social exclusion and Wayle was aware of this. Therefore, he insisted on an external confessor. In the end, not the crime, but his obsession was the problem and he had to leave his village. Witham became impoverished and had to face social decline and exclusion from his former rank.

Conclusion

According to the information provided by the authors of the First and the Second Continuations about their aims and the orientation of their works, differences in the sensitiveness to religious and political rules and the breaking of them could be expected.

---

49 RILEY, 1854, pp. 433-439.

The Prior Chronicler seemed to be less interested in politics and more in religious issues. The story about the greatest deviance from deserved piety, meaning the possession by an evil spirit, is logically the most elaborate. In the "Case Witham", the underlying purpose of the work becomes clear: one story tells about two deeds concerning the rights and claims of the abbey. Witham, one of the evil neighbours, is illustrated as a bad Christian in order to show the unlawfulness of his actions. Religious norms were employed to fortify legal claims.

The author of the Second Continuation was less interested in religion and more in politics. Therefore, even if religious remarks could easily have been inserted, he omitted them. Occasionally, religious or biblical references are given, but their function is political. In his view, the religious are clearly subordinate to the political aspects. In the political sphere, he proves his eye for detail. The notorious neighbours were, consequently, not illustrated as being despicable due to their unchristian behaviour, but because of their unnecessary brutality. Remarkably, the author of the Second Continuation does not describe direct consequences, e.g. social exclusion, for deviant behaviour. The consequences which had to be faced by the violent villagers are not mentioned.

In conclusion, the differences in the assessment and presentation of deviant behaviour are indeed traceable in the texts.

Literature

BLAKE, E.O./SAUER, H., Guthlac, in: Lexikon des Mittelalters vol. 4, Stuttgart 1999, col. 1803.

HANHAM, ALISON, The Mysterious Affair at Crowland Abbey, in: The Ricardian 18 (2008), pp. 1-11.

HICKS, MICHAEL, The Second Anonymous Continuation of the Crowland Abbey Chronicle 1459-86 Revisited, in: English Historical Review 122:496 (2007), pp. 349-370.

HICKS, MICHAEL, Crowland's World. A Westminster View of the Yorkist Age, in: History 90 (2005), pp. 172-190.

KELLY, HENRY ANSGAR, Canonical Implications of Richard III's Plan to Marry his Niece, in: Traditio 23 (1967), pp.269-311.

LYELL, LAETITIA/WATNEY, FRANK D. (eds.), Acts of Court of the Mercers' Company, 1453-1527, Cambridge 1936.

PRONAY, NICHOLAS/COX, JOHN (eds.), The Crowland Chronicle Continuations: 1459-1486, London 1986.

RILEY, HENRY T. (ed.), Ingulph's Chronicle of the Abbey of Crowland with the Continuations by Peter of Blois and Anonymous Writers (Bohn's Antiquarian Library), London 1854.

WILLIAMS, DANIEL, The Crowland Chroncile, 616-1500, in: England in the Fifteenth Century. Proceedings of the 1986 Harlaxton Symposium, ed. by Daniel Williams, Woodbridge 1987, pp. 371-390.

Online documents

http://www.crowlandabbey.org.uk/history/, 19.8.2015.
http://www.transportheritage.com/find-heritage-locations.html?sobi2
Task=sobi2Details&sobi2Id=238, 19.8.2015.

An enchantress, a saint and a prophetess

How religious deviance is described in Spanish Inquisition trials

MONIKA FROHNAPFEL-LEIS

1. Introduction

The meaning of "deviance" and who behaves in a deviant way is in the eye of the beholder, as is known. Deviationists are outsiders, and outsiders are those who are described as such.[1] What was it that was regarded as "the norm" concerning religious practices and what did deviant behavior look like during the Spanish early modern times?

In the wide field of guarding and watching Christian orthodoxy the Spanish Inquisition played a crucial role. According to its founding intention, this institution watched over deviationists. In this context, one sort of instruments used, namely the edicts of faith were a very important means in practical matters. Being a kind of catalogue that listed all forms of deviant behavior and heresy in a detailed way, they were read out loud during the visitation by an inquisitor, normally during high mass on Sunday.[2] Each and every member of the community was obliged to participate in this mass on pain of excommunication and other forms of punishment by the Holy Office.[3] The central point of the

---

1   BECKER, 1981, p. 8.
2   HENNINGSEN, 1980, p. 96; SCHLAU, 2013, pp. 9f.; PARKER, 1982, p. 523.
3   HENNINGSEN, 1980, p. 96.

edicts was that everyone who had the slightest knowledge of any circumstance described in the edicts was obliged to address the Inquisition in order to make a secret denunciation.[4]

As "forbidden" and therefore marked worthy to denounce were all manners of magical practices including all kinds of prophecies. The same was valid for the pretense of saintliness, meaning false saintliness, although it was not mentioned explicitly in the edicts of faith. When members of the community decided to submit a denunciation this happened – I suggest – because of a previous process of translation. This process I understand as some kind of social translation,[5] a translation of a certain behavior into a behavior, that one was obliged to tell the Inquisition's employees, because it was perceived as forbidden.[6]

This process of social translation is closely connected with knowledge and narratives of religious deviance: The narratives of religious deviance were supplied by a certain knowledge regarding conformity and deviance, which existed within the community – and this knowledge again was fed by the edict of faith, because this "anti-catalogue" contained detailed descriptions of the forbidden and therefore deviant practices, it labeled the opposite of the norm. But the knowledge also originated from oral traditions, which were passed on, especially in the case of sorcery, from one woman to another.[7]

---

4   IBID., p. 99.
5   Cf. FUCHS, 2009, pp. 21, 26f., 29. The quintessence of the social translation as described by Fuchs is that every dimension of social life is involved in translation. Fuchs' proposals concerning religion are confirmed by BACH-MANN-MEDICK, 2009, p. 10; see also: WOLF, 2012 as well as now HELLER, 2015.
6   This connection between social translation and labeling a certain behavior also describe BARBAGLI, 2003, pp. 34f. Although they do not name it as such, in describing the 'Bonding theory' presented by Travis Hirschi already in 1969 one can discover the same characteristics.
7   For sorcery as "daily life sorcery" as a typical female phenomenon see TAUSIET, 2004, pp. 306f., 465f., 508, 553; CARO BAROJA, 1992, vol. 1, p. 217.

2. An enchantress

The Spanish Inquisition trial records provide us with detailed information concerning the challenges of women's daily lives:[8] More than the accused themselves, the witnesses tell us how they perceived deviant behavior.

So what do witnesses in an inquisitorial process say about enchantresses – or, to be more precise: When do they speak of someone as an enchantress? Let us have a look at the case of Ysabel Rodríguez, who was charged with sorcery before the tribunal of the Canary Islands in 1607[9]: The following example was given by the witness Juan García, who knew the charged woman quite well, because he was her son's apprentice. When he was asked in court "what it was that Ysabel Rodríguez did or said concerning the Holy Office and its correct exercise", he reported: that it was about three years ago, and he was a shoemaker apprentice in the house of Francisco Montessa, the son of Ysabel Rodríguez, when Sebastiana Gonçalez, Ysabel's daughter-in-law, told him: "Juan, don't you know that my mother-in-law is a sorceress?" He replied: "How come that she is a sorceress?" And Sebastiana explained it was "because Ysabel Rodríguez went out to the courtyard by night in order to pray the prayer of the *Anima sola* [...] behind a big white clay jug that was located in the courtyard and behind it she sat down on her buttocks on a brick [...] with some wicks in her hands."[10]

That means: Sebastiana, his master's wife, told Juan something about her mother-in-law in a manner that suggested it to be an assured matter of fact, not a mere presumption. By describing a certain behav-

---

8   VOLLENDORF, 2005, p. 166.
9   The Process is documented in the Archivo Histórico Nacional, Madrid, and has the following signatory: AHN, Inq. 1824, Exp. 4, f. 1r-27r (AHN = Archivo Histórico Nacional; Inq. = Inquisición; Exp. [= expediente] = file; f. = folio; r = recto; v = verso).
10 AHN Inq. 1824, Exp. 4, f. 10v. The heterodox 'prayer' to the *Anima Sola* was used to achieve the return of an absent beloved person as well as to learn something concerning the outcome of a relationship, see MARTÍN SOTO, 2008, pp. 132, 545f.

ior, she created facts and labeled Ysabel as a sorceress, who did not fulfill the expectations for "normal" behavior.[11]

However, Juan wanted to be sure of Ysabel's practices, as he related the following in court: Because of the things which Sebastiana Gonçalez had told him before against Ysabel Rodríguez, he was eager to know whether they were true. Therefore, he looked through a hole in the wooden wall that divided the two flats of Ysabel and Sebastiana. One day, more or less shortly after midday, he saw that Ysabel drove all her sons out of the house, closed the doors and went into a chamber. Then she shut the house's main door and stayed inside. Juan did not see what she did inside, but he saw that she had some light with her in the chamber, and it seemed to him as if the light shivered. Further he described that in a very similar way he saw Ysabel by night in the courtyard sitting behind a big clay jug near some wood. Because he did not know what she was doing, he simply went to her and asked her: "Señora Ysabel Rodríguez, what are you doing, to whom are you praying", and she replied: "Juan, I am praying here because the boys disturb me." It may have been ten or twelve times that he saw Ysabel doing all this, and he presumed that he had been called by the Holy Office for this purpose.[12]

This means: Juan wanted to see "it", the deviant behavior, what had been told to him by Sebastiana before, with his own eyes. When he confronted Ysabel with her strange activities she answered him that the reason for her praying in the courtyard was quite simple: She sought silence and tranquility in a house that was frequented by a lot of people: Not only by her children, but also by her son's apprentices.

According to this description we can imagine that Ysabel lived together with her son's family in narrow confines.[13] This situation of living and working together in a very confined space was quite common

---

11   Concerning this labeling see BECKER, 1981, p. 8; SCHWERHOFF, 2011, pp. 35f. An example for a similar form of labeling a woman as sorceress from the early modern Italian context mentions Silvia Mantini for the case of Gostanza da Libbiano, see MANTINI, 2009, p. 147.

12   AHN, Inq. 1824, Exp. 4, f. 11v.

13   The witness Juan García related, that the wall that separated the two dwellings was no more than a wooden wall with holes in it, which both sides used in order to have a look on the other side (AHN, Inq. 1824, Exp. 4, f. 6r-v, 11v).

in early modern times: It was characterized by involuntary social gathering and effective vicinity, but also by real assistance. In this close form of cohabitation, a collective practice of control was very likely. The "house" consisted less by blood-relationship, but rather of the co-presence of kinsmen.[14] In this situation of close cohabitation it was almost impossible for the house members to do anything in the secret. Therefore, this constellation was excellently suitable for the creation of forbidden spaces[15] – for example when someone dared to close doors and windows by day.[16] This situation of more or less permanent surveillance by the neighbors limited the individual spaces beyond conform behavior. However, it was also suitable for the opening of spaces to perform religious practices out of a forbidden situation, e.g. when women like Ysabel carried out their opinion of religion in spite of the unwritten norms of society.[17]

3. A saint

From the perception of an enchantress, allow me to move on to the perception of persons with the reputation of saintliness – or false saintliness. I would like to concentrate on the female representatives of this phenomenon because, during the late 16th and the first half of the 17th century, the majority of persons charged with pretending holiness before Spanish inquisitorial courts were women.[18] One has to consider that having visions and other ecstatic experiences could offer women a way to participate in debates that traditionally where restricted to men.[19]

---

14 EIBACH, 2011, p. 642.
15 IBID., p. 652.
16 Again the example of Juan García's description of Ysabel Rodríguez' behavior, that seemed 'strange' to him, see AHN, Inq. 1824, Exp. 4, f. 6v as well as the case of Ysabel Martínez y Niguez, AHN, Inq. 2022, Exp. 38, f. 16r-v.
17 Concerning the terms of "space" in this context as heterotopia and forbidden spaces: FOUCAULT, 2012, especially pp. 320-322, 325f.; LÖW, 2001, especially pp. 158, 165f., 171, 177 as well as with a wider perspective: RAU/SCHWERHOFF, 2004.
18 SCHMIDT, 2004, pp. 155f.; ZARRI, 1991, pp. 14-30; HALICZER, 2004, pp. 46f.
19 KAGAN, 1990, p. 5.

In doing so, women opened and unclosed a form of space for religious expression and practice for themselves. This is what they had in common with the above described enchantress Ysabel.

Regarding saintliness, certain knowledge about this subject can be supposed within the community, which primarily arose from the numerous available descriptions of the lives of Mary and the saints as well as prints, paintings and theater plays on these topics which appeared increasingly right after the Council of Trent. Especially the sermons had a significant function in spreading the idea of an "ideal" form of behavior imitating Christ, Mary and the saints. The written, painted or performed descriptions of "good lives" could be understood as some kind of manuals on the way to obtain perfection and holiness, especially for religious women.[20] In this manner, the people's knowledge of holy behavior and its antipode was formed in one certain and only valid direction, which was the norm in this context. Especially by hearing and reading the description of the lives of the saints, the members of any early modern Spanish community knew how to recognize "real" holiness. When witnesses thought to have watched some of the following characteristics, they often described the accused women in inquisitorial trials as being of "holy perfection", meaning they labeled[21] her as being "saintly" and "perfect". Among others, the most important of these characteristics were: apparitions of Mary, God, Saints and Angels; visions concerning future events; extreme fasting, meaning not eating anything for months; recovery after severe illness.[22]

Let us have a look at the example of Teresa Valle de la Cerda:[23] Teresa was the prioress of the convent of San Plácido in Madrid. From her

---

20 HALICZER, 2004, pp. 43-47; SLUHOVSKY, 2002, p. 1401.
21 BECKER, 1981, p. 8; SCHWERHOFF, 2011, pp. 35f.
22 As such one can find it in the trials against Sor Clara de San Francisco and María de San Bartolomé before the Canary Island's inquisitorial court, 1640-1642, AHN, Inq. 1823, Exp. 1; see also BRAMBILLA, 2010, pp. 39-41; SLUHOVSKY, 2007, pp. 211f.
23 Her case is extensively documented in the AHN. I used the fascicle that contains only the accusation and the sentence and is kept at the Historical Library of the University of Valence: Biblioteca Histórica de la Universitat de València, MS 310/7: Acusación y sentencia de Doña Theresa Valle de la Çerda Priora del Monasterio de San Plaçido de Madrid. See also PUYOL BUIL, 1993; BARBEITO CARNEIRO, 1991; GONZÁLEZ DURO, 2004; SLUHOVSKY, 2002, pp. 1385f.

convent, which was situated within the center of Spain's capital, she maintained close connections to the court and the high nobility in general, especially to her former fiancé, *don* Jerónimo de Villanueva, who held the important office of *Protonotario* of Aragón, and to King Philipp IV's favorite, the *Conde-Duque* de Olivares. At least with Olivares she was connected by correspondence.[24] As a member of a very influential Madrid family, Teresa founded San Plácido in 1623 as *Monasterio de la Encarnación Benita*. This is remarkable, because it took place at a time, when further foundations of monasteries were forbidden because of the numerous, already existing religious houses in Madrid. That Teresa nevertheless obtained a special permit may be due to her own good connections and that Villanueva had won Olivares's favor as well.[25]

In her trial before the Inquisition's tribunal of Toledo she was accused, amongst other, of having assumed unjustified saintliness by claiming to have visions. Further, she was charged with having made plans for founding a new – female – apostolate with the aim to evangelize the world with her sermons until she would die a martyr – an act similar to a second redemption.[26]

So where did Teresa go wrong with her activities? When was she perceived as religious deviant? There seems to have been some kind of discrepancy between the perception of her direct social environment within and outside of the cloister and the Holy Office's employees: For example, during the process it is said that:

"Pieces of food, which Teresa had bitten off or which she had left, were spread among the people who venerated them like relics. Within and outside of the convent she was adored like another Teresa of Avila. And she al-

---

24 Concerning the correspondence between doña Teresa and Olivares: PUYOL BUIL, 1993, e.g. pp. 88, 150f.
25 BARBEITO CARNEIRO, 1991, pp. 99f., 125, 127; VOLLENDORF, 2005, p. 199.
26 Biblioteca Histórica de la Universitat de València, MS 310/7: Acusación y sentencia de Doña Theresa Valle de la Çerda Priora del Monasterio de San Plaçido de Madrid, f. 252v-253v; BARBEITO CARNEIRO, 1991, pp. 109f., 125f.

lowed them to call her 'the Great', 'the Saint' or 'Mother of the 12 tribes'."[27]

However, the Inquisition's opinion on her religions practice was quite different: "It is all deceit and deception and lie like the 40-days fasting, which she is rumored to have simulated without having eaten a mouthful just in order to be venerated as a great Saint."[28] Teresa, in contrast, said in her hearing "that she for her part had never made use of fiction or deceit or deception or delusion."[29]

The aspect of deceit seemed to be crucial not only for the question of conform religious behavior, but also for a religious practice that imitated the practices which people knew from hearing and reading the lives of the saints. By her promulgation of her direct succession of Christ together with her nuns and by her preaching, Teresa entered gender-specific spaces of religious practices, which were normally exclusively reserved for men, respectively for priests.

The tribunal not only condemned certain aspects of what she did, but her entire way of living: In the Holy Office's eyes, this was just not strict enough, and the fact that she did not follow the community in the choir and refectory, even when she was a novice, suggested that she led a very lax form of religious life.[30] We can only suspect the extent to which Teresa herself promoted the veneration by her direct social environment. Insofar, it could be understood as the continuation of an attitude she maintained from her life outside the cloister. Surely, her good connections to the court and her correspondence with members of the high nobility gave her the feeling of being not just a "normal" nun, but a special religious woman, like being chosen. In the Holy Office's documents, we can clearly see a deep mistrust toward her doings, which led to them being labeled false, deceitful and as such deviant.

Another example for a woman with the reputation of saintliness, but also of deviant religious behavior, is the tertiary nun Francisca Roselló in Valencia. As such a religious woman, she did not live within a mon-

---

27 Biblioteca Histórica de la Universitat de València, MS 310/7: Acusación y sentencia de Doña Theresa Valle de la Çerda Priora del Monasterio de San Plaçido de Madrid, f. 250v.
28 IBID., f. 265r.
29 IBID., f. 265v.
30 IBID., f. 250v.

astery, but practiced her religious life outside the cloister.[31] In her trial, a witness testified how another woman ("the wife of Barreter") had told him,

> "that many men, profane and [clerical] ones, had been in the house of the named Sister Francisca and kissed her hand and asked her for her advice concerning the things they had to do. And they venerated her as a Saint. And that to the named Barreter this appeared to be something bad and a dangerous thing [...]."[32]

That means, in this case, deviance was perceived as a behavior which was not in line with the expectations concerning a religious woman. It seems as if the categorization that Francisca was a woman was more important than the aspect that she was a *religious* woman. The expectation was clearly connected with her gender. Related to this facet is another point of the accusation, namely that Francisca seemed to treat priests in an unusual manner. In this sense, one witness related that some priests

> "frequented Francisca's house and usually called her 'mother' and she called them 'sons' and that they obeyed her in things concerning prayer and spirit by praying and reading devotional things in the form she told them."[33]

Thus, Francisca's behavior was described as that of a spiritual authority – a role normally fulfilled by a man, more precisely a priest. Ignoring this rule and obtaining this male role in spite of being female was a form of questioning traditional male dominance. As such, it could be

---

31   In Spain tertiary nuns were called *beatas*, see BARBEITO CARNEIRO, 1991, p. 28; KAGAN, 1990, p. 18 (annotation 26) quotes Sebastián de Covarrubias, who defines beata in his book 'Tesoro de a lengua castellana' (Madrid 1611, p. 293) like this: 'A woman in religious habit who, outside of a [religious] community and residing in her own house, professes celibacy and leads a retiring life, praying and doing works of charity'; see also LEHMANN, 2000, col. 1349-1352.

32   Archivo Universitario de la Universiad de Valencia, Varias 42/10: Declaración de testigos en el proceso (de inquisición) contra Francisca Rosello, beata, vecina de Valencia, acusada de haber cometido delitos en ofensa de Dios y contra la fé catholica (a. 1624-26), f. 14v.

33   IBID., f. 33r.

seen as a threat to regular authorities[34] – and as a deviant behavior. But what was the motivation for Francisca's divergent actions? She was probably aware of the consequences of her doings. Why did she nevertheless continue? I suggest that she did so in order to uncover space for her individual form of religious expression: That she created an open space for her religious practice which was normally reserved for men. By acting like a man or a priest, she entered a space which women were traditionally not allowed to enter. She behaved in a deviant way, because she broke with the prevailing opinions, the "common law" of her community, which often existed in an unwritten form.[35]

But there were also other perceptions, as we can see by the description given by a witness, who depicted her as a harmless and ignorant woman, obviously in order to defend her in court: according to the witness Fray Joan Ximénez, the priest *Mosen* Ruiz had stated that one had to worry very little about these things Francisca did and said, "because she was very simple and he had seen her making things like a woman lacking of comprehension".[36] He even specified his opinion: "that everything she did originated from ignorance and simplicity".[37] And in this sense this witness made very little fuss of her doing.[38] By labeling Francisca's forms of religious practice more or less as "nonsense", this witness labeled it as harmless, as no threat to society's order and therefore as nothing to worry about.

---

34 FERNÁNDEZ LUZÓN, 2000, p. 9.
35 SCHWERHOFF, 2011, p. 10.
36 Archivo Universitario de la Universiad de Valencia, Varias 42/10: Declaración de testigos en el proceso (de inquisición) contra Francisca Rosello, beata, vecina de Valencia, acusada de haber cometido delitos en ofensa de Dios y contra la fé catholica (a. 1624-26), f. 40v.
37 IBID., f. 41r.
38 IBID., f. 40v.

4. A prophetess

After this look at the perception of sorceresses and of (false) saintliness, let us finally turn to the perception of prophetesses, prophecies and dreams. One form of prophecies was the dream. Dreams were considered to have two different sources, a natural and a supernatural. Aristotele's explanations of dreams as a product of the mind's sensual perception while sleeping, was assumed to be the dreams' natural cause. Concerning the supernatural side, a diabolic or divine origin was possible.[39] These two provenances were also named for prophecies: The true were regarded as being inspired by God, the false and the scandalous propositions as inspired by the devil.

In spite of all the moral warnings concerning the dreams' doubtful reliability, most of the Spaniards were utterly fascinated by them – like most of the people in other parts of Europe.[40] One has to bear in mind, that the prophet was understood not to tell his own wisdom and opinion, but always to speak for someone else.[41] This leads to the question, for whom the seer spoke, meaning for God or for the devil. Conversation about the contents of dreams and how to interpret them was quite common in sixteenth century Europe, and it was not limited to the house. In this context, priests and confessors operated as dream interpreters; but they faced competition from other analysts, persons who claimed to have a deep knowledge concerning predications about the future. The majority of these dream experts were women, who were also engaged in other forms of fortune-telling.[42] One can therefore see that the performance of prophecies in the wider sense of any prognostics concerning future events was – like sorcery and false saintliness – also a primary female phenomenon.

The famous case of Lucrecia de León is the one of a young women living in Madrid by the end of the 16th century who claimed to have prophetic dreams since she was a little girl.[43] Lucrecia was born in the

---

39 KAGAN, 1990, p. 35. Generally regarding these aspects see also: JORDÁN ARROYO, 2001.
40 KAGAN, 1990, p. 35.
41 RIEDL, 2005, p. 9.
42 KAGAN, 1990, p. 37.
43 IBID., 1990, p. 43f., were Kagan also refers to other cases of female seers and visionaries whose activities begun at a very young age, e.g. Catherine

new Spanish capital in 1568 to her parents Ana Ordóñez and Alonso Franco de León, a solicitor with connections at court. Her family lived in the heart of the old Madrid in the parish of San Sebastián in a neighborhood of a number of famous writers and artists.[44] Lucrecia was quick in learning and had a good memory, so that she could save lots of information she received from many informal teachers, since she grew up in an astrologically affected environment.[45] Because her hundreds of dreams were written down by two trusted friars[46] and were published and widely spread[47], she was quite popular in Madrid, the town of the court. One of these friars was *don* Alonso de Mendoza. In him, Lucrecia had a mighty and influential supporter. In his eyes she was a divine prophet. As he was convinced that Lucrecia's visions contained divine messages of great importance for Spain's future, he began to transcribe her dreams in order to make her the new spokeswoman of Madrid's prophetic movement. He also offered her protection and financial help and arranged for fray Lucas de Allende to become her confessor, who also began to transcribe her dreams. It was Allende who also gave cop-

---

of Siena (10 years old), Joan of Arc (13) and Margaret of Ypres (5). Concerning Lucrecia's case in general see also: JORDÁN ARROYO, 2007 and FERNÁNDEZ LUZÓN, 2000. Concerning the function of dreams during the early modern period in general see: GANTET 2010 and SCHMIDT/WEBER 2008.

44 KAGAN, 1990, p. 14. For her father's connections at court see IBID., p. 30.
45 One of them was her friend Juana Correa, a *beata*; another was an unnamed *morisca* woman who lived as a boarder in the León household for 3 or 4 years. She told Lucrecia about the Moorish tradition of dreams and prophecy. Another one of these illustrious guests was Guillén de Casaos, who had a weakness for magical arts, especially astrology. With Lucrecia he discussed about dreams and prophecies and taught her about the stars. An interest in astrology, prophecies and dreams did also have their neighbor Martín de Ayala, a visionary as well. He told Lucrecia about the famous contemporary visionary Sor María de la Visitación. And – perhaps more decisive – he introduced the young woman to a group of people in Madrid who claimed to be faith healers and prophets, see IBID., 1990, pp. 26f.
46 Lucrecia's dreams were written down by the friar don Alonso de Mendoza, in whom she seemed to trust. He came to Lucrecia's house on a regular basis in order to write down what she had dreamt the previous night, see KAGAN, 1990, pp. 45f.
47 JORDÁN ARROYO, 2007, p. 4. Here it is stated quite clear that it was not Lucrecia's idea to have her dreams written down, but the one of the two learned men.

ies of her dreams to his powerful friends, presumably for further distribution at court.[48] Gradually, the number of courtiers interested in Lucrecia's dreams increased and soon she became a kind of "court celebrity".[49] As time went by, her dreams became more and more characterized by their blatantly critical content. For example, in dreams concerning the king Philip II, he was described like this: "He has tyrannized the poor"; "he is responsible for the evil and the ruin of Spain"[50]; "the cruelty of Philip's heart"[51], and the advice to "Stop work on the Escorial, as it is not pleasing God"[52] was given. For the most part, her critique concerned the monarch and his way of ruling. But, curiously, the Inquisition did not intervene for quite some time – possibly because Philip himself did not feel seriously threatened by the dreams of a young woman.[53]

The turning point came in spring 1590: The former secretary of state and one of Philip's former most trusted advisers Antonio Pérez was imprisoned in Madrid. When he escaped on 19 April 1590, the king feared that Pérez could use his "base" in Aragón to stir up opposition to royal authority. Because of the political trouble abroad, Philip could not afford any interior trouble. Pérez' escape and the crisis provoked by it raised new questions about Lucrecia and the group surrounding her: The fear was based on the idea that her predictions about new popular rebellions were nothing but constructs created by her, her allies and Pérez in order to plot against the king. In May 1590, the king's closest advisors thought it was time to stop Lucrecia, and the Inquisition started its procedures.[54]

Another example of the recounting of the deviant form of prophecy is María de la Concepción. She was a *beata* who lived in a village near Seville during the 1640s. In 1645, she had to face an Inquisition trial

---

48   KAGAN, 1990, pp. 28, 45, 48, 51, 60f., 109f.

49   IBID., 1990, p.125. Even a confraternity known as "The Holy Cross of the Restoration" was established after her dream of an army with white crosses marching against Spain's enemies, see IBID., pp. 127f.; see also JORDAN ARROYO, 2007, pp. 8-10.

50   KAGAN, 1990, p. 80; dreams of 15 and 22 January 1588.

51   IBID.; dream of 4 November 1588.

52   IBID., p. 81; dream of 15 January 1588.

53   IBID., pp. 128f.

54   IBID., pp. 88-94; to Pérez' escape see also OSBORNE, 2002, pp. 224f.

because she had caused scandals and disturbance in the city and the entire region of Seville by her predictions on the future.[55]

Until 1630, Seville was the largest town with respect to inhabitants in Spain.[56] It was characterized by an extremely heterodox social structure, which was marked by a high percentage of noble families. As a consequence, Seville was known as a particular rich town.[57] It is significant for the case that not only "common people" came to ask for her advice, but also members of the "lucent" upper class, of Seville's nobility.[58] This is important in a city like Seville with a great percentage of nobility. We can see this directly in the trials records which mention that María was supported and favored by many illustrious and influential persons. One witness stated: "Nobody dared to say anything of matter because the named *beata* was favored and assisted by such illustrious persons and of such authority."[59]

Just a few years before María scandalous predictions, in 1640, rebellions had broken out in nearby Portugal – which was indeed a serious matter because they led to Portugal's independence from Spain.[60] Many soldiers had to serve under the Spanish crown during the Portuguese rebellion, and the people were discontent and frightened because of the continuous economic crisis.[61] Against the background of the problematic and crisis-ridden year 1640, it seemed to be quite a good idea to avoid social and political disturbances. This fear was not unjustified

---

55   AHN, Inq. 2061, Exp. 12.
56   DOMÍNGUEZ ORTIZ, 1986, p. 79; this changed as a consequence of the great plague in 1649, see IBID, p. 73.
57   IBID., pp. 38f., 94, 96f.
58   In the trial acts it is said that: Countless persons consulted her, not only those belonging to the lower classes – what probably would have been more or less "normal" – but also "illustrious" and noble persons. The more: There seemed to be some kind of "hype" for her service, and for that purpose people came from a distance of more than 20 leagues to her village, see AHN, Inq. 2061, Exp. 12, f. 4r, 5r, 9v.
59   IBID., f. 6r-v.
60   PERRY, Gender and Disorder in Early Modern Seville, Princeton 1990, p. 43.
61   DOMÍNGUEZ ORTIZ, 1986, p. 72. This crisis resulted also from other factors, such as the expulsion of 7500 *moriscos* already in 1610 with negative consequences for the town. Furthermore, the war against France from 1635 on affected Seville in a severe way because of the great number of soldiers that were recruited from there, see IBID., pp. 71, 110f.

because social disturbances and revolts occurred in Seville owing to bad harvests and extreme rise in prices in 1652.[62] Just because the Inquisition long since knew about María's activities in fortune-telling and the already given reprimand,[63] this socio-historical background of the region of Seville is important in order to understand why the Holy Office did not intervene until the scandals became excessive. The increase was mostly due to the visit of an inquisitor in charge at her home. For the people as well as the Inquisition's employees, this seemed to be very strange. The inquisitor and the secretaries themselves had contributed to exacerbate the scandal.[64] The testimonies said that, after returning from María's house, the inquisitor and the secretary were frightened as never before. The inquisitor did not want to talk about the visit and the secretary publically requested to be transferred to another tribunal. Therefore, one thought that María's answer had not been too favorable and that they believed it.[65] Thus, María's behavior was translated as being religiously deviant at the moment, when she caused scandals with her predictions on future events and when she became a factor of insecurity because of it. It was extremely scandalous that not only people of a lower status were attracted by her prophecies, but also of the most "illustrious", as the trial records especially mentioned. This phenomenon even surged as the scandals increased after the inquisitor's visit and more clients than ever before came to consult María.

5. Conclusion

Recounting religious deviance in early modern Spain meant to describe the perception of a behavior which friends, neighbors and family members recognized from the forbidden practices they knew by listening to the edicts of faith or by hearing, reading and watching descriptions of the lives of saints. After having heard the edict of faith, the community had to make interpretations and social translations in order to perform the step of recognizing a forbidden practice and then prepare a denunci-

---

62 DOMÍNGUEZ ORTIZ, 1986, pp. 26, 113f.
63 AHN, Inq. 2061, Exp. 12, f. 3v-4r.
64 IBID., f. 9v-10v.
65 IBID., f. 8r, 10v.

ation. As we have seen, various forms of perception and recounting religious deviance can be derived from sorcery, false saintliness and in performing prophecies.

The enchantress Ysabel Rodríguez was named sorceress by her daughter-in-law and consequently by the rest of her social environment. She was a sorceress because she was declared as such. Her deviant behavior resulted from the label that was given to her. Recounting the stories of "holy women" often meant telling two stories: On the one hand the account of revelations, visions and spirituality, a life worth telling, a woman of true spiritual authority – and on the other hand, a story full of lies, falseness and vanity. Sometimes the perception of the accused woman herself and of the inquisitors had nothing in common and was therefore deviant in the wider sense of the word. In the example of *doña* Teresa Valle de la Cerda we have seen that even a religious life that was dedicated to the imitation of the lives of the saints as an approved, ideal form for religious women could fail in the sense that it was labeled as deviant. In Teresa's case, her connections to influential people at court in combination with her spiritual activities could have been perceived as a menace, so that the Inquisition stopped this kind of deviant behavior. In the case of the *beata* Francisca Roselló, she was labeled as deviant because of the assumption of male and clerical roles and, in the process, entering male spaces. When someone was charged by an inquisitorial court because of her or his prophecies, it not only recounted unsatisfied personal destinies: When the content of the predictions caused social uprising and the people performing them became a social and political risk, the simple deviant practice became a concrete menacing factor of insecurity – which authorities tented to avoid. The activities performed by Lucrecia de León and María de la Concepción seem to have ranged over quite a long period. The Inquisition knew about them, but did not intervene – until it could no longer tolerate them and begun an official investigation. The reasons have been quite similar in both cases: What the women had done had caused uproar and trouble within their respective community. With respect to Madrid and Seville, both cases were located within an urban society with a high percentage of members of the high nobility, a decisive factor concerning the relation between scandals, social uproar and political instability. The prophecies and prophetic dreams performed by María de la Concepción and Lucrecia de León caused these scandals because many of their clients were nobles. As the risk of social disturbances had become too high, the authorities had to intervene.

Literature

BACHMANN-MEDICK, DORIS, Introduction, The translational turn, in: Translation Studies 2,1 (2009), pp. 2-16.

BARBAGLI, MARZIO et al. Sociologia della devianza, Bologna 2003.

BARBEITO CARNEIRO, MARÍA ISABEL (Ed.), Cárceles y mujeres en el siglo XVII. Razón y forma de la Galera. Proceso Inquisitorial de San Plácido (Biblioteca de escritoras 21), Madrid 1991.

BECKER, HOWARD S., Außenseiter. Zur Soziologie abweichenden Verhaltens, Frankfurt am Main 1981.

BRAMBILLA, ELENA, Corpi invasi e viaggi dell'anima. Santità, possessione, esorcismo dalla teologia barocca alla medicina illuminista, Roma 2010.

CARO BAROJA, JULIO, Vidas Mágicas e Inquisición, two volumes (Ediciones Istmo, Colección Fundamentos 121 and 122), 2nd ed., Madrid 1992, vol. 1.

COVARRUBIAS Y HOROZCO, SEBASTIÁN DE, Tesoro de la lengua castellana, o española, Madrid 1611.

DOMÍNGUEZ ORTIZ, ANTONIO, La Sevilla del siglo XVII (Historia de Sevilla) (Colección de bolsillo 93), 3rd ed., Sevilla 1986.

EIBACH, JOACHIM, Das offene Haus. Kommunikative Praxis im sozialen Nahraum der europäischen Frühen Neuzeit, in: ZHF 38 (2011), pp. 621-664.

FERNÁNDEZ LUZÓN, ANTONIO, Profecía y transgresión social. El caso de Lucrecia de León, in: Historia Social 38 (2000), pp. 3-15.

FOUCAULT, MICHEL, Von anderen Räumen, in: Raumtheorie. Grundlagentexte aus Philosophie und Kulturwissenschaften (suhrkamp taschenbuch wissenschaft 1800), ed. by DÜNNE, JÖRG /GÜNZEL, STEPHAN, 7th ed., Frankfurt am Main 2012, pp. 317-329.

FUCHS, MARTIN, Reaching out; or, Nobody exists in one context only. Society as translation, in: Translation Studies 2, 1 (2009), pp. 21-40.

GANTET, CLAIRE, Der Traum in der Frühen Neuzeit. Ansätze zu einer kulturellen Wissensgeschichte (Frühe Neuzeit 143), Berlin 2010.

GONZÁLEZ DURO, ENRIQUE, Demonios en el convento. El conde-duque de Olivares frente a la Inquisición, Madrid 2004.

HALICZER, STEPHEN, Between exaltation and infamy. Female mystics in the golden age of Spain, Oxford 2004.

HELLER, LAVINIA (ed.), Kultur und Übersetzung. Studien zu einem begrifflichen Verhältnis (Interkulturalität. Studien zu Sprache, Literatur und Gesellschaft), Bielefeld 2015.

HENNINGSEN, GUSTAV, The Witches' Advocate. Basque Witchcraft and the Spanish Inquisition (1609-1614), Reno 1980.

JORDÁN ARROYO, MARÍA V., Francisco Monzón y "el buen dormir": la interpretación teológica de los sueños en la España del siglo XVI, in: Cuadernos de Historia Moderna 26 (2001), pp. 169-184.

ID., Soñar la historia. Riesgo, creatividad y religión en las profecias de Lucrecia de León, Madrid 2007.

KAGAN, RICHARD L., Lucrecia's dreams. Politics and Prophecy in Sixteenth-Century Spain, Berkely et al. 1990.

LEHMANN, LEONHARD, Terziaren, Terziarinnen, in: Lexikon für Theologie und Kirche, Bd. 9, Freiburg im Breisgau 2000, col. 1349-1352.

LÖW, MARTINA, Raumsoziologie (suhrkamp taschenbuch wissenschaft 1506), Frankfurt am Main 2001.

MANTINI, SILVIA, Gostanza da Libbiano, guaritrice e strega (1534-?), in: Rinascimento al femminile, ed. by NICCOLI, OTTAVIA, 3rd ed., Roma/Bari 2009, pp. 143-162.

MARTÍN SOTO, RAFAEL, Magia y vida cotidiana. Andalucía, siglos XVI-XVIII (Biblioteca histórica 12), Sevilla 2008.

OSBORNE, ROGER, The dreamer of the Calle de San Salvador. Visions of Seditions and Sacrilege in Sixteenth-Century Spain, London 2002.

PARKER, GEOFFREY, Some Recent Work on the Inquisition in Spain and Italy, in: The Journal of Modern History 54, (1982), pp. 519-532.

PERRY, MARY ELIZABETH, Gender and Disorder in Early Modern Seville, Princeton 1990.

PUYOL BUIL, CARLOS, Inquisición y política en el reinado de Felipe IV. Los procesos de Jerónimo de Villanueva y las monjas de San

Plácido, 1628-1660 (Consejo Superior de Investigaciones Científicas, Biblioteca de historia 18), Madrid 1993.

RAU, SUSANNE/SCHWERHOFF, GERD (eds.), Zwischen Gotteshaus und Taverne. Öffentliche Räume in Spätmittelalter und Früher Neuzeit (Norm und Struktur 21), Köln et al. 2004.

RIEDL, MATTHIAS, Einleitung: Prophetie als interzivilisatorisches Phänomen, in: Propheten und Prophezeiungen – Prophets and Prophecies (Eranos, Neue Folge Bd. 12), ed. by ID./ SCHABERT, TILO, Würzburg 2005, pp. 9-16.

SCHLAU, STACEY, Gendered Crime and Punishment. Women and/in the Hispanic Inquisition (The Medieval and Early Modern Iberian Word 49), Leiden/Boston 2013.

SCHMIDT, PEER, Inquisitoren – Mystikerinnen – Aufklärer. Religion und Kultur in Spanien zwischen Barock und Aufklärung, in: HARTMANN, PETER CLAUS (ed.), Religion und Kultur im Europa des 17. und 18. Jahrhunderts (Mainzer Studien zur Neueren Geschichte Bd. 12), Frankfurt am Main et al. 2004, pp. 143-166.

ID./WEBER, GREGOR (eds.), Traum und res publica. Traumkulturen und Deutungen sozialer Wirklichkeiten im Europa von Renaissance und Barock (Colloquia Augustana 26), Berlin 2008.

SCHWERHOFF, GERD, Historische Kriminalitätsforschung (Historische Einführungen 9), Frankfurt am Main/New York 2011.

SLUHOVSKY, MOSHE, The Devil in the Convent, in: American Historical Review 107 (2002), pp. 1379-1411.

ID., Believe not every spirit. Possession, mysticism and discernment in early modern catholism, Chicago 2007.

TAUSIET, MARÍA, Ponzoña en los ojos. Brujería y superstición en Aragón en el siglo XVI, Madrid 2004.

VOLLENDORF, LISA, The Lives of Women. A New History of Inquisitorial Spain, Nashville 2005.

WOLF, MICHAELA, Cultural Translation as a Model of Migration?, in: Translatio/n. Narration, Media and the staging of differences, ed. by ITALIANO, FEDERICO/RÖSSNER, MICHAEL (Edition Kulturwissenschaft 20), Bielefeld 2012, pp. 69-87.

ZARRI, GABRIELLA, ,Vera' santità, ,simulata' santità: ipotesi e riscontri, in: Finzione e santità tra medioevo ed età moderna, ed. by ID., Turin 1991, pp. 9-36.

Blasphemy on Trial
Splinters of deviant recounts from 17th century Venice

LUCA VETTORE

Introduction

In this brief report I intend to focus my attention on the particular form of deviance known as blasphemy. In doing so, or at least trying to do so, I shall break up the article in two parts: in the first, I will summarise the main lines of interpretation and problems emerging from literature pertaining to the study of blasphemy, adding some considerations over the geographical and chronological boundaries given in the title; in the second, I shall try to read comparatively different trials, focusing my attention on the image commonly stated before inquisitorial tribunals by the people deemed guilty of blasphemy – being blasphemy, as a crime, recounted as a quite fixed type –, suggesting some of the most common patterns we can establish between them, searching for clues on the practice of blasphemy outside the courts of justice, its life and uses in the urban milieu.

For sake of clarity, I shall provide initial, brief juridical information: even if the *Santo Uffizio* (Holy Office) was present and quite industrious in Venice, at least two other magistrates ruled upon blasphemy: the *Consiglio dei Dieci* (Council of Ten), and the *Esecutori contro la Bestemmia* (Perpetrators against Blasphemy). I shall briefly talk about these later in this speech, as we encounter them (mainly the first and the third of these courts): for now, I simply say that I shall use their original vernacular names in this paper, being the translation of *"Esecutori"* as "Perpetrators", an adjustment made by the author, incapable of finding an alternative in the literature and thus a translation without any base or intention of objectivity. Another terminological note: all-historical sources I have used are located in the Venice's State Archive: according to tradition, I shall cite them by their Italian initials ASV, *Archivio di Stato di Venezia.*

Much has been written about the topic of blasphemy, but there is still much work to be done. To create a solid framework of interpretation and use it for the purpose of analysing a theme spatially and chronologically so wide spread and yet somehow invisible, hard to pinpoint and to circumscribe thanks to its blurry and liquid nature, deeply embedded in the socio-cultural context of origin is an objective far from the present possibility of this small contribute. More realistically, I shall offer merely a sketch of the topic, trying to underline some of its most peculiar features in the late 17th century Venice, hoping that some of its sparks and suggestions could be worthwhile in the current effort of this workshop.

I. A few basic coordinates

The peculiar nature of blasphemy, standing between sin and crime since its beginnings, opens up to today's students as a tricky and blurry, yet fascinating field of research. Although most legally and theoretically solid formulations regarding this composite essence of blasphemy, destined to vast success especially in the English-speaking world's juridical tradition, are to be found in some mid-17th century trials held in England, especially that against John Taylor and the sentence formulated by Sir Matthew Hale,[1] we can trace this kind of link earlier:

---

1   "such kind of blasphemous words were not only an offence to God and religion, but also a crime against the laws, State and Government, and therefore punishable [...] for to say that religion is a cheat, is to dissolve all those obligations whereby the civil societies are preserved, and that Christianity is parcel of the law of England; and therefore to reproach the Christian religion is to speak in subversion of the law". From the sentence of Lord Chief Justice Sir Matthew Hale against John Taylor, 1672; LAWTON, 1993, p. 26.

the dominant school of thought on the subject links this peculiar nature to the origins of blasphemy, found in the Hebrew and Greek practice.[2] More prudently, I shall merely highlight this topic whit respect to what is to be found in some Venetian sources.

In 1537, the *Esecutori contro la bestemmia* were created as the first secular magistrate appointed exclusively to regulate the wide-spread and troublesome practice of blasphemy registered in Venice, "in order that the reverence toward God, upon which depends the advantage of public society and mostly of this Republic of ours, be always before our eyes";[3] in his 1613 scripture "Regarding the office of the Inquisition", Paolo Sarpi (the great theologian and juridical advisor of the early 17th century republic) proposed to split the jurisdiction over blasphemy between secular and religious magistrates, stating that "ecclesiastical punishments are not sufficient penances for such heinous action. [...]. [These laws we are proposing] do not deprive nor prevent knowledge and verdict of the Inquisition regarding the nature and the suspicion of heresy: but, leaving these matters to that tribunal, (secular magistrates) punish the crime otherwise not sanctioned".[4] Inside the dominant school of thought on the topic, blasphemy has been incorporated in the long and progressive course of change in the European way of thoughts, philosophies, manners and habits that, in short, we can call desecration or, using a more fitting term, scepticism or unbelief (a concept maybe more blurred than non-belief, relating more to a lack of interest than an atheist opposition to the world of the sacred, and for this reason preferred in this contribute), towards all aspects of associated life and cul-

---

2 As I have been able to find, the habit of starting the recount of blasphemy's history linking it to its most ancient origins is quite common. From one of the first study to be found focused on this theme (LEVY, 1981), this trend has been passed down to more recent studies (LAWTON, 1993; NASH, 2007 and 2010). Only recently this somehow troublesome topic of the origin of western blasphemy has been bypassed for more focused studies.

3 ASV, *Esecutori contro la Bestemmia*, b. 53: *"onde doversi haver sempre davanti li occhi il timore di Dio, dal quale dipende il beneficio pubblico e spezialmente di questa nostra Repubblica."*

4 *Sopra l'Officio dell'Inquisizione*, 1613, Paolo Sarpi: *"le pene ecclesiastiche non sono sufficiente castigo di così gran scelleratezza. [...] non levano nè impediscono la cognizione e sentenza dell'inquisizione per la qualità e la suspicione di heresia: ma, lasciata quella circostanza al giudicio di quel tribunale, puniscono il delitto che resterebbe impunito"*: GAMBARIN, 1958, p. 169.

ture, process that contributed to create the idea itself of "modernity", as perceived by women and men of the 21st century. About this vast topic, I shall recall merely the articles of David Wootton, *Unbelief in Early Modern Europe*, 1985 and Silvia Berti *At the Roots of Unbelief*, 1995. Especially the latter, pointing out the inconsequential (or at least not strictly consequential) link between unbelief and other more radical forms of irreligious behaviour, conviction and philosophy, has been enlightening about the topic of blasphemy, all too often presented as the first sign of inevitable atheism. However, over this quite linear link between blasphemy, radical unbelief and modern forms of speech, manners and thoughts is imprinted the speculation of most of the Anglo-Saxon research on blasphemy.

Furthermore, thanks to its somehow vague essence and absolute vernacular nature, blasphemy has been placed beneath more complex and articulated forms of secular or religious dissent in determining this long path to the modern world. It is difficult to clearly discern how different dimensions participated to form the early modern conglomerate of speeches, manners, believes and practices that was deemed blasphemous by early modern women and man: anthropological tendencies and basic needs of expressing frustration, envy and desire for revenge of the lower social groups against those above them mixed variously with leaked and misguided interpretations of new philosophical and religious tendencies, different manners and habits of social coexistence, bravado and common rudeness, practice and rituals of expressing rage, anger, honour. The balance between these and others polarities between different people changes greatly, or even between different acts of blasphemy committed by the same person. However, reading the proceedings and the summaries of the *Esecutori* verdicts (*Raspe*), we can see how the practice of blasphemy in Venice concerned the entire social spectrum, from nobles to the most humble of citizens. Even in the same proceeding, we can see the mixture between the social spectrum, and not surprisingly: blasphemy was especially uttered in those places (casinos, taverns, brothels) were social barriers easily tended to fall apart. Reasons, uses, punishments and the visibility of these different practices varied greatly, but the common milieu that hosted blasphemous practices tells us of a deep interconnected world. Peter Burke is enlightening with respect to the recreation of this dense context, especially for his contribution about the comic and the communication in early modern Italy.[5]

Although especially in the case of Venice, some studies regarding the practice of popular information and religious deviances have clearly stated that we can hardly consider early modern Italy (especially the urban context) to be clearly divided into an upper, exclusive culture and a low-class tradition mute one to the other, blasphemy is still considered the lesser son of greater sires. In recent years, the research of both Filippo de Vivo and Federico Barbierato helped to form a picture of the lagoon city much more plastic and dynamic than that generally considered before. While focused on different topics, their studies helped in the recreation of Venice as a complex, crowded and undisciplined system of different needs and interests, with social, economic and cultural boundaries so porous to be unable to block willing or unconscious trespassers, a trend increasing during the 17th century. A trend documented even by contemporary witnesses: all things considered, I think that when Ludovico Zuccolo wrote that

> "few are the men that, even if they never ruled, pretend not to be able to give an opinion over the administration of republics and empires [...] barbers and other more humble workers in their shops and in their gatherings use to speak and judge over the national interest and they believe to know when something is done for reasons of national interest, and when it is not"

the author was not merely vouching for an aristocratic perspective, but was witnessing a change (quite disturbing for him) that stretched from political discourse to a vast variety of collateral topics, making what was held too important to be popularized outside selected coteries a common topic of chatter and debate.[6]

---

5 BURKE, 1988 and 2000.
6 See the bibliography DE VIVO (2012) and BARBIERATO (2006); the quotation of Ludovico Zuccolo is to be found in INFELISE, 2011, p. VII; *"pochi sono quegli uomini i quali, benché non governasser mai, non pretendano di saper dar giudicio della amministrazione delle republiche e degli imperii [...] i barbieri eziando e li altri più vili artefici nele lor botteghe e nei lor ritrovi discorrono e questionano della ragion di stato e si*

It may be an old rhetorical trick to point out the complexity of the subject chosen, sometimes used mainly to gain support in the speech; nevertheless, I have to outline some of the limitations encountered in researching a shifting and uncertain topic as blasphemy, and more specifically blasphemy in early modern Italy, to better understand it.

First of all, it is striking how copious and various historical sources are to be found somehow related to blasphemy: legal proceedings, city and community constitutional charts and juridical codes, theological dissertations, novels and other published literature, private writings as diaries, letters, *memoires* as also more ephemeral but vastly spread and deeply rooted form of communication such as songs, printed or hand-written papers, jester's and later theatrical plays, not to mention blasphemy's ubiquitous presence inside the context of the oral world. The impression we harbour from many of the legal proceedings is of a society of chatters that disregards and hides the ubiquitous practice of chatting not only about common topics, but also about more relevant and delicate matters. Both Barbierato and De Vivo underlined the long process that made taboo and daring propositions or interpretations regarding the basic rules of religion, faith and political power (themes, we have to remember, deeply intertwined in the early modern period) wide spread topics of free and peculiar interpretation. Many proximities (of kin and family, but also related to dwelling, workplace, faith, socialisation and free-time occupations) emerge from these trials, underlying dense patterns and practices of oral communication that had the strength to bypass given limitations. Sometimes, even some sensible news travelled faster than would normally be allowed, as in the many cases when a witness or even the accused release a deposition at the tribunal (all blasphemy cases were held by courts of justice using the inquisitorial procedure, a strictly secret procedure) long before the trial is made public. But more important, we obtain the impression of a context nearly without boundaries of sorts: in the houses of the prostitutes and in the gambling dens found everywhere despite regulations, in the shops, in the streets, in private houses and even in churches we can see a constant coming and going of different people of different cultural, economic, juridical and social status mixing together disorderly, usually

---

danno a credere di conoscere quali cose si facciano per ragion di stato e quali no".

for a very brief time span, but enough to break the illusion of a strictly class-divided seclusion. A city-wide milieu of continuous cultural translation and adaptation, where "a circular course of images and themes, where what comes back is never the same of what was intended"[7] was the standard rule, not the exception.

Even if I had chosen to use the most traditional approach insofar, founding my research on trials and juridical theory, it is impossible to turn a blind eye to the other dimension of the topic, spanning beyond the courts of justice. Moreover, the use of trials in historical research changed greatly over time:[8] passed the habit of considering them an ill-mannered kind of historical research, the enthusiasm and later the scepticism over their use, now regarded prudently as peculiarly intertwined and deeply context-related exchange, a sort of play between the magistrates, the accused and all the witnesses ensued. To acknowledge early modern legal proceeding not as a pure expression of rationality but as a complex mixture of different needs, mediations, powers, fiction and truth (aspects differently perceived by different scholars) permitted to some historians to reconstruct and analyse deeply the rationality behind the norming and punishment of blasphemy by the great power of early modern Europe, the church and the rising secular state. For early modern Venice, two main studies that share this kind of approach and regarding the *Esecutori* are those of Gaetano Cozzi and Renzo Derosas. Both authors agree that the increasing presence of the theme of blasphemy in theological and juridical documents, found across all western Europe starting from the mid of the 16th century, has much to do not with an increase in its practice, but by the change in perception towards blasphemy by the established powers of the time. Both focused their work over the need manifested by the early modern state to regulate areas of interest traditionally perceived as an ecclesiastical prerogative, as part of a jurisdictional tension partially up with the times and the European context, partially in line with Venice's traditional fierce defence of its jurisdiction. While both emphasised the increasing need felt by the political and secular state to defend religion and to standardise and conform the indiscipline incarnated by the

---

7   BURKE, 1988, p. 148.
8   For the estate of the art in Italy, a good summary is given by DEL COL, 1994.

blasphemers, Cozzi deems this process a form of "paternalistic humanitarianism" consistent with the usual practice of power of an early modern state, while Derosas evokes (even if briefly) the change of perspective over the lowest cultural and social groups we can sense behind these changes and consequently, we may add, to the beginning of a new form of cultural identity chosen and elaborated by the political elites, less inclusive and less tolerant than before towards blasphemy.[9]

Secondly, however, this particular point of view had been mainly used proceeding exclusively upstream, starting from the juridical proceedings and aiming to define the logic of power behind and beneath them, presenting the trials as the direct manifestation of a form of power conceptualized as strong, linear and clearly established, variously divided between different religious and secular formal institutions. If we employ only this perspective, the examination of juridical proceedings could hide and simplify the topic we are trying to outline more than enlighten it: in the first place, because it reinstates in new forms a strict and separated partition between up and down, in which legal rationality product of the top of the political body is imposed to a downward class of subjects, free-willed only in the choice of whether accepting the system, or fleeing it; secondly, because it reduces blasphemy (along with other forms of deviance) to the field of justice and so forth to its definition as a crime. Historians experienced in political and juridical anthropology have done much to enrich the debate about power, justice and the application of the law in early modern Italy. In a recent article, Claudio Povolo presented the juridical theory as a "rhetoric of deviance [...] aimed at persuading, but also describing, listing, separating, and sanctioning the legitimate behaviour of those inside with respect of those outside", rationalisation of "the vast and uncertain social phenomenon known as criminality or deviance".[10]

Even if I mostly tend to agree with this interpretation, the logical fork between crime and accepted behaviour, if applied solely in this context, is somehow inadequate in a study of this kind, shadowing the process of deep mediation of powers and prerogatives intertwined with the practice of blasphemy. Only the most daring (or, we shall see, inconvenient) cases of blasphemy were reported to the authorities: all

---

9   COZZI, 2000, p. 86; DEROSAS, 1980, p. 446.
10   POVOLO, 2007, p. 36.

others were blunted and absorbed before they were recognised and sanctioned as crimes, entering the blurry field of acceptable deviance. The risk is to underestimate this slippery, yet pivotal angle of the problem. Somehow, this operation is justified by the legal definition of blasphemy during history; nonetheless, to reduce this deviant practice to its legal sanction only is greatly diminishing its scope. Deemed as a usually excusable *lapsus mentis* in medieval theological and juridical dissertations, blasphemy became "anti-cultural" it its essence during the end of the 17th and the 18th century.[11] This change in perspective reveals a profound shift in thought: from being one of the acceptable forms of deviance, normally nullified before becoming a crime, and thus under the jurisdiction of a magistrate, blasphemy became the complete opposite of civil coexistence and society. Regarding it as the opposite position of an identity perceived as whole and unique had been the main reason for its definition as a mere crime. There could not be a theoretical sanction of a blasphemous discourse, but only one made by subtraction: blasphemy became not a vernacular and usual element of oral culture and socialization, but exclusively the leftover of the process struggling to build a common identity, not something to regulate, but something to delete (this is, of course, in theory). This is somehow traceable in the so called *Raspe*, the summary of all the sentences pronounced by the court of the *Esecutori* in the two and a half centuries of its life: omnipresent in the proceedings, recalled and carefully measured by the prosecutor, blasphemy progressively became quite difficult to find in the final verdicts, until it practically vanished in late 17th century.[12]

Just as every linguistic act, blasphemy itself had very different meanings and functions, related to whom, where, when and why someone was pronouncing it. Although some more strict and intransigent theologians (Meister Eckhart *in primis*) deemed otherwise, some others and especially the forensic practice (and already in the 15th century in Spain[13]) paid great attention to determining where, in the presence of whom and possibly why blasphemous speeches were pronounced as late as during the 17th century. Some of the medieval justifications help

---

11 LAWTON, 1993, p. 119.
12 ASV, *Esecutori contro la Bestemmia*, b. 66-67.
13 FLYNN, 1995, p. 40.

to consider blasphemy as a "slip of the mind", a moment when what was said was parted from what was intended, were still considered by the courts of justice until the late 18th century, and largely used by the accused in their defence: drunkenness, anger, gambling, frustration, misfortune etc.[14] Moreover, as all linguistic acts, its precise meaning would have been impossible to understand outside of its precise context, and its uses encompassed a wide variety of possible functions in early modern (as well as modern) practice of communication. However, this variety of uses will become progressively more irrelevant in the penal discourse, as the courts of justice began to recognise all blasphemers as willingly rebels.[15]

Moreover, when blasphemy became increasingly identified (in the mind of the common people as well as the penal codes) not only as matter of word, but a composite mixture of practices, beliefs, ways of life and social status, the legal sanctioning of it encompassed only a small portion of the wide spectrum of its nature, focusing on more pressing and proven items and skipping the vaguest. Just to quote an example: on the 26th of November 1704 three men, all incarcerated at the time by the *Avogaria de Comun* (one of the oldest and originally the most prestigious penal tribunal in Venice), were accused of blasphemy before the *Esecutori contro la Bestemmia* by anonymous entities. The description of one of them, along with the progressive increase of fields of jurisdiction recognised to the *Esecutori* half a century from their creation,[16] tells us about the deep complexity of this practice, and the inevitable problems and hindrance of its regulation:

"Battista Pagiaro [...] uses to blaspheme every day with great frequency [...] not only when impatient or gambling, but ordinarily speaking and even joking [...] he is used to throw up from his heart endless blasphemies. [...] He is used to talk about sodomy, sometimes explaining the taste of this sin, some others joking about someone else in jail [...] his infamous tongue always speaking of scandalous sensuality, about men and women alike, and

---

14 NASH, 2007, p. 3.
15 Regarding the function of language, I retain to the *schema* found in JAKOBSON, 1960; for the progressive diminishing relevance of the mitigating circumstances, LAWTON, 1993, cpt. 4; CABANTOUS, 2002, cpt. 5.
16 COZZI, 1991, pp. 80-82.

many times he has shown himself completely naked, jesting over his male organ".

Also, as very precisely stated further, he does not respect religious rules of nutrition.[17] They are all full-condemned: shame punishment and whipping in *piazza San Marco*, with their tongue in a *mordacchia* (a sort of wooden vise) for six hours; a moderate fine (in absolute terms: but considering their conditions, it is unlikely they could easily afford it) and six months rowing in a state-owned galley each. They are deemed guilty and punished quite sternly (being the worst possible recorded penalty for blasphemy the cut of the tongue or, but it was extremely rare, the removal of a hand and an eye) not in regard of their moral and religious beliefs, which are just stated, but simply in regard of where their deviant behaviour was manifested, and the consequential danger of its implication. Their morality became inconsequential: or, to be more precise, their action poured necessarily from a willingly wicked and deviant disposition.

Thirdly, but I shall only speak briefly on this point, blasphemy in Italy is now-a-days quite different from blasphemy elsewhere in Europe. Quoting Maureen Flynn:

> "Among the most common interjections in the vernacular languages of the West are those that take the name of God in vain. [...] Although these expressions may appear to be meaningless today, sliced into our conversations for spice and momentary release from thought, they have not always been regarded as an innocuous form of speech".[18]

The shift in blasphemous speech, from sin to crime to manner of speaking, is certainly a fact to be kept in mind when examining the long run

---

17 ASV, *Esecutori contro la Bestemmia*, b. 3: *"Battista Pagiaro [...] è solito biastemar quotidianamente con frequenza [...] non solo in atto di impazienza, o nel gioco, ma nell'ordinario discorso e nelli parlari scherzevoli [...] è solito vomitar dal suo cuore inumerabili spergiuri [...] Che molto spesso suole muovere discorsi di sodomia, ora spiegando i gusti di questo peccato, e ora scherzando verso qualche altra persona di prigione [...] la di lui lingua infame che sempre parla sensualità enormi, tanto sopra femina che sopra maschio, e molte volte mostrorsi nudo affatto scherzando sopra il suo membro genitale."*

18 FLYNN, 1995, p 31.

of this practice (especially on the matter of profane swearing). However, if we can agree that no one at the present times would question matters of faith if a person expressed her/his stupor or other light emotional perturbation during the act of speech by saying *"my God", "oh Gott", "Dios Mios"* or *"Mio Dio"*, the situation in Italy would be quite different. I did not have the means to conduct a serious statistical study or an anthropological enquiry with respect to this topic, I shall therefore refrain from stressing it: I shall simply state that the contemporary use of blasphemy in Italy has retained something of its ancestor's features, in the way of being a low-regarded and despicable but quite widespread form of speech, daring in its literal form the moral and orthodox practice of faith but not perceived as such, often spoken out of deep emotional stress, often a form of use, a manner of speaking, full of meaning yet deprived of any significance.

Daring and troubling blasphemous acts of speech are in some ways linked to Italy since the 16th century. In 1526, the Spanish Inquisition takes to process a young servant born in Naples, known by the commoners as "Angelo the Holy" (*Angelo el sancto*) for his less than savoury habits: he used to mutter tremendous words. The obscene and repulsive formulation, mixing different types of offence against religion was quite common in Italy, as far as we can glean from the juridical sources: in fact, when confronted with the scandal of his propositions, he justified himself: "Back in Italy, one hears people in the streets utter foul proclamations like this for whatever frustration they might feel".[19] The defence before the inquisitorial tribunal could have been exaggerated: but reading the proceedings of the *Santo Uffizio*, the *Consiglio dei Dieci* and the *Esecutori contro la Bestemmia* reveals a verbal use of blasphemy in mid-seventeenth century Venice not too different from that described by Angelo in the early 16th century Naples. The lewdest, most scandalous and most daring assault on religiousness in all its

---

19 Angelo was denounced for the expression *"Rinego de Diu e de nuestra dona puta fututa en el culo cornuda."* FLYNN, 1995, p. 32. However, the fact that these "remarks which rang scandalously in the ears of the Castilian public" were truly so unbearable by 16th century Iberian audience could be exaggerated: even in Venice all the witness of blasphemous practice used to underline their distance and the scandalous nature of the blasphemy heard in front of the tribunal, only to be found often author of same or more daring speeches.

forms came under deep stress, but also naturally, as a manner of speaking, revealing a practice far beyond any real control by the city authorities and, we could say, sometimes even beyond the control of the one pronouncing them.

How this perception grounded itself and became so widespread, as well as its possible links to modern practices of blasphemy or peculiar habits of early modern Italian irreligious behaviour, stretches far outside the reach of my present study.

II. Blasphemy and Blasphemers

The deep complexity regarding nature and interpretation of blasphemy, which I have tried to loosely summarise in the first part of the article, has proved to be extremely difficult to represent and to theorise especially in writing, and this fact had hindered its fortune as a subject of study *per se*. Most of the scholars I have encountered confronting the topic of blasphemy mainly had to choose between two options to solve this issue: to reduce its complex and intertwined to a more plain status, or to take it to the extreme. Of course, this remark is not at all intended as an evaluation of the value of the past literature, and every scholar had faced the problem with different angles and perspectives: but, in wider terms, the decision had to fall somewhere in between these two trends.

In the first case, we have the researches (many of them have been cited previously) that favour only some characters or even perspectives regarding the topic and make them keys to its interpretation, shifting progressively the remaining aspects (the most peculiar, and most vague) far from the core of the new definition, deeming them as trivial. The conception resulting from this refining process is somehow monochromatic, but is sufficiently well-defined to be employed for geographically and chronologically wide-spanning narratives.[20] In the second case,

---

20 In this case the focus shifts (mainly) between the grand narratives established by the traditional schools of political and juridical history and history of thought. While we can relate Italian scholars (COZZI, DEROSAS) to the first trend and Anglo-Saxons authors (LEVY, LAWTON, NASH) to the second one, a strict division is somehow inappropriate: frameworks and

and this is by far the least followed method, the logic of peculiarity and distinctiveness regarding blasphemous cases, or even one single blasphemy case, has been enhanced to recreate the context-specific dimension where the fact took place. In Italy, this approach has been used by Giovanni Scarabello: his focus on topics deemed liminal by some of his contemporary colleagues, and the attention to the hosting milieu had influenced his perspective, leading to a book intended to recreate an early 18th century trial held by the *Esecutori* and the thick anthropological environment within which the facts recounted took place.[21] This procedure, however, not too different from that used by Carlo Ginzburg in his famous study over the Friulian miller *Menocchio*, along with the creation of a much more complex and rich picture of the theme of blasphemy, harbours risks and complications related to the uniqueness of the case examined: beyond the precise recount of a single event, similar to many others, which makes us sure we are succeeding in recreating a micro-cosmos, a complex system of ideas, ways of thoughts and beliefs somehow related to the general trend of the times, and not simply narrating a quaint anecdote?[22]

In this second part of the presentation, I shall attempt an approach half way between these two: as a comparison, I shall try to read some trials found in the archives of the *Esecutori* and the *Holy Office*. My intent is to focus on the practice of blasphemy and to suggest some communal features of blasphemers, something recurring in their description before the magistrates. As far as possible, I shall try to reason not about single unrelated people, but the blurry and sketchy definition that was necessary to consider someone the blasphemous type. In this sense, I hope that the cases I shall bring as examples, while obviously related to particular situations, enlighten a wider trend.

I shall start with some observations of blasphemous practice in speech itself. It is somehow striking how the injurious words reported to the *Santo Uffizio* and the *Esecutori*, found abundantly in the absolute majority of the trials, mainly conformed to four specific types. Moreover, three of them referred to God (Christ was blasphemed quite less

---

suggestions from both traditions are variously approached and reinterpreted by these scholars.

21 SCARABELLO, 1991.
22 GINZBURG, 1999, pp. XIX-XXII.

frequently, and the Holy Ghost hardly ever: in both cases, they took the place of God in the speech) and where aimed at the desecration of his all-mighty definition and the parody of the cardinal Catholic mystery, the transubstantiation; only one of them focused on the Holy Mary, and attacked another mystery of all Christianity, her virginity, in various and disturbing ways. Blasphemy was then articulated by its perpetrators in various pejorative forms: *Sangue, Sanguazzo, Sanguenazzo*; *Corpo, Corpazzo, Corponazzo*; *Cospetto, Cospettone, Cospettazzo, Cospettonazzo etc.* All these formulations, however, highly similar in our perception, were absolutely not interchangeable: they were all accounted for precisely by the magistrates, and also reported prudently by the witnesses, so we must presume they corresponded to different degrees of wicked behaviour. Sometimes, especially during long proceedings with many accused, the magistrates used to write down in two or three pages (usually half-way through the process) all the blasphemous words proved to have been pronounced by every accused, the exact formulation and the precise number of witness reporting the given blasphemy:[23] somewhere between a summary and a statistical analysis. The mathematical mentality beneath this process is mainly related to juridical practice: as in every inquisitorial trial, three concordant witnesses were required to render a statement valid, either as an accusation or as a defence, so a particular case whit less than the minimal concordant witnesses would have been ignored, if not proven differently – usually, the difference between an easily aborted proceeding and a more serious one was whether the accused was summoned before court; moreover, the difference between the previously stated forms of blasphemy were combined, forming a play of additions and multiplication we fail to precisely understand. A 17th century Venetian magistrate possessed and used a certain mental habit strict enough to allow comparison between blasphemies and to position them in a scale of magnitude, where the place was subject to the frequency-seriousness ratio.

The presence of such a small range of possible offences against the Divinity, in a city landscape, as we stated previously, so lively and rich

---

23 ASV, *Esecutori contro la Bestemmia*: b. 2, trial *"per Bestemie contra Francesco Pichioluto retento anni 5 in Galera; Giacomo Tirabosco retento anni 3 Galera; Battista Pagiaro Bandito"*; b. 3, trial *"contro Antonio Ianucci"*.

in different and deviant behaviours, deeply plagued by the sin of blasphemy – as stated and of course exaggerated by many official voices[24] – is somehow suspicious. In fact, if we examine the documents just a bit more precisely, we can see that the constant recurrence of common forms in the juridical proceedings is more apparent than real. As we glimpse into some particular trials, the arrays of blasphemous words and acts at the disposition of 17th century Venetians were much more varied.[25] But most importantly, we have the far more common cases of

---

24 ASV, *Esecutori contro la Bestemmia*, Capitulary (b. 54): "because Our Lord and Holy Mother Mary and the Saints are blasphemed, even in the public places, without any reverence or fear to offend our Maker and Benefactor, so we are called to fix these great sins, reason of the Divine Fury against our city and our people" (*"perciochè si biastema il Signore Dio Nostro et la Madre Vergine Maria, Santi, et Sante, etiam in li giudicij et lochi publici, senza alcuna riverentia, over timor di offendere il Creator, et Benefattor Nostro, tanto che si deve provveder a così grandi errori, li quali sono causa de procurar la Divina ira contro la Città, et popoli"*); "This council (the Council of Ten) whit the best interest to extirpate, to eradicate those who blaspheme the Holy Name of God, established punishments against them [...] to have always as a top priority the fear of God, by whom depends the well-being of our Republic" (*"Questo consegio col la ottima intenzion de estirpar, eradicar li biastematori del Santiss.o nome de Dio, ha statuito le pene contro di loro [...] onde douendosi hauer sempre avanti li occhi il timor di Dio, dal qual dipende il beneficio della Repubblica nostra"*).
25 ASV, *Santo Uffizio*, b. 124, trial *Contra Mario Tolomeo Nerucci*. The protagonist of this trial had a quite stratified and complex way to insult the divinity, other than the more common ones: "'If I had lived at the time of the Hebrews, I would have made my share against Christ; I want to go to Saxony to repudiate Christ, but in fact I have already repudiated him,' and then he added 'he was hanged as a thief!', talking about Christ. One time as he passed in front of a statue of Holy Mary he said she was a prostitute. I have heard him to say 'Christ, I would give you fifty wounds with a knife!'. And one evening going home from the gambling den near the Lovo bridge, in a little colonnade just down the stairs, where was placed an image with a crucified Christ, Holy Mary and other saints, he tossed a small silver coin to them, with maximum contempt. And another time he urinated over those images with deep disgust, saying 'Here! Here!'". (*"se fossi stato al tempo degli hebrei, avrei fatto la mia parte contro Cristo, voglio andar in Sassonia per renegar Christo, se bene è un pezzo che ci ho renegato, e poi soggiungeva, fu impiccato per ladro! riprendendo ciò al medesimo Christo. Et una volta passando davanti ad un'immagine della vergine disse bugiarona. Ancora ho sentito dire Christo ti vorrei dare 50 stilattate. Et una volta nel uscir dal ridotto al Ponte del Lovo, in un*

speeches that, even if characterised by propositions usually regarded as matter of inquisitorial scope, daring to the orthodoxy of Catholicism or to religion as a whole, and thus found in the *Santo Uffizio* archives (therefore called both by the juridical theorists, the magistrates and the witnesses "Heretical Blasphemies", *bestemmie hereticali*) referred to these themes in such a botched, partial and superficial way that separated these from the more accomplished of various faith contestants;[26] moreover, and we shall return to this point, the theatrical aim of these speeches sought to achieve, and often the presence of a state of deep emotional stress when they were uttered, are two characteristics to which we can relate the practice of blasphemy. Expressions such as "I renounce God", "The devil has my souls", "There is no soul", and many other similar cases were extremely common,[27] but to see them as the

---

portighetto giù delle scale, ove è l'immagine di un crocifisso, la madonna e altri santi, viddi che gettò con gran spezzo una moneta d'argento contro un'immagine del crocifisso. Ed un'altra volta sopra dette immagini orinò con gran sprezzo, dicendo tò tò").

26 In his work of legal and theological consultant for the Republic, Paolo Sarpi proposed a legal system in which all blasphemies had to be identified whether to be Ordinary, or to be Heretical. Both blasphemy types should have been jurisdiction of the civil magistrates as offences against the common interest of the State and the common well-being, while only the latter was passed also to the Inquisition, for the possibility of heretical beliefs underscored by these blasphemous formulations. The distinction between Ordinary and Heretical blasphemy is however too weak and vague to be of some use: "Heretical blasphemy is not the same than atrocious blasphemy: more atrocious is the one much more daring and of greater insult, heretical the one spurring much more suspicion of heresy, even if lighter" (*"bestemmia hereticale non è lo stesso che bestemmia atroce: più atroce è quella più grave e di maggior ingiuria, più hereticale quella da cui nasce maggior suspicione d'heresia, anche se minore"*, GAMBARIN, 1958, p. 170). Latter juridical doctrines (TIRABOSCO 1636, PRIORI 1738) will abandon this unclear division, abstaining themselves from a topic too blurry to be the key to the system.

27 This statements could be particularly colourful, symptoms of a blasphemous practice that had much to do whit the immediate experiences found in everyday life. As the one of Marina *Chiouzota* (Marina from Chioggia, near Venice) that used to state to have less soul of a pumpkin, especially when she was scolded for her blasphemous practices. "And what about your soul?", asked to her a fellow laundress. "Soul? Since when pumpkins have souls?" (*"'Mo l'anima?' E Marina rispose ad esse col dirle, 'Mo l'anima han le zucche?'"*): ASV, Santo Uffizio, b. 80.

evidence of a city ravaged by atheists is somehow inaccurate because it emphasises the willingness and ideological and moral commitment to the contents of blasphemy on one hand, and makes the expression of this supposed ideology the aim or the accidental result of the deviant speech on the other. In the Anglo-Saxon world, other than John Taylor, the other example to underscore the change towards blasphemy by the authorities is that of the Quaker James Nayler. His personal story, leading to his entrance in Bristol on the Palm Sunday of 1656, riding a mule bareheaded while his fellow adepts saluted him as the Messiah, sounds quite different from the story of the absolute majority of the Venetian cases: the precise consciousness, the solid theological knowledge and expertise he manifested while building his religiousness, and the life-long commitment to his ideals, willingly expressed and never denied, are all aspects I have still failed to appreciate, or to find in any Venetian trial for blasphemy.[28] To sustain this observation, I shall need to answer – at least briefly – the two questions mentioned above: where blasphemy was pronounced, and why? What kind of emotional state generated it?

First of all, blasphemy had not so much to do with its literal value as the context in which it was pronounced: in this sense, blasphemy was dramatized or, in some cases, *carnivalized*. At least in Venice, blasphemy occupied one of the steps (just like a common insult) in the anthropological ritual of early modern violence, a kind of alarm placed as the last device of a boundary not to be crossed, penalty as the necessary demonstration of material violence against the opponent, his family or his possessions. Donald Weinstein reconstructed the story of a verbal duel occurred in 1559 between the siblings of two great Pistoian's families, Lanfredino Cellesi and Pietro Gatteschi, led by the exchange of insults, friction between the two coteries and injurious cartels posted in the city's most frequented spaces. An episode like many others, but somehow symptomatic of the new practice of preserving and defending honour in early modern Italy: "A duel fought between two men over a question of honour, according to a formal scenario. In place of swords and daggers they fought with words, thousands of words over a period of many days"; a peculiar form of duel, was "the lengthy verbal display

---

28   LAWTON, 1993, pp. 62-74; NASH, 2007, pp. 119-122.

(was considered) just as effective in validating their honourable status as a trial of arms".[29]

In this case, we are presented with two rather similar people: they share a common cultural and anthropological ground due to them coming from a similar background, being both nobles from the same city also tied by a familiar bond (they were cousins). In a situation such as this, we can accept that they are fighting for something we can call "pure" honour. But honour with a capital H is rarely an absolute value, increasingly becoming a wide spanning construct, claimed with different emphases, pertinence and intention by different people, and mediating between different needs and drives:[30] also, thanks to the vernacular nature of the practice of blasphemy, honour tended to blend differently into different situations, mixing its prerogatives with others of another nature. It is a matter of honour that ignited the rudeness, the blasphemous speech and later the violence of the nobleman Gasparo Longo: not recognised as a noble by a ferryman, "despite the apologies of the ferryman, he was not satisfied by having offended him with the most gruesome words, and he said to him he had to get off the boat and dismount on land. Since the ferryman was reluctant, he drew his knife and holding the ferryman by his clothes he stabbed him twice".[31] At the other end of the social scale, honour was mixed with more practical concerns: it was the honour and good reputation among friends and relatives of Nicolò Pasina, captain of the ferry that took the people from the mainland to Venice, which was at stake during his trial for blasphemy, but also his trade; because, while he was held and interrogated for his supposed crimes along with the rowers of his ship, his false and

29 WEINSTEIN, 1994, p. 204 and p. 217.
30 I will not open here a dissertation over the matter of honour. I will only suggest some bibliography I used to set the frame of the discussion: a formulation regarding honour in early modern Venice and its socio-political implications, POVOLO, 1997; two study quite outdated but still well capable to clarify some of the different and changing values and practices regarding the theme of honour, MARAVALL, 1986 and PITT-RIVERS, 1977.
31 ASV, *Esecutori contro la Bestemmia*, b. 67: *"non ostante le giustificazioni del suddetto non contendo di haverlo ingiuriato con più vilanie gli disse, che dovesse smontar di gondola ed adare in terra dal che mostrando lui renitenza pose mano ad un stilo e questo preso per gli habiti gli diede nella sua barca due ferite."*

gossip-mongering enemies could destroy and sink his boat.[32] We have seen examples from the upper and the lower classes of the Venetian population; but again, a strict division between these two alternatives could be inappropriate because, the situation was sometimes far more complex than a partition between those who are above and those who are below. When in 1686 Mario Tolomeo Nerucci, a noble man from Siena known in Venice as *Count Mario*, was arrested by the *Santo Uffizio*, half a dozen of his fellow gamblers where called to testify during his trial. While three of them presented themselves as nobles, their habits and their means are somehow striking against the status they exhibited, sometimes proudly: just like Mario Nerucci, they were all foreigners who fled their native city to escape justice; they lived in humble and precarious accommodations; they did not mention to be employed in labours of any kind; two of them had already been prosecuted by the *Esecutori* in Venice; they were reported blaspheming, gambling and duelling all over Venice, usually for reasons of money or women.[33] These worn-out nobles where not only foreigners: mostly during the 17th century, the increasingly number of poor nobles became a serious issue for the Republic and a share of them, failing to accomplish themselves in any other way, dedicated to a life of petty offices and small endeavours, pledging themselves variously to more influential houses, went often to increase the number of regular client of brothels, casinos and taverns, forming up a loose layer of alienated.[34] This

---

32 ASV, *Esecutori contro la Bestemmia*, b.1. The fact of owing a ship and to act towards his men as a sea captain, even if only to a small ferry whit four rowers, put placed Nicolò Pasina in a peculiar position where his honour and good reputation had to be stainless. Sea captains, whether of a military vessel or a civilian one, were somehow appointed by the common sense, and later explicitly by the law, to take care of their men, to be responsible of their moral and behavioural actions and to maintain an impeccable and moderate reputation, just as the publican towards his patrons, or the master of a trade toward his assistants, in a link of moral supervision alike the one undergoing father and sons. That ships, taverns, workplaces and even homes where the places where blasphemy was more frequently reported is something to meditate about: NASH, 2007, pp. 12-14.

33 ASV, *Santo Uffizio*, b. 124, *Contra Marium Tolomeo*.

34 The political and social problem of impoverished nobles was not of course to be found exclusively in Venice, but the high number of Venetian patrician families and the economic decline of 17th century Venice made it especially daring. A distinction formed between richer and poorer families,

common trend had at least three consequences for the city: to further blur the already liquid boundary between people in a social, political and cultural context still perceiving itself as class-divided;[35] to display a negative example of wide-spread and tolerated deviancy, to the citizen of Venice and the subject territories, also recalling from abroad people in need or longing, even temporarily, for this kind of shady lifestyle; creating a type of wide and common sense of belonging for those sharing this way of life and behaviour, linking them together, even if loosely and not exclusively.

In these cases, we can accept that blasphemy, as stated above, associated with a deep stressful condition, exacerbated by the precarious fortunes sometimes shared by these people. The effects of anger about blasphemers, of which Maureen Flynn wrote, the sensation of a tongue momentarily removed from the rational and moral control of the speaker,[36] could apply to the practice of *Count Mario*, who used to utter his quite elaborate depravities while losing at the gambling table, but afterwards "many times he felt sorry, and despised his bad habit, praying that Christ would not make his tongue to fall off his mouth, as He should have, because what he said with his mouth he was not telling with is heart"; "I have spent time with this Tolomei outside of the gambling practice, and he is the best man I have ever met, and a good Christian, too, but when he is gambling he completely loses his temper, and he said he would pay with his blood to lose this taste for gambling, because then he would blaspheme no more".[37] We should not take every anger issue as a completely honest statement: still being of some legal

---

leading to a different stratification of offices and consequentially to a change in the balance of power inside the republican system, fragmenting the necessary concord definition of Venetian nobility. For a revealing example of this long process, Cozzi, 1996.

35 On the subject, Chojnacki, 2000 and Grubb, 2003.
36 Flynn, 1995, p. 36.
37 ASV, *Santo Uffizio*, b. 124: *"molte volte dopo si mostrava pentito, e detestava il suo cattivo abito, e che si dispiaceva, che Christo non gli facesse cader la lingua, come meritava, dicendo che ben chè lo dicesse con la bocca non il diceva col core/ io ho conosciuto detto signor Tolomei fuori dal gioco per il più buon signore che habbi conosciuto, e per buonissimo christiano, ma nel gioco veramente dà nelli spropositi, e l'ho sentito dire che pagherebbe tanto sangue per non aver il rischio del gioco, per non proromper né spropositi, e besteme che preferisse".*

value for the traditional medieval justification of the *lapsus mentis*, many of these blasphemers would have resorted to it as a persistent line of defence, being that the precise moral condition of the accused at the time when the blasphemous manifestation occurred was very difficult to prove: but, all things considered, I believe that blasphemy still had much to do with anger, especially when it posed as the guardian and instrument used in a ritual play imprinted around the concept of honour.

However, in its essence as a spoken practice, blasphemy had at least one other function. In 1672 Simone Petrachin, son of a quite rich and large family working in the production and selling of false pearls, was condemned with two other women by the Holy Office to forswear his heretical practices.[38] Other than the blasphemous speeches, including his certainty about the absence of a soul of any kind and his pact with the devil to whom he ceded his soul (two contradicting propositions, but commonly used together), he was found guilty of many different magical practices: he used to blacken the hand of a young boy with ashes and oil whom, while handling a candle in front of him, could summon a spirit and ask him questions; he used the jaw of a dead man for other forms of prescience; he used to have night walks with the devil, who used to tell him the names of the nobles that were going to be elected for the game of the *Piria* (a city-wide gamble about who should have been elected in the next mandate. Thanks to the elective nature of all the offices in the Republic and their short mandate, the game was always open and well organised);[39] he was in possession of some forbidden tomes of magic; he had some incantations written on some pieces of paper he always brought with him, containing spells to bind the loved person to himself. Moreover, he used not to go to the mass, which he considered a fake and a waste of time, spoke freely about his practice of sodomy and he lived *more uxorio* with a married woman, whose husband was in jail (Camilla Borghi, one of the other

---

38 The trial is the first in ASV, *Santo Uffizio*, b. 116. We can speculate over the prosperity of the house thanks to some elements emerging from the trial: the numbers of workers simultaneously employed by the father, more than a dozen at a time; the size of the workshop-house of the family; the fact that the father of Simone will be the guarantor in front of the *Santo Uffizio* for his son and the woman of his son, leaving a substantial amount of money (nine hundred *scudi*) as a fee and will pay the lawyer for them.

39 WALKER, 1999, p. 31.

two people condemned). After many charges of this magnitude, the accusation of blasphemy under the circumstance of a loss at the gambling tables seems the least troubling: the magistrate, on the contrary, was determined especially to unravel the precise cases and surroundings of every blasphemy uttered, paying less attention to the practices of magic. The third person standing accused is an old woman, Marietta Marchiora, also charged with these and other magical practices: she is not, however, charged with blasphemy of any kind.

Between the old prostitute and the young gambler (Simone was twenty-three at the time of his trial, Marietta sixty-two) existed a quite solid bond of trust and practice, maybe even a teacher-student relationship: but their line of defence was completely different. Due also to a previous charge of blasphemy, the old woman seems quite experienced in resisting the rhetorical tactics of the inquisitorial magistrate, but outside the juridical defence she presented in the trial she probably considered herself a practitioner of that kind of magical, superstitious devotion which characterised early modern faith, causing many people in Venice to ask priests and monks to bless their clothes, sacred images and little books of prayers, but also decks of cards and pens used to sign contracts. Some elements emerging throughout the trial, even if in some cases probably moulded to form a convincing defence, at least suggest us than the religiousness of Marietta was much more complex than the binary choice of whether or not to believe the Catholic dogma:[40] she never denies her practices, only she blurs and confuses the circumstances of their occurrence, making them very difficult to firmly assess by the magistrate, and tries to circumscribe them to the forms of acceptable deviance, which, although punished, were so wide-spread to become

---

40 It is extremely difficult to state something over the religiousness of Marietta, being her trial the only source of information over her behaviour. However, whit some caution something could be speculated: her house was full of images of Holy Mary, as confirmed by a search made by the guards of the Holy Office; she cures herself whit sorceries learned by a friar; she does not make the sign of the cross properly in front of the inquisitor, correcting herself only when forced. These and other elements seem to lean towards not an atheistic or satanistic behaviour, but to a personal faith tailored using sparks and suggestions from different parts, like a patchwork. ASV, *Santo Uffizio*, b. 116.

highly tolerated in the lagoon city.[41] On the contrary, Simone exploited the same defence tactic as Camilla, who was only charged with having witnessed and attended to some of these practices: they denied having performed most of the magical ceremonies, they admitted having requested only some of them from Marchiora (to know the names for the *Piria*, to find some stolen pearls, to resolve some love affairs), and Simone in particular firmly denied any involvement with magic, the devil or sorcery, admitting just the usual practice of blasphemy, but exclusively when angered, and some minor incantations. However, though he denied all these acts, he could not deny (due also to what was stated in the vast majority of the deposition given by the witnesses) to have spoken widely about them, to have in fact performed in front of his parents and some of his father's workers some petty ritual, or to be in possession (a search by the guards of the *Santo Uffizio* found them) of some forbidden tomes and some spells written on sheets of paper. Both Camilla and Simone stated to have believed these sorceries not truly, but *"per liegerezza"*, lightly, carelessly. In her first interrogation, Camilla is asked by the inquisitor "if she believes now or had believed to be proper to a good Catholic to held such sacrilegious experiments and to call upon the devil, and to wait from him a response", she replied "I did not really think it was a good thing, but not even that it was too bad, but now that I know better I have understood that this is a vile thing, and dangerous, and I will never do this again".[42] This statement

---

41 ASV, *Santo Uffizio*, 124: Maria Pelizzari is accused by Giacomo Filomena to have made a sorcery that compelled Giovanbattista, his son, to fall in love whit a prostitute. While many considered her insane, some others describe her as a pious woman, preoccupied for the well-being of all his friends: for this reason, Holy Mary manifested to her many times, and for the same reason she could not stay too long in one place, because the devil used to search for her and hit her for all the souls she drove away from his grasp. In her deposition she admitted that many people went to her for her service, but all she did was to pray deeply for them. As she did for Giovanbattista and Elisabetta, that although loving themselves were not permitted to marry by the relatives of the groom, and lived their lives in grave danger of carnal sin. After the deposition of Maria Pelizzari, the trial against her stops. Magic, superstition, sorcery and religion mixed together quite variously, but where held in clear distinction by the authorities: SEITZ, 2011, pp. 59-72 and pp. 219-244.

42 ASV, *Santo Uffizio*, b. 116: *"se creda o habbi creduto esser lecito a buon cattolico far simili esperimenti sortileghi con far ricorso al demonio, et*

of ignorance would not save them, as they were both sentenced to pay a fine and to endure a shame punishment and a few years in jail, as did Marchiora; furthermore, Simone will be briefly tortured in the final moments of the process, to prove the firmness of his quite unsuccessful line of defence, an occurrence quite rare in the late 17th century. But the lightness of belief in the devil's power was deeply intertwined with another argument throughout the process, secondary in the strategy of defence, central for the understanding of the event and, I believe, to the practice of blasphemy in those years as a whole.

Simone and Camilla used to live together for some time in the family house of the Petrachin, along with a servant, the family (father, mother, two sons elder than Simone and two daughters) and at least five other people, some of them servants, some of them workers. One of these men, Geronimo Gabrieli called *Furlan* reports in his statement an event: one morning Camilla asked him if he had heard some commotion the previous night. He, who had not been able to sleep due to "a great racket, like the house was going to fall apart", asked her what happened. In the presence of Simone and her servant, Camilla answered "that the previous evening, during that racket, three people entered her room, one in chains, another holding him back, and a boy with a lit torch in his hands, and the boy was dark. To them she said to be gone, in the name of God, because she saw that the boy was trying to grab Simone by a foot. The chained one said that, since Simone would not deny him, he was willing to tell him that *"il corrente maggio porta"*, and all three of them opened the door and jumped down the stairs".[43] The recount above is not the only citing this fact, but is just the most thorough: by the end of the trial five people, not counting Simone and

---

aspettar da lui risposta RT veramente mi pareva cosa che non stesse bene, ma non mi credevo po che fosse tanto male, e adesso mo che conosco la gravità del fatto, credo fermamente non sia lecito, e cosa cettiva, e non farò più certo ste cose".

43   ASV, *Santo Uffizio*, b. 116: *"come un rumor grande che mi parve fosse gittata a terra la casa"*; *"che la sera suddetta al tempi di quel rumor erano entrati tre in camera, cioè uno in catena, legato con tre catene, uno che lo teneva, e un putto che teniva un torcio acceso, ed era moretto, a quali lei disse che da parte di Dio partissero, perché vide che quel moretto voleva ciapar detto Simon per un piede. Quello incatenato disse, già che non vuole disconoscerlo, diseghe che il corrente maggio porta, e partirono tutti tre spalancando la porta e zo dalle scale."*

Camilla, testified this fact to the magistrate, all of them adding or missing some particulars, but all of them heard about this diabolic visit, and all of them heard of it from Simone or Camilla. Similarly presented to the magistrate by other witnesses is another fact, also recounted by Camilla and Simone too: one night, practising some of his spells, Simone was attacked by the devil, and nearly choked to death.[44] Both Camilla and Simone stated that the facts had not really happened: the first was dreamt by Simone who woke up in the night, and told it to Camilla; the second never happened at all. How the first occurrence was a matter of dream is however reported to the magistrate by the couple, but by none of the other witnesses, so we must presume they were not told about this being a matter of dream. And for good reason: because, in recounting it, Camilla testified that "when I recounted what I saw that night dreaming I added many details of my imagination, to have a laugh, and could be that I said that the chained one was someone sentenced to death. To the recount I added endless fantasies to enjoy myself, and to make the workers chatter". The magistrate asks for further explanations.

> "Half laughing she said: I will tell how it happened. After I had the dream I have stated before I began to imagine in my mind how to recount it, and so to make it plausible I thought I had to make a great racket, as I did with my feet on the floor, and the morning after I demanded to know (from the workers) if whether they had heard any noises, and if they heard me asking for a pen, because I had to write down some names. And all this is a fantasy of mine, and when they asked me if these things were real, I said yes, they are, and then in my bedroom I laughed at them".[45]

---

44 ASV, *Santo Uffizio*, b. 116: "while he was tempting the head of a dead man at a time he was almost choked to death, because in that room there was a great confusion" (*"scongiurando la testa di morto una volta era stato quasi soffocato perché in quella camera della testa vi era una confusion grande"*).

45 ASV, *Santo Uffizio*, b. 116: *"Quando raccontai ciò che viddi quella notte in sogno aggiunsi molte cose di mio capriccio, per prendermi spasso, e può essere dicessi anco che quell'incatenato fosse un giustitiato Al che raccontar aggiunsi infinite mie imaginationi per prendermi spasso, e far dir a lavoranti"; "Subridens. Dirò come che sta. Dopo ch'ebbi il sogno come sopra incominciai figurarmi nella mente a raccontar questo fatto, e così per renderlo credibile mi imaginai far fracasso, si come anco feci co piedi sul solaro, e poi la mattina dimandai se havevano sentito fracasso, e*

This is not the only circumstance of forbidden practices willingly used by the young couple as laughing matters: all the third questioning to Simone, the longest one, is willingly played around this topic and, if examined trough, most of the depositions portrait him as a quite a frivolous young man, with little interest in his magical practices *per se* and not deeply attached to them at all, but in the reactions and feedbacks that he was able to achieve obtain by narrating them, and the resulting reputation, or even celebrity, he hoped to achieve in front of his public, composed by the people encountered in his daily life, more or less deeply connected to him, whether willingly or not to hear the enhanced and embellished recount of his deviance. Moreover, laughter is only a part of what Simone (we cannot state this for Camilla) wanted to obtain from his recount: or, to be more specific, his recount of laughter at forbidden practices held another significance a part from the collateral *divertissement* obtained. Increasingly from the middle of the trial, Simone often stated that "in fact none I have recounted was real, but I used to recount it to be held *bravo*". *"Bravo"*, meaning mostly "good" or "able", had retained in some proverbs of nowadays Italian language its former significance of "daring", "courageous", and "reckless", in some proverbs of the current Italian language as in the English form "bravado": in the 17th century, this remained by far its first meaning.[46]

Conclusions

The exhibition of these sorts of behaviours, and others I have yet to appreciate and outline, was one of the core reasons behind the preparation of most blasphemy cases. The strict distinction between the function of verbal blasphemy I have outlined are by no means intended as strict and complete, impervious to one another: honour, laughter and

---

se mi havvano sentito a dimandar da scrivere, perché voleva notar delli nomi. E tutto questo è stata mia inventione. è ben vero che raccontando tali cose mi dicevo se fossero vere, e io li dicevo certo certo, et era così, et io poi in camera me ne ridevo".

46 ASV, *Santo Offizio*, b. 116: *"in verità niente di vero era in tutto ciò, e lo diceva per essere stimato bravo"*. For the significance of the term *"Bravo"* see BOERIO, 1867.

bravado mixed themselves together in different parts and contributed all to the same play, as they were all means of placing a person in a specific space inside his context, to characterize one's reputation in front of his public. Of course, I am not stating that nothing was genuine in the 17th century, that what all the people did was to play a part in the complex baroque theatre life had become. I am simply pointing out that much of what was expressed throughout blasphemous speech was intended to achieve a function different to that immediately perceivable as the literal sense of the message: signifier and meaning were not always in strict accord and were highly subjective. Elements of angry, honourable, vulgar, superstitious, brave, rude, sceptical, irreligious or even atheistic behaviour mixed themselves chaotically, and were used to express a wide variety of needs, aims and emotional status: to make a statement about a blasphemer is, therefore, extremely difficult. Ironically, it may have been this anarchic and boundless nature of blasphemy that placed the established powers on the alert.

Therefore, the courts of justice began progressively to punish not just the opinions expressed by the blasphemers, troublesome towards matters of faith orthodoxy and subsequently to the basic rule of social coexistence itself: when these opinions retained themselves to private or exclusive context, just as in the case of the *Ridotti* at the beginnings of the 17th century, where nobles and powerful citizens could quite freely talk (or, in some cases, chatter) about philosophy, religion and political affairs, they were commonly tolerated, or at least underscored by the authorities. As we stated before, the real problem arose when these principles became sparks and suggestions for the discourses of an increasing number of people: it was feared not only the potential deconstructing power shared by some of these theories, but the absolutely free and anarchic ways in which they were received, interpreted and articulated by whoever choose to make use of them, the unpredictable effect these would have had on the city's populace. In this sense, blasphemy became not a matter of words and convictions, but a matter of discourses:[47] or, to be more specific, blasphemy became the particular articulation that the deviant discourse could assume. But, simultaneously to this radicalisation, this pattern of speech became somehow fashionable for an increasing part of the population: a trait of distinctive-

47 LAWTON, 1993, pp. 110-147.

124

ness, of intellectual stature, a way to differentiate and to enhance the position of the individual in respect of the masses thanks to this transgressive behaviour.[48] It is not my intention, of course, to state that transgression was invented in late 17th century Venice, or even that, in Venice, transgression was considered as a positive value for the first time, a way to enhance and to mark the individuality of someone: the dynamic between the establishment of a rule and its violation is at the base of all cultures, and one of the founding needs of mankind is the labelling of the boundary between what is to be allowed and what to be forbidden; I will shall simply state that, during this century, the leniency toward deviancy spread far more widely than before in a city somehow accustomed to deal with the deviant practices originating from its composite and multicultural nature, widely enough to alert the political and religious authorities. Following these trends, I have tried to picture blasphemy in Venice's late 17th century, intending it as a guideline to the process. From its practice and sanctions, I think we could learn something about the place, or better the different places and functions, that orthodox and divergent behaviour occupied in the lagoon city, and how they interacted together in ways far from fully rational, or linear.

At the end of this brief presentation, I acknowledge that much has been left unsaid. The length of this exposition prevented me from deepening the analysis of other themes here and which had presented themselves during the discourse, overlooking them in order not to weight down the panel with too many hints about badly sketched topics. Being aware of the absolute insufficiency of this work, and the seriously limited number of angles and perspectives offered to appreciate the topic of blasphemy, to speak about conclusions is highly questionable: thus, I have to say that it was never the ambition of this paper to build a solid framework of interpretation. More concretely, I hoped just to present the issues emerging from the study of blasphemy, or at least those perceived by a study which is just in its infancy, and to establish a minimum common ground, even if absolutely temporary and partial, to face the theme this congress is going to discuss. To see blasphemy as a form of recount permitted me to underline its constructed cultural nature as a form of expression so similar to others that it could not easily be identified *per se* but only through an in-depth comparison between different

---

48 BARBIERATO, 2006, pp. 170-189.

perspectives, and to focus on the multiplicity of the characters, the functions, and the places and the reasons of its use. To consider blasphemy as a peculiar form of deviance and to use blasphemy as a key of interpretation of the concept of deviance helped to deepen its analysis, ranging from different degrees and issues of willingness, toleration and logics behind its use, topics usually overlooked but produced simultaneously, as Jörg Rogge anticipated in his speech, questions and uncertainties over the opposite concept of norm. Blasphemy is not a static concept, as I have tried to prove: but, what changed on the opposite side of the cultural spectrum? If the 17th century elaborated a different kind of behaviours, rules, laws and mind-frames regarding what was not allowed, how this was related to a necessarily parallel process outlining what was still allowed? All I can say at this point is that the deviant behaviour called blasphemy, traditionally tolerated and nullified inside in the daily cultural practice, during the 16th and mostly the 17th increased its presence and most of all his its status in the everyday life of an increasing number of people, shifting decisively toward what was not tolerated, even if commonly practised.

Literature

Sources

ASV, *Esecutori contro la Bestemmia*:
- Buste n° 1-2-3-4 (Trials: 1662/1703)
- Busta n° 54 (Capitolari: 1523/1737-1739/1797)
- Busta n° 66-67 (*Raspe di Sentenze*: 1716/1735; 1692/1719, 1719-1769)

ASV, *Sant'Uffizio*:
- Busta n° 116 (Trial, *Contra Simone Petrachini*)
- Busta n° 124 (Trial, *Contra Mario Tolemei Nerucci*)

BOERIO, GIUSEPPE, Dizionario del Dialetto Veneziano, Third Edition, Reale tipografia di G. Cecchini, Venezia 1867.

PRIORI, LUDOVICO, Pratica criminale secondo le leggi della Serenissima Repubblica di Venezia, Venezia 1738.

TIRABOSCO, MARCANTONIO, Ristretto di prattica criminale che serve per la formatione de processi ad offesa, Venezia 1636.

Secondary Literature

BARBIERATO, FEDERICO, Politici e Ateisti. I percorsi della miscredenza a Venezia tra Sei e Settecento, First Edition, Unicopli, Milano 2006.

BERTI, SILVIA, At the Roots of Unbelief. In: Journal of the History of Ideas, 4 (1995), pp 555-575.

BURKE, PETER, Scene di vita quotidiana nell'Italia moderna. 1st Italian Edition, Laterza, Roma-Bari 1988.

ID., Sogni, gesti, beffe. Saggi di storia culturale, First Italian Edition, Il Mulino, Bologna 2000.

CABANTOUS, ALAIN, Blasphemy. Impious Speech in the West from the Seventeenth to the Nineteenth Century, 1st English Edition, Columbia University Press, 2002.

CHOJNACKI, STANLEY, Identity and Ideology in Renaissance Venice. The third serrata, in: Venice Reconsidered, the history and civilization of an Italian city-state, 1297-1797, Baltimore 2000, pp. 263-294.

COZZI, GAETANO, Religione, moralità e giustizia a Venezia. vicende della magistratura degli Esecutori contro la Bestemmia, secoli XVI-XVIII, in: La società veneta e il suo diritto, ed. by GAETANO COZZI, Venice, Fondazione Giorgio Cini, 2000, pp. 45-148.

ID., Giustizia 'contaminata'. Vicende giudiziare di nobili ed ebrei nella Venezia del Seicento, Fondazione Giorgio Cini-Marsilio, Venezia 1996.

DEL COL, ANDREA, Alcune osservazioni sui processi inquisitoriali come fonti storiche. In: Metodi e Ricerche, 13 (1994), pp 85-185.

DEROSAS, RENZO, Moralità e giustizia a Venezia nel 500-600. Gli Esecutori contro la Bestemmia, in: Stato, società e giustizia nella Repubblica Veneta, ed. by GAETANO COZZI, Jouvence, Roma 1980, pp 433-528.

DE VIVO, FILIPPO, Patrizi, informatori, barbieri. Politica e comunicazione a Venezia nella prima età moderna, Feltrinelli, Milano 2012.

FLYNN, MAUREEN, Blasphemy and the Play of Anger in Sixteenth Century Spain, in: Past & Present, 149 (1995), pp 29-56.

GAMBARIN, GIOVANNI (ed.), Scritti Giurisdizionalistici of Fra Paolo Sarpi, Laterza, Bari 1958.

GINZBURG, CARLO, Il formaggio e I vermi. Il cosmo di un mugnaio del '500, 3rd ed., Einaudi, Torino 1999.

GRUBB, JAMES SAMUEL, Elite Citizens, in: Venice Reconsidered, the history and civilization of an Italian city-state, 1297-1797, Baltimore 2003, pp. 339-364.

INFELISE, MARIO, Prima dei giornali. Alle origini della pubblica informazione, 2nd ed., Laterza, Roma-Bari 2011.

JAKOBSON, ROMAN, Closing Statement: Linguistics and Poets, in: Style in Language, ed. by THOMAS E. SEBEOK, The Technological Press of Massachusetts Institute of Technology, 1960.

LAWTON, DAVID, Blasphemy, University of Pennsylvania Press 1993.

LEVY, LEONARD WILLIAMS, Treason against God. A history of the offence of blasphemy, Schocken Books, New York 1981.

MARAVALL, JOSÈ ANTONIO, Potere, onore, elites nella Spagna del secolo d'oro, Italian Edition, il Mulino, Bologna 1986.

NASH, DAVID, Blasphemy in the Christian World. A History, First Edition, Oxford University Press, Oxford 2007.

PITT-RIVERS, JULIAN, The Fate of Shechem or the Politics of Sex. Essays in the Anthropology of the Mediterranean, Cambridge University Press, Cambridge 1977.

POVOLO, CLAUDIO, L'intrigo dell'onore. Potere e istituzioni nella Repubblica di Venezia nel Cinque e Seicento, Cierre, Verona 1997.

ID., Retoriche della devianza Criminali, fuorilegge e deviati nella storia (ideologie, storia, letteratura, iconografia), in: Acta Histriae, 15 (2007), pp 1-51.

SCARABELLO, GIOVANNI, Esecutori contro la bestemmia. Un processo per rapimento stupro e lenocinio nella Venezia popolare del secondo Settecento, centro internazionale della grafica di Venezia, Venezia 1991.

SEITZ, JOHNATAN, Witchcraft and Inquisition in Early Modern Venice, Cambridge University Press, Cambridge 2011.

WALKER, JOHNATAN, Gambling and the Venetian Noblemen c 1500-1700, in: Past & Present, 162 (1999), pp 28-69.

WEINSTEIN, DONALD, Fighting or Flyting? Verbal Duel in Mid-Sixteenth Century Italy, in: Crime, Society and the Law in Renaissance Italy, ed. by TREVOR DEAN/K. J. P. LOWE, Cambridge University Press, Cambridge 1994.

WOTTOON, DAVID, Unbelief in Early Modern Europe, in: History Workshop Journal, 20 (1985), pp 82-100.

"... fossimo presi per incantamento"
Witchcraft and love deviances in the trials of Venice's *Santo Uffizio* in the XVII century

GIULIA MOROSINI

In this article I shall refer to some examples of deviant love relationships, on basis of which I shall try to understand the connection between deviant love and witchcraft accusations in XVII century Venice. In particular: what was the role attributed to witchcraft in explaining deviant love? When and why the deviant labelling applied to love relationships lead to witchcraft accusation and, therefore, to denunciation and trial? This article is based upon ongoing research and aims at merely proposing some ideas as causes for a reflection, which, to be complete, will surely require a wider horizon in terms of both primary sources and disciplinary sectors, including the fields of literature, sociology, anthropology etc. The primary sources used to pursue these aims are the trials in front of the Inquisition court, the Venice's *Santo Uffizio* (Holy Office), from late XVI century to late XVII century.[1] Thanks to long depositions, direct conversations and vivid tales, these sources allow us a glimpse of scenes from everyday life in a Modern Italian city. More importantly, in order to understand the deviant love repression, the witchcraft trials serve as a privileged source, due to the fact that love magic and divination were some of the major aspects of XVII

---

1   Various examples of Holy Office trials can be found in the works of Marisa Milani. See: MILANI, 1989; 1994a; 1994c. See also MURARO, 1976.

century popular magic. On the other hand, this type of documents must be treated with caution: the impression of reality and spontaneity given by the direct conversations is in fact an artifice. Therefore, is necessary to always bear in mind the institution which produced the documents and, at the same time, the filter which is applied to the text during the court transcripts. Even if these documents can bring us closer to the people who stand and speak in the court, we always look at them from behind the inquisitorial desk.

In the context of this article it is not possible to analyze the particular rituals and the phenomenon of witchcraft, for which I refer to more detailed studies.[2] However, it is interesting to point out the several purposes for which men and women turned to magic[3]: to know if the person with whom they were in love was feeling the same way and was not cheating on them or if the distant lover was going to come back to them; to keep their husbands and wives from seeing someone else, to know if their marriage was going to be a happy one, to bind someone to them or make their loved one visit them, to take revenge on a former lover or his/her new partner, and so on.[4] In particular, some of the rituals performed most were those practiced to gain someone's love and bend him to his/her will. Rituals such as the *dar martello* (to give hammer) which could be defined as a psychological hammering, a relentless form of thinking about the other person. These magic rituals were practiced using many different objects, such as magnets, mirrors, pots, needles and wax statues, holy objects such as host, oil and church candles; casting broad beans and the *cordella* (a small rope, mainly of red color); burning salt, potassium alum and herbs in the kitchen fireplace; reciting prayers, religious orations, magic words, invocations and much more.

This love magic was a popular cultural field dominated almost exclusively by women who performed the rituals for a fee as a profession. These witches were, in almost all cases, illiterate and passed on their

---

2   DI SIMPLICIO, 2005; BALDINI, 2014; ZANETTI, 1992; MONTER, 1983; MARTIN, 1989 (in particular about the *cordella* and the bean-casting see pp. 121-124); O'NEIL, 1987.

3   A very interesting study which focuses on the love, the obedience and the feelings in the XVIII century Venice is: PLEBANI, 2012.

4   About the concept of *Voler Bene* in the XVII century see: NICCOLI, 2000, pp. 119-122. Stories of young lovers in Early Modern Italy can be found in: CORAZZOL/CORRÀ, 1981.

knowledge in an oral form, which caused slight differences in the techniques, objects and ingredients used in the rituals.[5] They were not the evil witches who lay with the devil and flew to the Sabbath, or the sinister figures that wander in the night at the crossroads. On the contrary: they were women in possession of a popular knowledge and used to protect from the unpredictable, evil and darkness, well integrated within society and the neighborhood. Nonetheless, from the late XVI century, the post-Tridentine church tried to apply greater control over the lay population and a clearer division between sacred and profane and, therefore, to those who had authorized access to supernatural. As written by Seitz:

> "This effort was part of a larger trend among early modern authorities (Catholic and Protestant alike) to 'discipline' the public, to try to force broad population to conform to the ideals endorsed by the political and religious leadership. [...] Time-honored religious practices were, in relatively short order, reclassified as illegitimate or prosecuted with a new vigor by ecclesiastical authorities"[6].

Therefore, XVII century society may have, in part, suffered the reorganization of the Counter-Reformation, which aimed to strike the irregular use of the Christian symbolism and those social figures who possessed a popular knowledge (about alternative and popular medicine, herbs, superstitious practices, magic unguents etc.) that was no longer tolerated both by laical and religious power.[7] The more controlled environment and the new pressure on the denunciation of the witches shed a

---

5   DI SIMPLICIO, 2005, pp. 62-71.
6   SEITZ, 2001, pp. 5-9.
7   About the Council of Trent see the studies of: PRODI, 1973, 2010; PRODI/REINHARD, 1996. About the disciplining and the control of the society operated by the Church and the political power during the XVI and XVII century, as well as about the prosecution of heresy and the role and function of the Roman Inquisition, there is a long and fruitful historiographical debate that cannot be reported in this article. Following are listed some of the major studies. About the Roman Inquisition and the justice in Early Modern Italy see: PASCHINI, 1959; PRODI, 2000; PROSPERI, 2003; COZZI, 2000. On the prosecution of heresy and the disciplining of the society see: MARTIN, 1987 and 1993; TEDESCHI, 1990 and 1991; PRODI, 1994; CARAVALE, 2003; CAVARZERE, 2011; LAVENIA, 2004.

light on the diffusion of the magic rituals, as testified by the great number of Inquisitorial trials.

Most of these practices, especially love magic, were not perceived as witchcraft by the contemporaries and were sought by both noble men and lower classes, due to the fact that popular magic represented a fundamental part in everyday life of the XVII century society.[8] The relatively recent condemnation of love witchcraft created an atmosphere of confusion in which old practices continued to be performed, arousing suspicion and concern in some and indifference in others.[9] During the Holy Office inquisition, the witchcraft accusation based upon love magic rituals, such as the *cordella* or the broad beans, sometimes caused astonishment and surprise. For example, in 1671, Camilla Borghi was taken to trial for witchcraft and admits: "Several times I had cast the *cordella* from various silly women when I was alone, to know various things". When asked "If she believes or have believed that it is legit for a good catholic to do such practices and witchcraft appealing to the devil, and wait for his answer" she replied: "Actually it seems to me that was it improper but I thought it wasn't that bad, and now that I know the seriousness of the fact, I firmly believe that it is not legit, and is bad, and I will never do these things again for sure"[10]. Camilla Savi-

---

8　For example, in ASV, SU, B77 (Trial of Bettina Loredana, Giulia Pisana, Vienna and Giulia Terzi), 1622, about the reputation and witchcraft of Vienna, Caterina Ricci stated: "A lot of people came to her to do witchcraft. and also she went in other houses to do witchcraft" ("Veniva anco da lei molta gente a far fare strigarie. et lei anco andava in altre case a far strigarie"). Lucrezia also stated: "I saw a lot of people went to her house, both men and women [...] they went there to do witchcraft, because mostly they were living doing witchcraft" ("Ho veduto molta gente andarli per casa homeni et donne [...] vi andavano per occasione di strigarie, perche per il più vivono con far strigarie").

9　The deposition given by Berto Stracciarolo, in 1590, about the reputation of Orsetta Padovana, testifies the confusion about what represented witchcraft and what did not: "I'm not aware that she practices witchcraft, but I heard that she practices the bean-casting" ("Io non so che faci strigarie, ma ho inteso raggionar che la butta le fave"). ASV, SU, B66 (Trial of Orsetta Padovana).

10　ASV, SU, B116 (Trial of Simone Petrachini, Camilla Borghi and Marietta Marchiora): "Di più diverse volte da diverse donnette ho fatto trar la cordella quando stavo da me sola, per saper diverse cose"; "*Interrogata* se creda o habbi creduto esser lecito a buon cattolico far simili esperimenti sortileghi con far ricorso al demonio, et aspettar da lui risposta. *Respondit*

oni was even more astonished when asked to explain her appeal to witchcraft, answering annoyed: "Since when is casting the *cordella* witchcraft? I made it cast for me several times thinking it wasn't bad"[11]. Similarly, Zanetta said: "I thought it was not a sin. [...] Since I was a small [I know how to cast the *cordella*], I learned it from my teacher at school when I was a child"[12]. The confusion about the official and legal status of these practices is testified by the fact that some of the accusers, in their denunciation against women who practice love magic, stated that they turned to magic as well.[13] Like the voluntary denunciation deposited by Barbara in 1670, in which she stated: "I taught the afore-mentioned secret to Bartolo Zentei [...], and I learn that this friend of mine has taught the secret to his wife Anzola; because this Anzola has told me, and to my mom, that she did that secret; but after she confessed it, she did not want to do it anymore, because the confessor told her that it was a diabolical act"[14]. As can be noted in the previous statements, these magic "secrets" were repeatedly handed down from one person to another, whether they were simple friends or old women (known in the neighborhood as witches), who passed their knowledge to some younger girl.[15] Vienna Terzi represents a perfect example: in

---

veramente mi pareva cosa che non stesse bene ma non mi credevo po che fosse tanto male, e adesso mo che conosco la gravità del fatto, credo fermamente non sia lecito, e cosa cattiva, e non farò più certo ste cose".

11 ASV, SU, B80 (Trial of Camilla Savioni): "Mo che il buttar la cordella è strigaria? Mi ho fatto butar la cordella diverse volte, pensando che non fosse male".

12 ASV, SU, B80 (Trial of Camilla Savioni): "Mi teneva che non fosse peccato. [...] et da picola in suso so questa cosa, che imparai dalla mia mistra a schola che ero puta".

13 For example, in ASV, SU, B124 (Trial of Apollonia Tessera known as Dandola), in the denunciation against Apollonia, Antonia asserted: "Equally she taught me how to force men to come" ("Parimente ha insegnato a me far venire delli homini").

14 ASV, SU, B116 (Trial of Simone Petrachini, Camilla Borghi and Marietta Marchiora): "Io poi ho insignato il suddetto secreto a Bartolo Zentel [...], e veddo che detto mio compare habbi insegnato il suddetto secreto a Anzola sua moglie; perche essa Anzola ha detto a me, e a mia madre di haver fatto tal secreto. ma che essendosene confessata, non voleva farlo più havendole detto il confessore che era cosa diabolica".

15 It can also be noted how the protagonists have found out about the diabolic nature of the practice only after the confrontation with the priest or the confessor.

1622 she was accused, among other things, to have taught her rituals to a little girl, as stated by Lucrezia: "[Vienna] had a little girl in the house called Cattina, to whom Viena used to say 'my daughter if you will be good I will teach you these virtues of mine'". In the following questioning of Vienna, she tells the inquisitor: "I was taught [how to cast the *cordella*] by an old woman 40 years ago [...] her name was Zuana Grega and she was a 100-year-old woman. *Interrogata:* for which purpose did they use to cast the *cordella* [?] *Respondit:* for the lovers, to know if they loved, and if the guy would come or not". In a further questioning she said: "I haven't taught how to cast the *cordella* to anybody, even though everybody cast it"[16]. These few trials' quotations, to which could have been added many others, show how permeating the love magic practice was in the Venetian society.[17] Furthermore, the pervasiveness of these rituals, turned to by different social figures, decreased their sensational character compared to the tales of the terrible witches' powers (such as kill livestock and infants, cause storms and natural disasters, dance with devils at Sabbath etc.), as stated by Vienna who admits: "I look if the lovers have to come, and other trifles of small importance"[18]. Nonetheless, their intrinsic supernatural factor and their effectiveness on reality were a certainty in the XVII century people's mentality, but the usualness of their practice has turned them into everyday rituals, performed regularly during women's meetings and by demand, as narrated by Meneghina, in a 1621 deposition: "A long time ago, a woman that I do not know, finding herself on the door of Madonna Bastiana, cast the *cordella* for a laugh, to see if a baby girl

---

16 ASV, SU, B77 (Trial of Bellina Loredana, Giulia Pisana, Vienna and Giulia Terzi): "[Vienna] haveva una putella in casa chiamata Cattina, alla quale Viena diceva; fia mia se sarai buona te insegnerò queste mie virtù"; "[Buttar la cordella] mi fu insegnato da una vecchia già 40 anni, [...] lei si chiamava Zuana Grega et era vecchia di 100 anni. *Interrogata* a che effetto si butava la cordella. *Respondit* per li morosi, per vedere se li vogliono bene, et se il tale ha da venir si o no"; "non ho insegnato a butar la cordella a persona alcuna, se bene tutti la buttano".

17 For example, about the magic books diffusion in Venice during the XVII and XVIII century see: BARBIERATO, 2002.

18 ASV, SU, B77 (Trial of Bellina Loredana, Giulia Pisana, Vienna and Giulia Terzi): "guardo se li morosi hanno da venir, et simili bagatele di poca importanza".

had to be loved. And that's it"[19]; more, in the deposition of Lucrezia: "I have seen this Pisana cast the *cordella* several times with other women who came there"[20].

Despite the post-Tridentine suspicious climate, the inquisitors were well aware of the traditional-popular nature of some magic rituals practiced by these witches, whose effectiveness in most cases originated from superstition rather than proper supernatural powers. Therefore, various inquisitorial manuals recommended the collection of a great number of "objective" evidence, for example written in the *Instructio pro formandis processibus in causis strigum, sortilegiorum et maleficiorum* (probably circulated around 1620-1625)[21], to avoid the incrimination of innocents (due to prejudice or rush to reach a verdict). The inquisitors, although still far from the sharp division between popular magic and diabolical pact reached by Illuminism, were more cautious to attribute the "Witchcraft" label to these rituals, in particular love magic, acknowledging the role that suggestion may have been performed in a magic field that was so close to the emotional and intimate spheres. This rationality was present also within the society, where a common opinion "about how they [women] easily believe[d] to chitchat" was "that all women are the same"[22]. Love magic was often indicated by

---

19 ASV. SU, B77 (Trial of Giacoma and Sabbatina, mother and daughter): "Già pur assae una donna che non conosco, trovandosi su la porta di madonna Bastiana così per rider butò una cordella per veder se una fantolina haveva da haver ben. Et non fu altro".

20 ASV, SU, B77 (Trial of Bellina Loredana, Giulia Pisana, Vienna and Giulia Terzi): "Ho veduto detta pisana parechie volte a butar la cordella insieme con delle altre donne che venivano la".

21 In the *Instructio* it is written: "The judges be aware that, although some Woman remains adamant, or confesses to have performed Enchantments or Sorcery *ad amorem*, or *ad sanada maleficia*, or whatever other effect, does not necessarily follow that she is a formal Witch, due to the fact that the Sorcery can be done without formal apostasy to the Devil". Quoted in: ZANETTI, 1992, pp. 91-93. For inquisitorial manuals present in Italy during the XVII century see: Fra Nicholas Eymerich's *Directorium Inquisitorium* (EYMERICH, 1998) and Eliseo Masini's *Sacro Arsenale,* the first manual in Italian *volgare*, printed for the first time in Genova in 1621 (MASINI, 1730). See also the collection of texts in ABBIATI/AGNOLETTO/LAZZATI, 1984.

22 ASV, SU, B80 (Trial of Camilla Savioni), deposition of Marco Dardani, 1625: "Quanto a creder facilmente alle ciancie, mi credo che tutte le donne siano ad un modo".

inquisitors as "superstitious", term that "mainly referred to those practices that assigned supernatural powers where they did not belong"[23]. Love magic practices, acknowledging the ability of the utilized objects to coerce the will of the target or to discover future events or other person's feelings, connected divination with coercion and, for this reason, clashed with the inquisitors' certainty regarding the impossibility of telling the future or force the human will.[24] Hence, the mistrust of some inquisitors about the real effects of these magic practices.

From prostitute to witch: a love journey

Especially prostitutes performed the witchcraft *ad amorem*, and made use of rituals such as bean-casting and casting the *cordella* to discover the devotion of their lovers, who represented their economic livelihood. Therefore, it is no surprise that most of the women charged before the Holy Office court of having performed or sought love magic were prostitutes.[25] Equally, while reading the Holy Office documents, it can be observed that love magic was just one of various deviant aspects of the lives, behaviors and relationships of prostitutes indicated as "witchcraft". In the next pages I shall attempt to identify some of the cases and the causes for which the sentimental life of the prostitutes came under the category of witchcraft and the connection between witchcraft accusation and deviant love.

---

23 SEITZ, 2001, pp. 13-14. This superstition accusation was often present in trials of women healers, who combined the use of objects or herbs with orations and magic formulas. To believe that the effectiveness of these practices depended on the invocation rather than on the strictly therapeutic qualities of the object itself, was considered superstition. For some examples of trials against healers see: MILANI, 1986.

24 About the Inquisitors' inclination toward superstition see: MARTIN, 1989, pp. 166-180. About the perception of the superstition see: PROSPERI, 1996, pp. 368-399.

25 In Early Modern Venice the term 'harlot' implied "all the unmarried women who have sexual practice with one or more men [...] the married women who did not live with their husbands and have sexual practice with other men" as stated by the Venetian Senate in 1543. Quoted in: MILANI, 1994b, pp. 14-15.

The high number of accusations could have been in part determined by the increasing condemnation, among both the laical and political powers and then within the society, of prostitution and concubinage[26], or by the rise of the number of prostitutes in Venice from the second half of the XVI century.[27] The prostitutes (whose job was considered as an important social function a few years earlier) began to be increasingly accused of causing social disorder, such as spreading diseases and lust or supporting adultery, and became a part of the "criminal" population.[28] In the same way, unmarried couples started, in part, to be seen and prosecuted as a threat to society's structure, in opposition to the sacred Christian family. Accordingly, illicit relationships were treated with less tolerance, and the consequences of these new cultural and religious trends on the society can be illustrated by the words spoken by Maria da Bassano, a former prostitute and prosecuted witch: "She used to say [...] that the Lord himself has spoken to her, and He said that she should have roamed around the world, and the cities, and if she has found any prostitute, she would have converted her, leaving the sin"[29]. The sin, in particular, pinpointed as the evil, "was defined as a consequence of human deficiency, as a sign of the divine will to test the believers"[30]. Illicit couples, in particular if composed of a prostitute and an ordinary man represented the sin with which the community had to

---

26 This phenomenon was also linked to the perception and legislation about sexuality and the repression of concubinage. On this subject see: MATTEWS GRIECO, 1991, pp. 73-93; WIESNER, 2003, pp. 56-73; SOLÉ, 1979, pp. 167-193; FERRANTE, 1996; DI SIMPLICIO, 1994, pp. 187-195; BYARS, 2008. About the sexuality and its different forms in Venice see: RUGGIERO, 1988.

27 It has been calculated that the prostitutes should have composed one third of the entire venetian female population on the second half of the XVI century. For a summary on this subject see: MILANI, 1994b, pp. 7-20.

28 MATTEWS GRIECO, 1991, p. 75. See, for example, the *Orazione contra le cortegiane* (Oration against the courtesans) by Sperone Speroni of Padova, written in 1572.

29 ASV, SU, B124 (Trial of Pelizzari and Maria da Bassano), deposition of Caterina, 1686: "Diceva [...] che il signor dio in persona li haveva parlato, e anco disse che dovesse andar per il mondo, e per le città, e ritrovando qualche donna di mal affare, s'haverebbe convertita, fattala lasciar il peccato". In the questioning of Girolamo, he told: "I know Giulia Pisana for 4 or 5 years, as a prostitute, with whom I had sex [...] I used to go to her, she had [as her man] Francesco Cuchi, and she was telling me that she loved this Francesco".

30 DI SIMPLICIO, 2005, p. 130.

live and confront. Subsequently, a growing number of illicit couples tried to align with the religious directives, as in the case of the cohabitation of Fausto and Margherita: "Fausto has not yet married [Margherita], due to his sister, but he hopes he will be able to marry her soon"[31]. Sometimes "working relationships" turned into actual love relationships between public prostitutes and ordinary men (most of the time younger than their women), and in the witchcraft trials it is common to notice their existence, as narrated by Giulia Pisana in 1622: "Francesco Cuchi [...] is my boyfriend [...] and for now I don't have any other boyfriend, he comes [has been coming] to me from 3 or 4 years"[32].

As outlined before, the concealment of the sin and the marriage of illicit couples, in particular between prostitutes and ordinary men, were heartfelt (but still confused) issues within the society.[33] Sought after by the prostitutes as a way out of their condition[34], marriage was opposed by the groom's families, particularly if they were of a social class higher than the women.[35] A means that was at disposal of the families to

---

31 ASV, SU, B77 (Trial of Margherita Bottonera), deposition of Lucrezia, 1622: "Detto signor fausto non l'ha ancora sposata [a Margherita], per causa di una sua sorella, ma ha speranza di sposarla presto".

32 ASV, SU, B77 (Trial of Bellina Loredana, Giulia Pisana, Vienna and Giulia Terzi): "francesco cuchi [...] è mio moroso [...] per hora non ho altri morosi, sono 3 o 4 anni che lui vien da me".

33 On Early Modern marriage legislation, and its transformation after the Council of Trent, see: WIESNER, 2003, pp. 73-82; DI SIMPLICIO, 1994, pp. 327-357; ZARRI, 1996; FERRANTE, 1994. For an analysis of marriage and divorce which takes account of the couples's disputes and the irrationality of emotions, and their role in the phenomenon see: SEIDEL MENCHI/QUAGLIONI, 2000 and 2001.

34 As stated by the mother of an inquired witch, both prostitutes: "I live with my daughter, who is a woman of this world [meaning, a prostitute], and a merchant comes to her, and she hopes that maybe he will marry her". ASV, SU, B77 (Trial of Bellina Loredana, Giulia Pisana, Vienna and Giulia Terzi).

35 About a marriage occurred between a Venetian nobleman and a courtesan narrates also Marin Sanudo in his *Diarii*: "In questo zorno [11 aprile 1526], se intese *publice* di un paro di noze fatte di sier Andrea Michiel di sier Francesco *da san Canziano* vedovo, in una Cornelia Grifo vedoa meretrice somptuosa et bellissima, qual è stata *publice* a posta di sier Ziprian Malipiero, et hora era di sier Piero da Molin *dal Banco*, e stata di altri, rica, qual li ha in dota dà ducati ... milia. Et fu fatte le noze nel monasterio di S. Zuan di Torcello; che è stata gran vergogna a la nobiltà veneta". Marin Sanudo, *Diarii*, vol. XLI, c. 166. On this subject see: COWAN, 2007.

oppose this kind of marriage was the witchcraft accusation, in which sorcery was used to explain the compulsory nature of the relationship, and therefore to nullify the marriage. The personal and social justification which originated from the attribution of obligatory characteristic to the relationships shall be discussed later in this article. For now, a good example of this kind of marriage, and the reactions toward it, is that between Giovan Battista Filomena and Betta Borella, which was brought before the Holy Office: "The 9th of March in this city was officiated an unexpected, unforeseen and incredible marriage between Giovan Battista, son of *messer* Girolamo Filomena, and a certain Betta Borella, public harlot and innkeeper"[36]. This denunciation summarizes, through the words of Giovan Battista's father, the different justifications adduced by the families to prove the magic nature of the marriage:

> "First, I consider the age of my son, who's just 26 years old, and on the contrary the age of the innkeeper who is more than 47 years old, hoary, partially bald and deformed. [...] I consider my son of respectable values, always very sensitive to distinction, who surely in any case would have sacrificed his life to the reputation, and on the other hand this innkeeper who is a public harlot. These considerations lead at first blush and efficiently to conclude that such unforeseen and unexpected change goes against nature and it was leaded by an unknown violence or by demons themselves"[37].

"Unforeseen" and "against nature" were the adjectives used to describe the love and the marriage of a prostitute. In spite of this condemnation,

---

36 ASV, SU, B124 (Trial of Pelizzari and Maria da Bassano): denunciation of Giovan Battista's father: "è seguito il di 9 marzo passato in questa città improviso impensato e fuori d'ogni credenza matrimonio tra Giovan Battista figliolo di messer Girolamo Filomena, et una tal Betta Borella pubblica meretrice e locandiera".

37 IBID.: "Primieramente considero l'età di mio figliolo a pena arrivato ad anni 26, et all'incontro l'età avanzata della locandiera che hormai eccede gli anni 47, resa canuta, calva in parte e deforme. [...] Considero il figliolo di costumi honorati, delicatissimo sempre ne sensi d'honore, che certo haverebbe in qualunque caso ancor lui sagrificato la vita alla riputatione, e d'altra parte essa locandiera pubblica meretrice. Queste consideratione portano di primo aspetto ad efficacemente concludere che così impensato, et improviso cambiamento va contro il corso della natura, e guidato da violenza ignota, e da demoni stessi". See: COWAN, 2007.

the sincere love of the groom is testified in the trial by the family's friend Ludovico Seroghetti: "[Giovan Battista] approached me and was complaining about his father because he was saying around that he suspected that the marriage depended on some sort of magic or sorcery, and he asserted that this was not true, on the contrary, he married his wife on personal initiative"[38]. Anyway, most of these women were not as lucky as Betta and spent many years involved in relationships with married men, or with men who refused to marry them.[39] In 1625, Marina of Chioggia, for example, was prosecuted as a witch and accused of having bewitched her former lover Girolamo, and his just married wife Marietta, due to the fact that he had promised to marry Marina and instead chose another woman.[40] Marina reacted violently to the news of the marriage (as will be seen in a moment) and fought publicly with Marietta, uttering curses and blasphemies. "Hence for all these words me and Andriana have scolded her, telling her to be careful of the soul, and that this Marieta was Girolamo's wife and was right and she should calm down. And she answered us that Girolamo had promised to marry her, and that we should keep our advices to ourselves"[41]. In these few

---

38 IBID.: "Esso s'introdusse meco a dolersi di suo padre perche andava dicendo che dubitava fosse il suo matrimonio seguito per qualche malia, o magia, asserendo non esser ciò vero mentre esso haveva sposata sua moglie per suo genio". In the deposition of Maria Pelizzari is stated: "[The marriage] happened because this young man was sinfully enjoying Betta for a long time, and he was very much in love with her, as he is now. So much that he said that he would not trade that woman for all the gold in the world if he would have her in God's grace".

39 See the case of Livia Azzalina narrated in: MILANI, 1989, pp. 49-57.

40 ASV, SU, B80 (Trial of Marina of Chioggia). Deposition of Pasqualina: "She used to say that Girolamo Battagia, who was said was her man, had married a young girl daughter of Andrea Rubbin; and she said that she didn't want that Girolamo would enjoy her, and that the young girl was not going to survive the year [...]. And she said that when she was complaining with a neighbor called la Rozza, telling her that Girolamo had promised Marina to take her as wife and then he threw her away". Deposition of Giovanni Bergomeni: "[Girolamo] told me [...] that woman had ruined him with witchcraft because he got married, and because he promised her to take her as wife". About the role of the promise within the marriage legislation see note 33.

41 IBID., deposition of Fiordelisa: "Onde per tutte queste parole fu ripresa da me et da madonna Andriana, con dirli che guardasse l'anima, et che ditta Marieta era moglie di Girolamo et haveva ragione et dovesse aquietarse. Et

lines the society's perception of an unfulfilled promise of marriage made to a prostitute is evident and, therefore, the consequent status-difference between a married woman and a prostitute, since the public complaining of Marina was "not right" and dangerous, compared to the "right" of Marietta, obtained by being the official and legit wife of Girolamo. The inquisitors were well aware of the fact, believed by the contemporaries, that jealousy and the desire for revenge could have led women to revert to witchcraft, as indicated in the *Malleus Maleficarum* about those men who are bewitched in their "generative power" after a marriage: "Since they [the witches] hoped to be married and they feel cheated, they cast witchcraft upon men in order to make them incapable of joining other women"[42].

The abandon, the unfulfilled promise, the rejection are some of the moments in which the overlapping between prostitute and witch takes place. The anger of these women was pinpointed as the cause of subsequent misfortunes that may befall their former lovers or wives.

"The rational of the witchcraft's repression by the Inquisition had a public value. It was inspired by the undermining of the Christian values intrinsic in the diabolic pact. The rational of common people's reaction had, on the other hand, a private value. The pact was ignored: people were afraid of the evil spell, of the personal damage inflicted by the vile witches"[43].

In this way the conception of the prostitute-witch who ruins men and women, and deserves to be accused before the Inquisition, is formed. In most cases, the men were wrecked by damaging wealth and health. Therefore, there are many trials in which women were accused to have forced their men to spend everything they had: "These are the witches that have driven Giovan Battista di Zanchi crazy and made him lose his mind, and spend all that poor son has in the world with witchcraft"[44].

---

lei di più ci rispose che Girolamo l'haveva tenuta con promessa di sposarla, et che dovessimo tener li nostri consegi per noi".

42 INSTITOR (KRÄMER)/SPRENGER, 2003, part 2, chapter 2, pp. 290-294.

43 DI SIMPLICIO, 2005, p. 112.

44 ASV, SU, B77 (Trial of Isabella Greghetta). 1622 denunciation: "Queste sono quelle strige che à fato perder il cervello e deventar mato Giovan Battista di Zanchi elia fatto spender tuto quello chel povero figliollo aveva al mondo con le sue arti diaboliche".

The conception of prostitutes as a social disaster, as chaos's carriers through the spreading of sin, is confirmed by their labelling as witches: "This Isabella is the cause that his nephew does not take care of his business, and that she will be the cause of his downfall"[45]. Camilla (here taken as an example) had a relationship with Andrea Marcello of 11 years, even though they bickered of late, and was accused by Andrea's brother of having bewitched her lover based on two facts: first, Andrea was in bed ill (of syphilis[46]) and, second, he decided to leave to her in his testament a thousand ducats, due to the affection he was feeling for this no longer young woman:

> "My brother Andrea Marcello is seriously ill [...] I suspect he might have been bewitched by Camilla Savioni [...] with whom Andrea had sexual intercourse, which woman is old and ugly, and with her talents she enticed Andrea to have a relationship with her for ten or eleven years, and he was never able to get rid of her. [...] He keeps repeating Camilla's name, and he has written his will, and he leaves her a thousand ducats"[47].

The sincere or specious denunciation of Andrea's enchantment gained legitimacy and became realistic since it presented witchcraft as consequence to the quarrel (between Andrea and Camilla), as a cause of An-

---

45 IBID., interrogation of Bartolomeo: "Ditta isabella è causa che detto suo nepote non attende alli fatti suoi, et che lei sarà causa della sua ruina".
46 For a study about syphilis and its impact on the Venetian's society see: MCGOUGH, 2011.
47 ASV, SU, B80 (Trial of Camilla Savioni). Girolamo Marcello's denunciation, 1624: "Ritrovandosi il signor Andrea Marcello mio fratello gravemente ammalato, [...] dubitando che lui possa esser stato amaliato et stregato da una signora Camilla Savioni [...] con la quale detto signor Andrea haveva havuto comercio carnale, qual donna è vecchia brutta, et con sue doti haveva allettato dicto signor Andrea ad haver comercio con lei per il spatio di dieci o undici anni, né mai ha potuto liberarsi da lei. [...] non fa altro che nominar questa Camilla, et ha fatto testamento, et le lassa mille ducati". In a following interrogation Girolamo stated: "4 or 5 days before my brother getting sick, Camilla asked him to who he would have leave his goods in case of his death, and my brother answered that he would leave everything to her, because he didn't care about anybody, nor his brother, nor his nephews, but her; and then it has been discovered that he has left her all that fortune".

drea's infirmity, and as a force which had driven Andrea to make a nonsensical choice in his testament.

On the other hand, there were vociferous arguments between the women and the prostitutes over the men, as well as the jealousy felt by the prostitutes toward other women, and furthermore some of the wives who felt that their ailing health had been bewitched by the prostitutes ("Camilla asked for Zanetta to cast the *cordella* for her because she had *martello* that Andrea was seeing other women, because in that time he used to go to Cecilia Valier"; "You blame me because you hate me. Where not you found in bed with my husband, by my little girl?"[48]). In the same way as men, women who suffered an inexplicable misfortune were quickly ready to indicate the prostitutes' witchcraft as its primary reason, as happened to Annetta: "[Lucia] called me and she said that Annetta did magic against her on her doorstep […]. She didn't say why she was blaming Annetta, but Lucia used to say that Annetta had Lucia's husband as her man"[49]. Due to the double nature, amorous and economic, of the long-lasting relationships between prostitutes and their lovers, it is not difficult to imagine the prostitutes bawling threats in public to protect their love and/or livelihood, as did an unnamed harlot, lover of a former priest named Barnaba Valavilla: "She's proud of having let him abandon religion with her magic, promising to never leave each other […] She threatens to kill with witchcraft other women who stare at him, and if he would leave her for another woman she will have him burned alive because he's an apostate and excommunicated priest"[50].

---

48 ASV, SU, B80 (Trial of Camilla Savioni). Interrogation of Agnesina: "La signora Camilla ricercò dicta Zanetta che li buttasse la cordella perché haveva martello che il signor Andrea andasse da altre donne, perché quella volta lui andava dalla signora Cecilia Valier"; In the direct comparison, during the trial, between Agnesina and Zanetta, here is how Zanetta answered to Agnesina's accusations: "Mi incolpate, perché mi volete male. Non sete stata trovata dalla mia puta in letto con mio marito?"

49 ASV, SU, B77 (Trial of Annetta de' Fornesi). Deposition of Francesco Rossetti, 1622: "[Lucia] mi chiamò et mi disse che detta Annetta gli haveva fatto strigarie à lei dinanzi la sua porta […]. Non mi disse perche incolpasse così Annetta, se non che Lucia diceva che Annetta teneva il marito di lei per suo homo".

50 ASV, SU, B77 (Trial of Don Barnaba Valavilla). Denunciation of canon Giovan Battista, 1621: "Se avanta haverlo ella con suoi strigamenti cavato fuor della religione con promessa l'uni all'altro mai abbandonarsi […] mi-

As previously mentioned, the connection between the intimidations and the evil spell was so rooted in the contemporaries' minds as to acquire the value of a casual factor. Thus, public quarrels between women, embellished by threats, insults and shouts, would not have been rare. In fact, the witchcraft trials are scattered by statements of publicly having heard some threats, or of having been threaten in public by someone. The tale of the fight between Bellina on one side, and Giacomina and Laura on the other, depicts a vivid scene of a neighborhood's life:

> "I heard from my house, which is close, a loud yelling and shouting coming from Giacomina and Laura's house. And after the clamor, I saw an old and short woman, who I don't know, saying 'Now you are warned, if something happens it will be at your own damage'. As soon as she left, Giacomina and Laura came out and they said that woman was come to threaten them about how they should not give shelter to a certain Frate, who previously was [Giulia's] man"[51].

A lot of the accused women are described, during the trials, as quarrelsome such as, for example, the aforementioned Marina of Chioggia (whereof is said "I've heard her angry screaming with this and with the other"[52]) who, due to the mentioned marriage, reacted in a violent manner: "When she had word of this marriage, Marina came to my home, thinking that Marieta was my daughter, and started yelling at me saying 'take this Battaglia whoever he wants as wife, anyway they'll not enjoy

---

nacciando l'altre donne, che lo guardano, farle morir con suoi strigamenti, se per altra donna l'abbandonasse lei, et lui lo faria brusciar vivo essendo apostata et sacerdote scomunicato".

51 ASV, SU, B77 (Trial of Bellina Loredana, Giulia Pisana, Vienna and Giulia Terzi). Deposition of a neighbor called Vienna, 1629: "Da casa mia che è vicina, sentei un gran strepito di gridare che si faceva in casa di ditta Giacomina et Laura. et doppo il gridare, viddi che uscì fuori una donna di tempo piccola, qual non conosco qual sentei che disse questo 'Basta che ve lo faccio avisato, se ne intravenirà qualche cosa à vostro danno'. Partita che fu la suddetta donna, uscirono fuori dalla casa detta Giacomina et Laura et dissero che quella donna era andata à protestarli che non dassero recapito ad un certo tal Frate, per che era prima moroso [di Giulia]".

52 ASV, SU, B80 (Trail of Marina of Chioggia): "L'ho ben sentita in colera à gridar con questa et con staltra".

each other' [...] and at that time there were some women of the neighborhood at my doorstep"[53].

These statements provide evidence that the public nature of the incidents is always underlined, how it took place in the middle of the street, where everyone could see and hear. Exceedingly exuberant conduct, speaking too loudly, and other unusual gestures could have corroborated the witchcraft accusation, since they characterized the perpetrator as deviant compared to the norm, which restated the values of decorum, dignity and measure.[54] The prostitutes' public manifestation of their relationships and their feelings, highlighted by words and gestures, increased the neighbors' suspicion and annoyance toward these women. Sentences like "Andrea does whatever he wants, anyway he'll be mine", and the fact that these love relationships were displayed ("I complained with her and with everybody. And everybody knew"[55]) together with quarrels and yells, created the increasingly justified reputation among the prostitutes of being witches. The public esteem of a person expressed an ethical evaluation of a higher level, and this norm operated as a fundamental principle of distinction. The reputation, in the small community, such as the neighborhood, was a tyrannical standard.[56] The following statements have arisen from this type of social background: "Meneghina Viola said in public that she wants Cochio to go to her house in spite of all his family"[57]; "How the indecent and dishonest prostitute [...] said personally a lot of times to want to spend all of her money to make her boyfriend come back from his

---

53 IBID., deposition of Olivia: "Hebbe notitia di questo matrimonio, lei vene a casa mia credendo che Marieta fosse mia figlia et si messe a strepitare con dire 'togia detto Battaglia chi vuole per moglie che ad ogni modo non si galderanno'. [...] et all'hora vi erano delle donne de corte alla mia porta".

54 On the reform of gesture and behaviors in Italy see: BURKE, 2000, pp. 79-98; BOTTERI, 1997.

55 ASV, SU, B80 (Trial of Camilla Savioni): "Faccia pure il signor Andrea quel che vuole che ad ogni modo sarà mio"; "Mi son lamentata con lei et con tutti. Et tutti lo sapevano".

56 DI SIMPLICIO, 2005, p. 168. About the matter of the honor in the Most Serene Republic in XVI and XVII century see: POVOLO, 1997, pp. 355-412.

57 ASV, SU, B124 (Trial of Marietta and Meneghina Viola). Unbound denunciation, 1685: "La suddetta Meneghina Viola a deto in publico che vuole che detto Cochio vaghi in casa sua al despeto di tuti li suoi di casa".

travel"[58]; "In the middle of the street he [Lunardo] publicly said that Marina bound him, and due to that, he wanted to kill her [...] and then, with a blade, he beaten her up with serious risk of killing. And she was praying him to stop"[59].

In the end witches, and in these cases prostitutes, were incapable of feeling true love, only lust. To affirm that a man's love toward a prostitute was uniquely caused by witchcraft deprived these women of an achievable acknowledgment of their feelings. Indeed, hurling the witchcraft accusation against these relationships removes all meaning from both men's and women's love, since it was a common notion that witches could not arouse true love in men, but only bind them with lust and with the arts of the body.[60] In this manner, the "honest" love remained a prerogative of good Christians, far from the sin and the filth of the corporeality, defined on the basis of the new rules of marriage, and claimed by a women's category that surely had to face less freedom and independence than the prostitutes.[61] Anyway, the illicit relationships continued to exist within society and were definitely more in numbers than those which were denounced. Then what was it that triggered the witchcraft accusation?

As written by Di Simplicio: "The tolerance toward indecent situations would continue for years only if an affair did not become unbearably 'showy' for the prevalent moral sensitivity". Following this line of interpretation, during questioning, the underlining of the public nature of love's demands by the prostitutes became the justification and the trigger of the denunciation. "In addition to disobedience and sin, in

---

58 ASV, SU, B77 (Trial of Bellina Loredana, Giulia Pisana, Vienna and Giulia Terzi). Denunciation against Bellina, 1615: "Come l'impudicca donna meretrice disonesta [...] ha detto più volte di sua boccha di voler spender tutto il suo per far rettornare di viazzo un suo moroso".

59 ASV, SU, B80 (Trial of Marina of Chioggia): Deposition of Adriana: "[Lunardo] in mezzo il terrao disse pubblicamente che ditta Marina l'haveva legato; et che perciò voleva ammazzarla. [...] Et all'hora col pugnal nudo la percosse con pericolo di ammazzarla. Et lei lo pregava à non darli più". The violence against the acknowledged prostitutes or witches, its legitimized implementation and how it was recounted proudly by the aggressors, is an extended subject that cannot be analyzed in the space of this article. See a summary in: NICCOLI, 2000, pp. 123-127.

60 See: INSTITOR (KRÄMER)/SPRENGER, 2003, part 1, question 7, pp. 97-102.

61 See for example: COWAN, 2007, pp. 135-150.

which anyone could have succumbed to *tamquam fragilis*, is abhorred the high profile kept by the offender within the public union: the look not downward, postures which clash and seem to offend the other's right expectations"[62]. The prostitutes were not expressing themselves with shame but with *jattanza* (haughtiness, arrogance), they were bragging, yelling and fighting. In other words, they made their sin so much known that society could no longer assimilate or tolerate it. While claiming a validity which was not entitled to their feelings, the prostitutes who were in love emerge from the boundaries of an accepted deviance, failing to fulfill the role attributed to them by society; they upset the social order which required by necessity that society should be imbalanced, unequal, and held together by deviance itself.

As a further proof of the perception of the inopportuneness of the "in love" prostitutes is given by the numerous sonnets and rhymes about courtesans, most of them of ironic and satiric nature, which circulated in Venice during the XVI and XVII century.[63] For example, in this ode in Venetian dialect entitled *Insegnamenti alle puttane* (teachings for prostitutes) it is written:

"[...]Per ultimo consegio/ no ve inamoré mai,/ ché avanti dei so guai/ il filar la lana è megio:/ l'amor alle puttane/ le manda in Carampane./ Chi è inamorà è sfedia,/ el vogio replicar:/ no ve lassé ingannar/ da questa frenesia,/ ché chi refonde amanti/ vien pasto da furfanti./ Mi ghe ne sè qualche una/ de queste poverette,/ che se trova in le strette/ de amorosa fortuna,/ che giera belle e riche/ e adesso sé mendiche. [...]"[64].

---

62 Dɪ Sɪᴍᴘʟɪᴄɪᴏ, 1994, pp. 218-219.
63 See, for example, the famous works of Pietro Aretino like the *Sonetti Lussuriosi* (1524) and the comedy *La Cortigiana* (1525), or *La Puttana Errante* and *Il trentuno della Zaffetta* (1532) by Lorenzo Venier.
    "For last I suggest to never fall in love, because better is to spin yarn than to have love troubles: love sends the whores to Carampane. Who is in love is bound, and I want to tell you again: don't fool yourselves with this craze, because who reciprocates the lovers becomes food for scoundrels. I know some of these poor things, who find themselves in the whirlwind of love, who were beautiful and rich and now are mendicant". Quoted in: Mɪʟᴀɴɪ, 1994b, pp. 81-86.

"Da rabia, da dolor e da martello"[65]: Witches and Lovesickness

One of the abilities attributed to the witches, and therefore to love magic, was the power to induce different kinds of illnesses on their lovers or their love rivals, as seen in the preceding lines. In the XVII century, a person who suffered an unexpected and odd misfortune explained it with a psychological method, in which the direct knowing (of emotional kind) predominated over the cognitive aspect of reality. Therefore, the sick person sometimes presented himself as a victim of a witch's magical aggression directed toward him. In a personalist system, a misfortune happens due to a social fracture between the people or the groups involved. Consequently the emotional elements prevail in the minds, which lead to not search for a medical cause for the illness, but to a personalization of the event that ascribes the blame to somebody.[66]

Some manifestations of love feelings, when were rationalized and narrated in the depositions in front of the inquisitor, were described as the arising of ailments, passions and diseases. This pattern can be especially noted in cases which involved illicit relationships.[67] In the trial against Isabella is stated: "Once I went upstairs to Isabella and I saw that the mentioned Zanchi was in trouble, because he was indignant with her, as far as she told me, and then we took him and we toss him on the bed, and a little later the ailment went away, and he woke up and started to laugh"[68]. About the sickness of Lunardo Gardin, who was a former lover of Marina of Chioggia and was unable to "enjoy" his new lover Agnesina, we can read: "[Lunardo] was lying on Agnesina's bed after dinner, and he was screaming out loud saying 'Oh dear I'm burning because of the witchcraft Marina did to me'; whence I brought him a bucket of water, and he drank almost half of it and it seemed that he

---

65 From the *Rime* of Maffio Venier, quoted in: MILANI, 1994b, pp. 55-74.
66 DI SIMPLICIO, 2005, pp. 130-133.
67 About adultery in Early Modern Europe see: MATTEWS GRIECO, 1991, pp. 93-96.
68 ASV, SU, B77 (Trial of Isabella Greghetta). 1622, deposition of Orsetta: "Una volta andai di sopra da detta Isabella, et vidi che detto Zanchi era andato in fastidio, perche si era sdegnato con ella per quanto essa mi disse, et lei et io lo prendessimo et butassimo sul letto, et de li a poco li passò il fastidio, rivenne et si messe a rider".

was recovering his senses, and then he raised himself and went away"[69]. As another example, Andrea de Gaspero stated: "In those times I was such consumed I looked like a spike, because of the pain for not going to my woman's house"[70]. Especially when a lover's one-sidedness determined to stop spending time with the other, the distance could have generated a feeling described as yearning for the other person. This particular feeling was depicted as an inside fermenting, a warm and painful claw that was scratching into the chest, the so-called *rabbia al cuore* (the anger in the heart). Due to the illicit nature of the relationships, the men could decide to put distance between themselves and the mistress whenever they wanted. The decision was binding for those who made it, and could be matched by a religious vow. 22-year-old Pietro Moretti, when called to testify against a woman, who practiced love magic, narrated his relationship with a prostitute named Benetta:

> "It is also true that I was indignant with Benetta for some time and I did not go to her that much; and then I went, and at the time of jubilee, I confessed and received communion, and I swore not to see Benetta anymore, nonetheless fifteen or twenty days later I felt a great anger in the heart and I could not help to go back to her. [...]. And when I went back to Benetta I told her about how I felt that anger in the heart and I suspected that she might have bewitched me. But she said no, and she told me that she wanted me to keep going to her though"[71].

---

69 ASV, SU, B80 (Trial of Marina Chioggiotta): Deposition of Lucrezia: "Butato sul letto di ditta Agnesina di dopo disnar, et gridando ad alta voce con dire 'oimè mi bruso per le strigarie fattemi da Marina'; onde io gli portai un secchio di acqua, et lo beve quasi mezzo et parse che revegni, et poi tolse su et andò via de longo".

70 IBID.: "Et io in quei tempi ero talmente consumato che parevo una spiera, dal dolor che non li andavo in casa de ditta mia donna".

71 ASV, SU, B80 (Trial of Camilla Savioni): "È anco vero che son stato qualche tempo sdegnato con ditta Benetta che non andavo tra tanto da lei; et poi son andato, che fu a ponto del tempo del Giubileo, che essendosvi confessato et comunicato, et havendo fatto fama risoluta di non andar più da Benetta suddetta, nientedimeno che da lì a 15 o 20 giorni mi vene et mi sentei una gran rabbia al cuor che non potei far di manco di tornar da Benetta suddita. [...] Et quando tornai da Benetta gli dissi che havevo sentito quella rabbia al cuor et che dubitavo che essa Benetta mi havesse fatto qualche strigaria. Ma lei mi disse si no, dicendomi però che voleva ch'io seguitasse andar da lei".

Thus, the departure could be hard and painful but, due to the fact that the genuine love between prostitutes and ordinary men was not acknowledged in the cultural and social context, all the feelings experienced and expressed by men after leaving were attributed to witchcraft. Another symbolic example is given, again, by the story between Girolamo Filomena and Betta Borella, occurred in 1686, when he tried, convinced by his father, to leave his wife and reach out to Vienna. After two days of travel with Pietro Antonio Visentin, a servant of the family, the young Girolamo decided that he was incapable of take a step further. Pietro Antonio, in front of the inquisitor, recounted the incident:

"He told me that surely he could not resist doing this move of leaving the mentioned Betta, his wife. I encouraged him to continue the travel, and when we arrived to a place called Longarone, this Giovan Battista told me unswervingly that he could not continue to travel anymore, but that at any rate he wanted to go back, because he felt a shortness of breath, a suffering, and a pain in the chest, that was eating him, whence he needed to go back. In fact he unswervingly wanted to go back although I tried to persuade him of the opposite. [...]. In the travel to Cadore, I observed that this Giovan Battista has always been passionate, without any desire to eat and he did not slept at night. And because I spent time with this Giovan Battista for 10 and more years and I saw him talking to young girls, nevertheless I have never seen him falling in love in a manner like how he is in love with the mentioned Betta, who is an old woman, bald in the head, infamous and an innkeeper. Whence I suspect he might have been bewitched"[72].

---

72 ASV, SU, B124 (Trial of Pelizzari and Maria of Bassano): "Egli mi disse che certo non potrebbe resistere a far questo passo di abbandonar detta betta sua moglie. Io l'esortai a continuar il viaggio, a quando fossimo gionti ad un luogo detto longaron, esso giovan battista mi disse risolutamente che non poteva continuar più il viaggio, ma che ad ogni modo voleva ritornar indietro, perche si sentiva un affanno, una passion, e dolor nel petto, che lo rodeva, onde bisognava tornasse a dietro. Come in fatti risolutamente volse ritornare, non ostante che io procurassi persuaderlo all'incontrario. [...] Nel viaggio facessimo verso cadore, osservai che detto signor giovan battista stete sempre come appassionato, senza voglia di mangiare e la notte non dormiva. et perche io ho pratticato detto signor giovan battista per 10 e più anni e l'ho veduto conversar con delle giovene ho di nulla di meno non l'ho veduto mai innamorarsi in modo como pare sii innamorato della suddetta betta, quale è donna vecchia pelata in testa, di mala fama, et locandiera. onde io dubito che li possi esser stata fatta qualche stregaria".

These representations of restlessness were well-established in the collective consciousness of the Venetian society, and used as a means to understand and recount deviant behavior. In fact, we can notice the use of the same terms in the *a posteriori* descriptions of the beginning of illicit relationships. Serving as last example is the recount of the love relationship between Giustina and Tommaso, described in the trial against Orsetta Padovana. The witnesses narrate how Giustina, a young married woman of 28 years, was forced by Orsetta's witchcraft to fall in love and have sexual intercourse with Tommaso (four years before the trial). In the denunciation registered on May 26, 1590, Antonio described the incident in these terms: Orsetta, at Tommaso's request, who desired to possess Giustina, delivered some fishes to her, which fishes must have been bewitched, due to the fact that – as soon as Giustina had eaten them – she could not resist to go to see Tommaso, and make love with him. When Giustina was questioned on June 5, she started saying: "This [Tommaso] was never my beloved, nor he has never practiced me carnally, I've never been to his house"[73]. After being demanded before and grilled by the inquisitor, she started to narrate the circumstances: "I liked him, but I have no *martello* for him, and I liked Tommaso, and he liked me, and you can imagine what happened between us […]. At the beginning, when I had seen this Tomaso only once in the house of Orsetta, one day when I was at home, it came to me a something to the heart, and I couldn't quieten, and I've never felt a thing like that"[74]. Suddenly, all the memories about that day started to re-emerge, and Giustina recounted the circumstances with all the right specifics. Describing how she and Paola (Giustina's servant and wife of the accuser, Antonio) went to Orsetta's house she told: "When I was going to Orsetta's house I was speeding so fast that Paola could not keep up to me. I

---

73 ASV, SU, B66 (Trial of Orsetta Padovana): "Questo [Tommaso] non è stato mai mio inamorato, ne ha mai havuto da far meco carnalmente, non son stata mai in casa sua".

74 IBID.: "Io ho voluto ben, ma non ho suo martello, et a Tomaso ho voluto bene, e lui ha voluto ben a me et fra noi potete considerar quel che è successo […] nel principio, che io non havevo visto se non una volta questo thomaso in casa de questa orseta, un di stando in casa me venne non so che al cuore, che non mi poteva acquietarse, che mai habbi una tal cosa".

ran like a crazy one, and I didn't know what I was doing"[75]. According to Giustina's tale, once arrived to the house, "this Thomaso went into the house and came upstairs, and I was like crazy, and I hugged him, and I kissed him, [...] and that pain ceased, and after a snack I had sexual intercourse with Tommaso"[76]. The same day Paola testified about these facts, giving an even more detailed deposition about the physical effects of Orsetta's magic: "Giustina's head was collapsing, and she changed color and started to say 'I feel an anger in the heart to go to this Orseta, necessarily I must go there to see Tomaso'. I told her to be patient [...] and she told me 'I want to go, I cannot stay'"[77].

"But she takes him the cake, steeped, as it were, in the other's suffering, and kept warm by her love. He has hardly bitten it when he is overtaken by an odd emotion, by a feeling of dizziness. Then as the blood rushes up to his heart he turns red and hot. Passion fastens anew on him, and inextinguishable desire"[78]. These few lines taken from *La Sorciére* by Jules Michelet could summarize the brief story of Giustina, her restlessness and her yearning. She, just like all the other examples given so far, illustrates her actions and feelings as the result of being under the spell of someone, and so ascribes them to witchcraft. In all these ill love manifestations, on one hand, the victims describe themselves as forced to satisfy someone else's will ("Giustina was forced to go there, and to caress him and to do his will, as said by Giustina"[79]), and therefore incapable of taking control over their own actions ("I'm

---

75 ASV, SU, B66 (Trial of Orsetta Padovana): "Nell'andare che io faceva a casa della detta orseta, io correvo tanto che Paula non mi poteva seguitar. Io correvo come una matta, non sapevo quello che mi facesse".

76 IBID.: "Detto thomaso intrò in casa et venne di sopra, che io era come matta, et lo abbracciai detto thomaso, et lo basciai, [...], et mi passò quel dolore, et doppo marenda hebbi commercio con detto thomaso".

77 ASV, SU, B66 (Trial of Orsetta Padovana): "Iustina che se accasciava il capo, se mutò di colore, e cominciò a dire, 'mi sento una rabbia al cuore da andar da questa orseta, le forcia che li vada per veder thomaso sopraditto'. Io le dissi che havesse pazienza [...] lei me disse, 'Io voglio andare, non posso star'".

78 MICHELET, 1862. Book I, chapter X. The quotation from Michelet is recalled here only for its great literary value. His interpretation of witchcraft as the result of a gender conflict is not adopted nor discussed in this article.

79 ASV, SU, B66 (Trial of Orsetta Padovana). Deposition of Margherita Manchiana: "Essa Iustina fu forciata andarci, et farli carezze et far la voluntà sua per quanto ne disse Iustina".

carried, I can't do otherwise"[80]), on the other hand they impute their compliance and their agitations to witchcraft ("And I thought she was practicing witchcraft against me"[81]). Due to the witchcraft accusation, all these victims can easily go back to their previously abandoned lovers, or continue their illicit love relationships, without failing their social role. Consequently, love magic operated as a social justification applied to deviant behaviors, which removed responsibility from the deviants and allowed them to maintain conducts perceived as illicit by the society, within the society itself. The certainty that witches could have a coercive effect on someone's will was used as justification which freed the society and the deviants from responsibility.

Was this justification used consciously or unconsciously? The case of Giustina allows supposing a conscious application of witchcraft accusation: when Orsetta was accused in 1590, Giustina was having an affair with Tommaso for four years. Orsetta was not only a plausible witch, due to the fact that she (legally) distributed a medicinal unguent and practiced the traditional love rituals (discussed in the first part of this article), and therefore fitted the profile of the witch as a woman who possessed a no longer allowed popular culture; she was also the former lover of Tommaso, who was the father of at least one of her daughters, and because of the just established relationship between Tommaso and Giustina, the latter and Orsetta, who were once friends, fought in the middle of the street and had stopped talking to each other since then.[82] In Orsetta's case then are summarized many of the aspects underlined so far. Another kind of accusation, which allows the suppo-

---

80 IBID.: "Son portata, non posso far altro".

81 ASV, SU, B80 (Trial of Marina Chioggiotta). Deposition of Andrea de Gaspero: "Et giudicavo che facesse delle strigarie contra di me".

82 Orsetta has explained the accusation as an Antonio's reaction to her denial of a sexual intercourse. She narrated that a couple of months before the trial, one night Antonio was drunk and went to her house asking to sleep there with her. As soon as she denied him to stay he started to curse and then, afraid that she was going to denounce him to the Holy Office, he accused her first. Therefore, the story of the spell cast on Giustina served as an excuse to protect himself. Regardless what really happened (if the incident was actually occurred or if the deponents were instructed to narrate a fictionalized tale), which we will never be able to know, the description of the incident summarizes the society's inclination toward the recount of deviant love relationships.

sition of a rationalized use of witchcraft as a support for the trial, is when the illicit relationships, often between a young male and an older woman, was reported by the victim's family, as seen in connection with the prostitutes who ruin men's health and the families' opposition to the marriage, like in this 1685 charge: "I [Sebastiano] testify to this Holy Office how Zuanne *quondam* Giovanni Cochio, my nephew, about a year ago started to have bad practice with a certain Meneghina Viola, daughter of Marietta Viola [both prostitutes], to whom my nephew Zuanne said, when he was at home, that he felt forced to go to the mentioned Meneghina, and to leave his wife"[83].

Conversely, the use of terms and expressions to explain and rationalize someone's feelings, which consequently lead to witchcraft accusation, could be the result of the application of an interpretative framework, derived from the cultural background, wherewith interpret reality. In other words, witchcraft and its physical results operated as a cultural set of words, phrases and explanations used to understand and recount deviant love's feelings, and this cultural set was available to the entire society, especially the lower classes. Therefore, if on one hand witchcraft became a cultural framework wherewith explain someone's illicit love feelings, on the other hand it served as a social justification of someone's illicit actions.

Conclusions

What was the role attributed to witchcraft in explaining deviant love? When and why did the deviant labelling applied to love relationships lead to witchcraft accusation and, therefore, to denunciation and trial? These are the questions posed at the beginning of this article. In the context of this workshop about "recounting deviance" I tried to start exploring the Early Modern illicit love on a very circumscribed documentary basis. Without any doubt, the subject requires a more analyzed

---

83 ASV, SU, B124 (Trial of Marietta and Meneghina Viola): "Depongo a questo santo offitio, come Zuanne *quondam* Giacomo Cochio mio nepote, ha preso circa un'anno fa, prattica cattiva con una tal meneghina Viola figliola di Marietta Viola, a quale detto Zuanne mio nepote in casa ha detto che si sente sforzato ad andar da detta meneghina, et abandonar la propria moglie".

study from different perspectives and various documents. However, from what has been noticed so far it is possible to outline an introductory interpretation of the connection between deviant love and witchcraft accusation.

In the path leading to the accusation[84] are added together different characteristics and situations that concern deviant love. First of all, the female gender, which was connected to the witch labelling from centuries.[85] Second the knowledge, the practice and the request of the witchcraft *ad amorem*, and its diffusion within the traditional popular culture. Another characteristic was the harlot profession because, as written in the *Malleus Maleficarum*, the women who surpassed other women in terms of superstition and witchcraft were those who were dominated by infidelity, ambition and lust, in particular the adulterers, the fornicators and the concubines. A further cause was the public manifestation of the deviant and sinful behavior compared to the current norms, which prevented the community from absorbing and tolerating the deviance. Lastly, the exploitation of the physical effects of the love encouraged, consciously or unconsciously, the witchcraft labelling. Even though each one of these motivations individually represented a passable deviance tolerated within the community, the confluence of two or more of them could have triggered the accusation. However, in some cases it was not the deviant label which brought these women before the Holy Office. It was their attempt to legitimize themselves, to shake off the deviant label, which was intolerable to those who applied that label in the first place.

---

84 An attempt to schematize the formation of witch's idea within the small communities is made by: DI SIMPLICIO, 2005, pp. 168-191.
85 See: SALLMANN, 1991, pp. 455-469; WIESNER, 2003, pp. 245-333; BAROJA, 1990.

Literature

ABBIATI, SERGIO/AGNOLETTO, ATTILIO/LAZZATI, MARIA ROSARIO, La stregoneria. Diavoli, streghe, inquisitori dal Trecento al Settecento, Arnoldo Mondadori Editore, Milano 1984.

BALDINI, ERALDO, Tenebrosa Romagna. Mentalità, misteri e immaginario collettivo nei secoli della paura e della "maraviglia", Società editrice (Il Ponte Vecchio), Cesena 2014.

BARBIERATO, FEDERICO, Nella stanza dei circoli: Clavicula Salomonis e libri di magia a Venezia nei secoli XVII e XVIII, Sylvestre Bonnard, Milano 2002.

BAROJA, JULIO CARO, Witchcraft and Catholic Theology, in: Early Modern European Witchcraft. Centers and Peripheries, ed. by ANKARLOO, BENGT/HENNINGSEN, GUSTAV, Clarendon Press, Oxford 1990, pp. 19-43.

BOTTERI, INGE, Oltre le barriere confessionali: i manuali sul comportamento e i percorsi della loro diffusione nell'esempio degli "avvisi delle buone creanze", in: I tempi del Concilio. Religione, cultura, società nell'Europa tridentina, ed. by MOZZARELLI, CESARE/ZARDIN, DANILO, Bulzoni Editore, Roma 1997, pp. 327-352.

BURKE, PETER, Sogni, gesti, beffe. Saggi di storia culturale, Il Mulino, Bologna 2000.

BYARS, JANA, The Long and Varied Relationship of Andrea Mora and Anzola Davide: Concubinage, Marriage and the Authorities in the Early Modern Veneto, in: Journal of Social History, vol.41, 3, (Spring, 2008), pp. 667-690.

CARAVALE, GIORGIO, L'Orazione proibita. Censura ecclesiastica e letteratura devozionale nella prima età moderna, Olschki Editore, Firenze 2003.

CAVARZERE, MARCO, La prassi della censura nell'Italia del Seicento. Tra repressione e mediazione, Edizioni di Storia e Letteratura, Roma 2011.

CORAZZOL, GIGI/CORRÀ, LOREDANA, Esperimenti d'amore. Fatti di giovani nella Feltre del Cinquecento, Libreria Pilotto, Feltre 1981.

COWAN, ALEXANDER, Marriage, Manners and Mobility in Early Modern Venice, Ashgate, Aldershot 2007.

COZZI, GAETANO, Religione, moralità e giustizia a Venezia: vicende della magistratura degli Esecutori contro la Bestemmia, in: La società veneta e il suo diritto, Venezia, Marsilio, Fondazione Giorgio Cini, 2000.

DI SIMPLICIO, OSCAR, Peccato, penitenza, perdono: Siena 1575-1800. La formazione della coscienza nell'Italia moderna, F.Angeli, Milano 1994.

ID., L'autunno della stregoneria: maleficio e magia nell'Italia moderna, Il Mulino, Bologna 2005.

EYMERICH, FRA NICOLAU, Manuale dell'Inquisitore, Edizioni Piemme, Casale Monferrato 1998.

FERRANTE, LUCIA, Il matrimonio disciplinato: processi matrimoniali a Bologna nel Cinquecento, in: Disciplina dell'anima, disciplina del corpo e disciplina della società tra medioevo ed età moderna, ed. by PRODI, PAOLO, Il Mulino, Bologna 1994, pp. 901-927.

ID., Il valore del corpo, ovvero la gestione economica della sessualità femminile, in: Il lavoro delle donne, ed. by GROPPI, ANGELA, Laterza, Roma-Bari 1996, pp. 206-228.

INSTITOR (KRÄMER), HEINRICH/SPRENGER, JAKOB, Il martello delle streghe: la sessualità femminile nel transfert degli inquisitori, Spirali, Milano 2003.

LAVENIA, VINCENZO, L'Infamia e il Perdono. Tributi, pene e confessione nella teologia morale della prima età moderna, Il Mulino, Bologna 2004.

MARTIN, JOHN, Popular Culture and the Shaping of Popular Heresy in Renaissance Venice, in: Inquisition and Society in Early Modern Europe, ed. by HALICZER, STEPHEN, Croom Helm, London/Sidney 1987, pp. 115-128.

ID., Venice's Hidden Enemies. Italian Heretics in a Renaissance City, University of California Press, Berkeley/Los Angeles 1993.

MARTIN, RUTH, Witchcraft and Inquisition in Venice 1550-1650, Basil Blackwell, New York 1989.

MASINI, ELISEO, Sacro Arsenale ovvero Pratica dell'Uffizio della Santa Inquisizione, Stamperia di S. Michele a Ripa, Roma 1730: https://books.google.it/books?id=Xt7bhnKGCZQC&printsec=frontc over&hl=it&source=gbs_ge_summary_r&cad=0#v=onepage&q&f= false, 26.08.2015.

MATTEWS GRIECO, SARA F., Corpo, aspetto e sessualità, in: Storia delle donne in Occidente. Dal Rinascimento all'età moderna, ed. by DUBY, GEORGES/PERROT, MICHELLE, Laterza, Roma-Bari 1991, pp. 53-99.

MCGOUGH, LAURA, Gender, Sexuality and Syphilis in Early Modern Venice: the disease that came to stay, Palgrave Macmillan, Basingstoke 2011.

MICHELET, JULES, La Strega, trad. it. CUSUMANO, PAOLA/PARIZZI, MASSIMO, Rizzoli, Milano 1977.

MILANI, MARISA, Antiche pratiche di medicina popolare nei processi del S.Uffizio: Venezia 1572-1591, Centro stampa palazzo Maldura, Padova 1986.

ID., Piccole storie di stregoneria nella Venezia del '500, Essedue Edizioni, Verona 1989.

ID., Streghe e Diavoli nei processi del S.Uffizio: Venezia 1554-1587, Ghedina & Tassotti, Bassano del Grappa 1994a.

ID., Contro le Puttane: rime venete del 16 secolo, Ghedina & Tassotti, Bassano del Grappa 1994b.

ID., Due processi per stregoneria a Venezia 1574, Centro stampa Palazzo Madama, Venezia 1994c.

MONTER, WILLIAM, Ritual, Myth and Magic in Early Modern Europe, The Harvest Press, Brighton (Sussex) 1983.

MURARO, LISA, La signora del Gioco: episodi della caccia alle streghe, Feltrinelli Editore, Milano 1976.

NICCOLI, OTTAVIA, Storie di ogni giorno in una città del Seicento, Laterza, Roma-Bari 2000.

O'NEIL, MARY, Magical Healing, Love Magic and the Inquisition in Late Sixteenth-Century Modena, in: Inquisition and Society in Early Modern Europe, ed. by HALICZER, STEPHEN, Croom Helm, London/Sidney 1987, pp. 88-114.

PASCHINI, PIO, Venezia e l'Inquisizione romana da Giulio II a Pio IV, Editrice Antenore, Padova 1959.

PLEBANI, TIZIANA, Un secolo di sentimenti, Amori e conflitti generazionali nella Venezia del Settecento, Istituto veneto di Lettere ed Arti, Venezia 2012.

POVOLO, CLAUDIO, L'intrigo dell'Onore. Poteri e istituzioni nella Repubblica di Venezia tra Cinque e Seicento, Cierre Edizioni, Verona 1997.

PRODI, PAOLO, The Structure and organization of the church in Renaissance Venice. Suggestion of research, in: Renaissance Venice, ed. by HALE, JOHN RIGBY, Faber and Faber, London 1973, pp. 409-430.

ID., (ed.), Disciplina dell'anima, disciplina del corpo e disciplina della società tra medioevo ed età moderna, Il Mulino, Bologna 1994.

ID., Una storia della giustizia. Dal pluralismo dei fori al moderno dualismo tra coscienza e diritto, Il Mulino, Bologna 2000.

ID., Il paradigma tridentino. Un'epoca della storia della Chiesa, Editrice Morcelliana, Brescia 2010.

PRODI, PAOLO/REINHARD, WOLFGANG (eds.), Il Concilio di Trento e il Moderno, Il Mulino, Bologna 1996.

PROSPERI, ADRIANO, Tribunali della Coscienza. Inquisitori, confessori, missionari, Giulio Einaudi Editore, Torino 1996.

ID., L'Inquisizione romana. Letture e ricerche, Edizioni di Storia e Letteratura, Roma 2003.

RUGGIERO, GUIDO, I confini dell'Eros. Crimini sessuali e sessualità nella Venezia del Rinascimento, Marsilio Editori, Venezia 1988.

SALLMANN, JEAN-MICHEL, Strega, in: Storia delle donne in Occidente. Dal Rinascimento all'età moderna, ed. by DUBY, GEORGES/PERROT, MICHELLE, Laterza, Roma-Bari 1991, pp. 455-469.

SEIDEL MENCHI, SILVANA/QUAGLIONI, DIEGO, Coniugi nemici. La separazione in Italia dal XII al XVIII secolo, Il Mulino, Bologna 2000.

ID., Matrimoni in dubbio. Unioni controverse e nozze clandestine in Italia dal XIV al XVIII secolo, Bologna, Il Mulino, 2001.

SEITZ, JONATHAN, Witchcraft and Inquisition in Early Modern Venice, Cambridge University Press, Cambridge 2011.

SOLÉ, JACQUES, Storia dell'amore e del sesso nell'età moderna, Laterza, Bari 1979.

TEDESCHI, JOHN, Inquisitorial Law and the Witch, in: Early Modern European Witchcraft. Centers and Peripheries, ed. by ANKARLOO, BENGT/HENNINGSEN, GUSTAV, Clarendon Press, Oxford 1990, pp. 83-118.

161

ID., The Prosecution of Heresy. Collect Studies on the Inquisition in Early Modern Italy, State University of New York at Binghamton, Centre for Medieval and Early Renaissance Studies, 1991.

WIESNER, MERRY E., Le donne nell'Europa moderna 1500-1750, Giulio Einaudi Editore, Torino 2003.

ZANELLI, GIULIANA, Streghe e società nell'Emilia e Romagna del Cinque-Seicento, Longo Editore, Ravenna 1992.

ZARRI, GABRIELLA, Il matrimonio tridentino, in: Il Concilio di Trento e il Moderno, ed. by PRODI PAOLO/REINHARD, WOLFGANG, Il Mulino, Bologna 1996, pp. 437-483.

Representations of Deviance

Inquisitorial Practices and Feminine Divergence in Venice between the 17th and 18th Centuries

FEDERICO BARBIERATO

As it is known, discussions regarding deviance in modern times have a clear gender dimension. In the past – and also today – settings, where gender determined what was considered to be legitimate existed. This is obviously clear. However, it is interesting to consider the settings where the same societies have created different stories on deviance.

In the following discussion, I intend to focus on a very particular and perhaps marginal problem, which nonetheless can provide extra information to create a more dynamic picture of the discussions on deviance in Modern times. The point of observation that was certainly partial is given to us by the Roman Inquisition's behavior towards women – in particular that of the Sant'Uffizio in Venice. The timeframe considered focuses on the 17th and 18th centuries.

The attention towards the documentation produced by the ecclesiastical trials evidently reduces and selects the field of interest from the very beginning. It has to do with crimes that deal with cases of conscience and that, more than others, refer to the complex link between belief and action. However, I believe that such perspective could give us a wide variety of examples of different behaviors exhibited by the institutions towards men and women.[1]

The interest in this theme began with the attempt to establish whether or not it was possible to think of a female *esprit fort*, just as the grand majority of historiography affirmed. In fact, one of the elements which dominated the historiography regarding libertinism is the acknowledgment, on behalf of libertines, of the implicit association between women and their physical and intellectual weaknesses. It has to do with a strongly misogynous point of view. Indeed, evident proof can be found in libertine literature in the sixteen hundreds Italian setting.[2] Nevertheless, if analyzed from the point of view of the Inquisitorial documents, I believe the issue is at the crossroad between a series of different and often contradicting elements.

First of all, it is worthwhile to once again underline the additional problem represented by the resources. The Inquisitorial trials, as is known, are sources that have had much success among historians in the last decades. No one can hide the problems that such sources present. In our case, in particular, it should be pointed out that – as it almost always happens – these sources are exclusively male, which is to say created by a magistrates composed of only men, for the most part religious men. Moreover, this resource reports investigations and judgments regarding cases of conscience. Therefore, a source that, first of all, presents what is believed to be dangerous at a certain moment and that may change based on the variation in the perception of such danger.

We have to deal with what the Inquisitors considered dangerous and hence decided to prosecute. Returning to the initial problem: was the figure of the libertine and disbelieving woman part of the female representation of the Inquisitors and, more generally, of the male culture in Modern times? In the Venetian Inquisitorial trials, women's voices are present and they speak about visions of the world also marked by extreme incredulity that could lead to atheism. They are less numerous cases compared to similar episodes that have men as protagonists; nev-

---

1   The literature regarding the use of Inquisition sources is broad. See, for example, GINZBURG, 1980, p. xvii; OSBAT, 1994, pp. 375-391. See also CORAZZOL, 1997.
2   A series of examples in SPINI, 1983.

ertheless, they are quite frequent.[3] But what should be noted immediately is the minimal attention paid by the judges to these manifestations of female dissent. It is almost as if women were not able to present a systematic speech and therefore were not perceived as a threat.

It is a matter of feminine identity, created by the Inquisitors.[4] Women, children and "idiots" all belonged to a triad that is constantly evoked to define social groups believed to be incapable of elaborating complex and autonomous intellectual thoughts. Therefore, those who belonged to such groups were believed to be able to detach themselves – if not merely superficially – from the Church's teachings. But it also had to do with an identity built by the libertine culture: women, just like children and ignoramuses were unable to see reality behind the false beliefs induced by the Churches and the established power forced upon them.

In both cases, it is a male projection: as I mentioned before – I will use some examples – there were women who built their own identity on deviance. With this identity, they often used a language that was at least partially different from that used by men. For example, women frequently substituted heretic blasphemy widespread among men with "disdaining images", that is to say desecration of sacred images. Therefore, there were crushed and broken crucifixes, the images of Madonna figures and torn saints, sacred objects soiled with excrement and so on.

What seems to be distinctive, based on certain points of view, is that there was no such thing as "one" heterodox discourse. On the contrary, heterodox discourses and deviant words all had a gender. Women were less indicative to create a tie between words and thoughts; they were evidently considered to be unfamiliar with or little inclined to do so. But women were not considered a threat because of this inability which made them less believable and less persuasive. From a paternalistic point of view, women were considered less dangerous.

---

3   For an initial bibliographic approach and pertaining to the sources, see BARBIERATO, 2012.

4   It is not possible to delve into a parallel discussion here. Perhaps what is even more interesting regarding the female agency is this: the widespread knowledge of the mechanisms and of the institutional cultures that led women to knowingly use a defensive position based on relative innocence and superficial thoughts, because of their femininity. The study of this perhaps unaware instrumental use could say a lot about the strategies women used to defend and represent themselves.

Therefore, on one hand, we have scholarly libertinism that uses women as an element of comparison in a negative way that assimilates her to the ignorant and easily fooled commoners. On the other hand, the Inquisitors who – thanks to the goodness of their heart – decided to not prosecute or to only partially prosecute the women who had stained themselves with divergent discourses. In some aspects women were lucky, but it is certainly not very reassuring from a cultural point of view.

However, I would like to clarify that using gender categories to define mental inadequacy is, first of all, implemented by the ecclesiastic institutions. This is evident in the Inquisitors' behavior with respect to female sexuality: the implicit premise of such conduct is that women cannot "choose" rationally to follow their instinct. Simply because of their weakness, they cannot repress doing so. But they regret being this way: they go to the Confessor and they confess. On the contrary, men have the ability to control themselves but, in their self-constraint, know that they would be going against natural laws, and therefore choose not to act upon their instincts.

Feminine divergence, according to the Inquisitors, tends to be perceived at best as the result of being taught by men to not believe. This way, women are paternalistically identified as victims of persuasion, and not considered able to elaborate on their own. And, for this precise reason, when the Inquisitors decided to proceed with the trial, they looked for the male figures who could have given them the divergent elements in their investigations.

I do not want to imply that the Inquisitors were always mistaken: a constant attempt to teach deviance by men existed and was widespread. It is evident that this could happen for delectable sexual purposes: I try to convince a woman that sins don not exist or that sexual relations are not a sin. This way I can convince her to have sex with me: it was a common technique especially used by confessors. However, there are many cases in which this detail does not seem to be present or at least relevant.

Allow me to give an example: in the 1720s, friar Lodovico Molin, a Zoccolante, was employed as spiritual guide to the 14-year-old commoner Margherita Marcuzzi. He taught her not to believe in the Trinity, "but that there was only one person, that is the Father, and only one

God, adding that only the Father had created the world."[5] In itself, the idea did not make too much of an impression on Margherita: another friar from the same order had already told her the same thing. He urged her "that I should not believe anything about Incarnation, and that believing in this mystery is total madness". She did not give it too much importance, but after listening to Lodovico's words and combining all this information, she was ready to follow the friar in his successive teachings.[6]

These teachings provided a complete course of heterodoxy. First of all, according to the friar, the young girl did not have to pay too much attention to her virginity, since God appreciated marriage – and marriage was obviously a very broad term to define all types of sexual relationships – much more than chastity. To prove it, he exhibited his own personal cosmology that made a great impression on Margherita's imagination:

"He told me that it is not true that there is only one paradise, but there are seven paradises, in the first of which there is God alone, and even if we are righteous, we do not go there, confessors go to the subsequent paradise, all those who are married go to the sixth, along with those who are unmarried and have children, and the virgins go in the last paradise, that is to say the seventh, with that he concluded stating that virginity is less appreciated by God than marriage."[7]

The friar's position may have exhibited a certain carnal interest, although Margherita, in the many trial appearances, never referred to any tentative seductions. What he taught her, or better yet what Margherita learned, was strictly tied to the devotional aspect of her life. In fact, it should have made it easier for her to transfer her thoughts into actions instead of proceeding in abstract reasoning: in this way she learned that the Holy Communion was a meaningless ritual, since Incarnation did not exist. She experienced this, thanks to her spiritual guide, by communicating without fasting and violating the host by placing it in her

---

5   ASV, *Sant'Uffizio*, b. 140, trial against friar Lodovico Molin, spontaneous appearance by Margherita Marcuzzi on 20 August 1726.
6   *Ivi*, spontaneous appearance by Margherita on 12 September 1726.
7   *Ivi*, spontaneous appearance by Margherita on 20 August 1726.

handkerchief after having received it. According to Molin, the Church wanted that communication was observed by fasting, so much so that breaking this rule was a grave sin. He therefore suggested the young girl to eat something before the Communion. Then it was only a question of waiting: if God had punished her, it would have been the true sign that God existed in the Holy Communion. He was certain that if Christ did not exist, all would go smoothly. It was the Church that "taught this, although it was not true." Moreover, after receiving the host, she was told to spit it in her handkerchief: here as well "if God had immediately punished me, it would be a sign that our Savior's body and blood would have been in the blessed host, and if I was not to be punished immediately, it was a sign that our Savior's body and blood was not to be found in the blessed host."

Once the experiences had been tested and "seeing that there was no divine punishment, I became deviant". She saw everything as being fabricated, an imposture. Margherita considered Christ's own genealogy, having been born by a virgin, as highly unlikely.[8] Being able to doubt, and being able to do so by possessing vocabulary and tools – no matter how uncouth – the friar had to skillfully imbue her with pride, and she was repeatedly told that "if I lived in the way and form that he was teaching me [...] I would be equal to God in greatness, wisdom, happiness and in all divine perfection, so that when a man dies, there is no difference between God and man"[9]. For his part, like many others, the friar also tried to move closer to God through magic and sacrament abuse. To do so, he habitually asked the young girl and many others to help him.

---

8   *Ivi,* spontaneous appearance by Margherita on 27 August 1726. The custom of spitting out the Host and keeping it as a charm, *agnus dei* or element of magic rites was quite common. Besides being a fundamental element of the repertoire of advanced domestic magic – it was always a gesture that entailed the abuse of sacraments –, it seems that it was a common habit also among prisoners and soldiers, according to the testimony to the Sant'Uffizio in Treviso by a friar of Lendinara, returning from the East: ASV, *Sant'Uffizio,* b. 151, *Miscellanea processi* file, spontaneous appearance by friar Giovanni, on 27 April 1681, at the court in Treviso, sent to Venice for reasons of jurisdiction.
9   ASV, *Sant'Uffizio,* b. 140, trial against frair Lodovico Molin, spontaneous appearance by Margherita on 5 September 1726.

For eight years, Margherita kept believing in Lodovico's teachings, at least until the new confessor insisted that she report it to the Sant'Uffizio. For eight years, she had repeated them to her family and to the younger children with whom she spoke, thereby creating a chain of communication that extended from the friar to a progressively larger number of people. Its effects spread like wildfire and with completely unpredictable results.

The aforementioned example can provide the impression that female divergence is a by-product of the male divergence. It is, however, a mistaken impression. Instead, it shows that we are facing religious dissidence that is created by multiple channels. The conveyance could be exclusively female: towards the end of the seventeenth century the German noble Maria Desmit explained to the maids that people were child-like and needed to be frightened to be good. Therefore, it was simply ignorance that kept them subservient: "we who are ignorant imply these things"[10].

Instead, in 1647, Faustina Cortesia did everything on her own: she believed "that everything is random" and that "I would even become Turkish to heal" from the disease that was afflicting her and which was the reason why she turned to God. Her frame of mind had also made her "very perplexed regarding the immortality of the soul"[11]. She was ill, and therefore, she entrusted herself in the hands of God, the Virgin Mary, and the Saints. It seems that she had done so with a certain conviction. However, in the end "by not granting my wish, I said that there is no God, no saintly Virgin nor Saints, that these things do not exist, because it is impossible that my wishes were not granted"[12]. Furthermore, "discussing […] with mine at home, in matters of faith, I said it is now prohibited to discuss faith, because perhaps the reasons are unfounded and conversing on religions could lead to discover that I was right"[13]. It is evident that the empirical data of the verification of God's

---

10 ASV, *Sant'Uffizio*, b. 126 trial against Maria Desmit, spontaneous appearance by Lucrezia Palamon on 12 June 1692.
11 ASV, *Sant'Uffizio*, b. 103, Salvatore Caravagio file, trial against Faustina Cortesia, spontaneous appearance by Faustina del 28 April 1647.
12 ASV, *Sant'Uffizio*, b. 103, Salvatore Caravagio file, trial against Faustina Cortesia, spontaneous appearance by Faustina on 28 April 1647.
13 ASV, *Sant'Uffizio*, b. 103, Salvatore Caravagio file, trial against Faustina Cortesia, spontaneous appearance by Faustina on 28 April 1647.

absence, based on the unfamiliarity shown towards one's own affairs, was joined by a different kind of reflection: it was the theory of political imposture of religions that was emerging. The firm belief that "speaking about something" could be transformed into free thinking, which was opposed by the Church.[14]

In the 1690s, according to the scribe, Domenico Cavagnin, religion was an invention of the princes

"To keep men obedient, seeing that weapons were not enough [...] Numa Pompilio was the first to discover such invention [...] but that was forbidden to common men, it was allowed to princes, other things were forbidden to women, and to prove this, he said that the King of France was allowed to order the killing of many people, and if it were true that Hell existed, the confessors would be the first to go because they deceive through religion."[15]

Reality was a world governed by rapports of force and where all means were justified to be used. But then, man was not so different from animals. The only difference between man and capons was that "we eat the capons, and they don't eat us"[16].

Cavagnin expressed a characteristic concept of non-religious conformity that was not just Venetian. A concept that in Venice – for various reasons – was extremely widespread. The already prevalent anticlericalism, expanded during the fifteen hundreds driven by the impetus of the Reformation and by the many heterodoxy groups who appeared even briefly in the Republic's territories. In the course of the sixteenth century, a more systematic vision matured and began to be used in view of the fact that a full blown and structured attack was no longer only against ecclesiastic institutions, but it often spread to Christianity in its

14 Regarding the theory of charlatanism of religions, see SPINI, 1983; PAGANINI, 2001; BIANCHI, 1999, pp. 21-36; GINZBURG, 1986, pp. 190-198; GINZBURG, 1976, pp. 28-41; GINZBURG, 1998; MOREAU, 2000, pp. 179-216 CAVAILLÉ, 2005, pp. 27-42.
15 ASV, *Sant'Uffizio*, b. 126, trial against Domenico Cavagnin, spontaneous appearance by Elena Cavagnin on 11 September 1692.
16 *Ivi,* spontaneous appearance by Francesca Canciani on 13 March 1692. The extensive similarities between man and beast were a recurring theme in anti-Christian and irreligious thought. See, for example, the position expressed in chapter II of the essay VI of *Theophrastus redivivus*. On this aspect GREGORY, 1979, pp. 83-84 and 190-191.

entirety, and sometimes to religion in general.[17] Becoming gradually stronger, especially compared to the previous century, the clergy started to be considered as a social group that, thanks to the phantoms of punishment or of rewards after death, strictly kept society on track. It maintained control over the sexual realm, behavior in general, and over peoples' thoughts. It was widely accepted to act as a necessary surveillance to keep the social fabric intact. However, this led people to foremost consider religion as a means of domain, a set of dogma, norms and regulations completely detached from any unearthly hypothesis.

It was a matter of fact that the view of religion as an essential means of social control was almost a universally accepted fact for both the libertines and the supporters of the Counter-Reformation. But few came to the conclusion that the sets of norms and dogma guaranteed by some heavenly authority had given life to useless or damaging institutions, and therefore needed to be removed.[18] But identifying the power mechanisms in historical religions – necessary or not – implied self-awareness, which would have gradually lead people to strip religion of any meaning that would exceed earthly experiences, and in the case of Catholicism refute the role played by the Church of Rome as the custodian of any transcendent truth. Religion ended up being considered a matter of exquisitely mundane and political status – or rather as a "political guise"[19].

Therefore, some things were forbidden to men and others to women. They served political purposes. So, according to Cavagnin, it was really the religious political imposture that could explain the difference be-

---

17 On Italian anti-clericalism see NICCOLI, 1998, in particular pp. 62 and 83-88 and especially IBID., 2005; DYKEMA/OBERMAN, 1993. See also BRAMBILLA, 2000, pp. 321-343. Anti-clericalism often took the form of the literary *topos* that presented friars and the clergy in general as parasites and cheats: see PASQUINI, 1984.

18 On the history of this concept and its decline, in addition to SPINI, 1983, see WOOTTON, 1983, pp. 56-80 and IBID., 1986, pp. 58-77. In a letter to Guy Patin, Gabriel Naudé explained how Cesare Cremonini had confided to some friends that he did not believe in the existence of God or the devil, let alone the soul was immortal. However, he made sure his manservant was a good Catholic, "de peur, disoit-il, s'il ne croyot rien, qu'un de ces matin il ne m'esgorgeseat dans mon lict" : quoted in PINTARD, 1983, p. 172.

19 ASV, *Sant'Uffizio*, b. 132, trial "of 5 March", deposition by Antonio Partenio on 8 April 1705, cc. 8*r bis*.

tween men and women, differences that were based on social order, deceit and certainly not on "the laws of nature".

Sexual behavior was considered a kind of common ground where men and women could, with the same authority, manifest their own distance from dogma, which they could practically rely on divergent behavior and conception of religious faith as a mere convention.[20] In this sense, religious indifference was as much an application of principle and "carnal use" was not a sin and the senses had to be indulged, as much as its premise. Therefore, it was possible to use it as a kind of theoretical justification, for both oneself and for those who had to be convinced. For example, in 1681, Matteo Roder was convinced "that God commanded him to womanize to help them"[21], and anyway the opinion that "the sin to womanize is the least of mortal sins" was quite widespread. Vittoria Lusdafer, in 1682, claimed to have "heard it many times, by many"[22]. In 1702, the cook of a doctor from San Trovaso explained to Margherita Mezanelli, who went even further: "bodily sins are not sins". Actually, questioned again by Margherita a few weeks later, she extended her reasoning: "when one falls in love with someone, and one desires that person, satisfying oneself [...] wasn't a sin". These were not new concepts for Margherita, because they confirmed what she had heard some years before in Verona from a girl named Angelica Quinta in a "community of women". They had spoken "about impure dishonest acts among whores", and Angelica claimed that although the confessor maintained the contrary, in her opinion they were not sins, "because they were not done out of malice, but only for goodwill"[23].

The belief that copulation between "an unmarried man and an unmarried woman" was not a sin was fairly widespread throughout the period in question. In its broadest and least assertive formulation, such theory provided a fundamentally political explanation for the re-

---

20 Interesting considerations on the lack of regulation of sexual habits in modern Italy in DAVIDSON, 1994, pp. 74-98.
21 ASV, *Sant'Uffizio*, b. 122, trial against Matteo Roder, spontaneous appearance by Giovan Carlo Malipiero on 27 February 1681.
22 ASV, *Sant'Uffizio*, b. 123, trial against Francesco Muselani, deposition by Vittoria Lusdafer on 23 July 1682, c. 4*r*.
23 ASV, *Sant'Uffizio*, b. 130, abbot Menoncour file, spontaneous appearance by Margherita Mezanelli on 28 November 1702.

strictions on sexuality, seen not as based on Scripture but introduced later on by a Church that followed earthly logic like every institution throughout history.

The spread of the idea that considered religions as fraud reached a wide consensus thanks to this type of transference to a concrete aspect of prescriptions and obligations: it had to do with experience; therefore, it was virtually open to both men and women. But only for men and women who could elaborate thoughts of heterodoxy and could publicly express them.

A failed cover-up, hence: in Venice with respect to the social classes I am focusing on, libertine elitism was more a claim specifically for oneself than a social matter; an attempt to classify society not based on social classes, but based on the freedom of thought. However, it was an attempt that used the tools at hand, those of social inequality and the identification of the idea of the people – not of the female realm – and with the means of vague ignorance. And it was members of the populace who tried to make this distinction. In principle, nobody questioned the thesis that politics, knowledge, culture, literature and deviance were matters for a few chosen people, and if it were to become common heritage, it would be its downfall. As with political secrets, it was commonly considered separate and a protected area: secrecy was kept as the premise for both the public officials of "high" level knowledge, and beneficiaries of these discussions. The fact was this: starting from the mid-sixteen hundreds, a gradually increasing number of individuals felt they were able to be a part of this tight-knit group and become part of the circle of those who detached themselves from the masses. The implicit covenant was that the existing issues that others were not supposed to speak about, restricted and hidden areas of knowledge, were limited to only a few. Nevertheless, the process of exclusion was widespread but always other-directed.[24]

---

24 What was written for the seventeen hundreds Parisian setting can in some way be extended to the Venetian setting: "Chacun s'autorise de dire et de penser; dans cette permission que chacun se donne à lui-même, ponctuée par une répression qui ne la fait jamais faiblir, s'invente non pas tant de nouvelles formes de subversione qu'un affinement des capacités cognitives et réflexives. L'originalité de cette période tient plus aux formes prises pas la discussion et la critique qu'au contenu même de la critique": FARGE, 1992, p. 265.

In the 1640s, "a large number of great and literate people" told Orsola Ciuran, a junk dealer, that hell did not exist, that the sacraments were ineffective and that the soul was mortal. So many that they were described as "almost the whole world". Orsola shared these truths with her fellow tenant Maddalena, and "they both decided to refuse the holy sacraments"[25]. It was an attempt to imitate educated people. "One really needs to say something in order not to come across as a baboon", was Grando de Grandi's justification in 1692, after he had been reprimanded for suggesting that the soul was mortal and that the afterlife did not exist, along with a personal variation on the imposture of religion.[26] These are only a few examples. But one thing is clear: putting forward ideas of "witty spirits" that introduced an element of diversity, creating a distance between the proponent and "the baboons" that were unable to understand them.

The references to define the juxtaposition of one's own identity of "esprit forts" can each time be the categories of animals ("baboons"), social (common people), of age (children), definitions of not intellectual excellence (normally "idiots") and so on. Never women. Why not?

It is an interesting fact because, if we read theological literature on female weakness instead, we would think it was a widespread topos. One could think about how youngsters, women and idiots were not allowed to read the Latin Vulgate Bible during the inquisitorial rulings. However, in 1754 when Marco Dizziani reproached Marianna Fabris and the priest Giorgio Capuccio, claiming that banned books could be read only after having the approved license, these people, a man and a woman, started laughing. He went on to say that "banned books can be read without a license and that the Church only requires a license so that people submit"[27]. It mattered little whether they were men or women. And, I repeat, it was a generally divergent man and woman to remember that in unison.

It is evident that this is a scholarly case of discrepancy between popular libertinism. Just think about the submissive behavior towards

---

25   ASV, *Sant'Uffizio*, b. 103, Ludovico Fugarola file, trial against Orsola Ciuran, spontaneous appearance by Antonia Sgambozza on 5 June 1646.

26   ASV, *Sant'Uffizio*, b. 127, trial against Grando de Grandi, spontaneous appearance by Zanetta de Grandi on 3 September 1692.

27   ASV, *Sant'Uffizio*, b. 145, trial against don Giorgio Capuccio, spontaneous appearance by Gaspare Dizziani on 7 March 1754.

"female mood swings" reserved – always in the Venetian area – for Arcangela Tarabotti on the part of members of the Academy of the Unknown. Members who had little to learn about the practice and theory of libertinism from their colleagues beyond the Alps.

This certainly does not mean that popular Venetian dissent was *gender sensitive*: in 1736, Andrea Pisani, a doctor, revisited the stereotype of the virtuoso applied to sexual liberty, defined in different terms than those seen earlier. In his opinion "whoring was not a sin", and he envied the Turks who could have a large number of women. If he had been a prince, he would have done the same. But he believed that marriage "was something for fools and that only ignoramuses and idiots get married, and that philosophers and educated people, just as he was a philosopher, never get married but keep many women for their pleasure, because this was not a sin". After all, "in the law of nature" men had several women, because they had been created by God "for the enjoyment and pleasure of men"[28].

We are not even remotely speaking about women's social status perceived as equal. I would like that to be clear.

I see things from a particular viewpoint, namely from a particular city as Venice, with its unique urban and social fabric. I do not wish arrive at general conclusions, but I have come up with the idea that libertinism among the popular classes did not discard a priori the possibility of feminine divergence. It did not consider it the most plausible hypothesis, but did not exclude it.

Perhaps in terms of common circulation, where the oral dimension and usually not the written manifestations of dissidence prevailed, it had to be a matter of a more predictable behavior. The problem of establishing inequality was less felt than the educated elaboration, which is typical of libertinism. Often, the academic and written dimension was at least limited, if not completely forbidden to women. In sixteen and seventeen hundred Venice, the sources to build one's dissidence and own divergence were not limited to the *Accademias*. They did not cir-

---

28 ASV, *Sant'Uffizio*, b. 142, trial against Antonio Pisani, spontaneous appearance by Angelo Mazzon on 21 August 1736. Anti-matrimonial themes were part of libertine trends advocated first by Vanini and then by Antonio Rocco, above all in *L'Alcibiade fanciullo a scola*. See SPINI, 1983, p. 165 and Cavaillé, 2006.

culate only in secret books. They were discourses that spread everywhere: in houses, in sermons. Everywhere. In male and female spaces.

In these cases, deep down, the specialist, the *esprit fort*, were considered in this manner not really for what was said, but for being the one who said it – whether it was a man or a woman.

Literature

BARBIERATO, FEDERICO, The Inquisitor in the Hat Shop. Inquisition, Forbidden Books and Unbelief in Early Modern Venice, Farnham 2012.

BIANCHI, SILVIA, Unmasking the Truth. The Theme of Imposture in Early Modern European Culture, in Everything Connects: In Conference with Richard H. Popkin. Essays in his Honor, ed. by FORCE JAMES E./KATZ DAVID S., Leiden 1999, pp. 21-36.

BRAMBILLA, ELENA, Alle origini del Sant'Uffizio. Penitenza, confessione e giustizia spirituale dal medioevo al XVI secolo, Bologna 2000.

CAVAILLE, JEAN-PIERRE, Antonio Rocco, Alcibiade enfant à l'école. Clandestinité, irréligion et sodomie, in: Tangence, 81 (2006), pp. 15-38.

ID., Imposture politique des religions et sagesse libertine, in: Littératures Classiques, 55 (2005), pp. 27-42.

ID., Le prince des athées, Vanini et Machiavel, in: L'enjeu Machiavel, ed. by SFEZ GERALD/SENELLART MICHEL, Paris 2001, pp. 59-72.

ID., 'Pour en finir avec l'histoire des mentalité', Critique, 695 (2005), pp. 285-300.

ID., Libertinage, irréligion, incroyance, athéisme dans l'Europe de la première modernité (XVIe-XVIIe siècles). Une approche critique des tendances actuelles de la recherche (1998-2002), available online at the address:
http://www.ehess.fr/centres/grihl/DebatCritique/LibrePensee/Libertinage_0.htm.

CORAZZOL, GIGI, Cineografo di banditi su sfondo di monti. Feltre 1634-1642, Milan 1997.

DAVIDSON, NICHOLAS, Theology, Nature and the Law: Sexual Sin and Sexual Crime in Italy from the Fourteenth to the Seventeenth Century, in Crime, Society and the Law in Renaissance Italy, ed. by DEAN, TREVOR/LOWE, KATE J.P., Cambridge 1994, pp. 74-98.

DYKEMA, PETER A./OBERMAN, HOYCO A. (eds.), Anticlericalism in Late Medieval and Early Modern Europe, Leiden 1993.

FARGE, ARLETTE, Dire et mal dire. L'opinion publique au XVIIIme siècle, Paris 1992.

GINZBURG, CARLO, The Dovecote has Opened his Eyes. Popular Conspiracy in Seventeenth-Century Italy, in: The Inquisition in Early Modern Europe. Studies on Sources and Methods, ed. by HENNINGSEN, GUSTAV/TEDESCHI, JOHN/AMIEL CHARLES, Northern Illinois University Press 1986, pp. 190-198;

ID., The Theme of Forbidden Knowledge in the Sixteenth and Seventeenth Centuries, in: Past and Present, 73 (1976), pp. 28-41.

ID., Occhiacci di legno. Nove riflessioni sulla distanza, Milan 1998.

ID., The Cheese and the Worms, Baltimore 1980.

GREGORY, TULLIO, Theophrastus redivivus. Erudizione e ateismo nel Seicento, Morano 1979.

MOREAU, PIERRE-FRANÇOIS, La crainte a engendré les dieux, Libertinage et philosophie, 4 (2000), pp. 179-216.

NICCOLI, OTTAVIA, La vita religiosa nell'Italia moderna. Secoli XV-XVIII, Rome 1998.

ID., Rinascimento anticlericale. Infamia, propaganda e satira in Italia tra Quattro e Cinquecento, Rome-Bari 2005.

OSBAT, LUCIANO, L'Inquisizione e la storia dei comportamenti religiosi, in: Storia dell'Italia religiosa, II, ed. by DE ROSA GABRIELE/GREGORY TULLIO, Rome-Bari 1994, pp. 375-391.

PAGANINI, GIANNI, Legislatores et impostores. Le Theophrastus redivivus et la thèse de l'imposture des religions à la moitiè du XVIIe siècle', in: Sources antiques de l'irréligion moderne: le relais italien, ed. by CAVAILLE JEAN-PIERRE/FOUCAULT DIDIER, Toulouse 2001, pp. 181-218.

PASQUINI, EMILIO, Clero e pubblico parrocchiale nei testi letterari, in Pievi e parrocchie in Italia nel basso Medioevo (secoli XIII-XV), Roma 1984.

PINTARD, RENE, Le libertinage érudit dans la premère moitié du XVIIe siècle. Nouvelle édition augmentée, Genève-Paris 1983.

SPINI, GIORGIO, Ricerca dei libertini. La teoria dell'impostura delle religioni nel Seicento italiano, Florence 1983.

WOOTTON, DAVID, From Duty to Self-Interest, in: Divine Right and Democracy, ed. by ID., Harmondsworth 1986, pp. 58-77.

ID., The Fear of God in Early Modern Political Theory, in:
Historical Papers, 18,1 (1983), pp. 56-80.

"Miscellaneous remarks"

Recounting deviance in Early Modern travel accounts

SEBASTIAN BECKER

The vast number of sources on the history of travel in the form of private diaries, personal letters and printed accounts of literary travelers from the 16th to 18th century offers a wide range of approaches to the phenomenon 'Grand Tour', an educational trip that was at first traditionally undertaken by the European nobility, later on applied by a European upper class, mainly from England. Since the beginning of the 1980s, cultural historians have recognized numerous approaches to these sources, generally described as the genre of *"Reiseliteratur"*.[1] A major part of present studies stressed educational history in general, the education of nobles or, with a broader scope, the history of travel in a wider sense.[2] During the last ten years, a growing number of scholars took into account the perception of traveled lands and their inhabitants or more generally the perception of spatial relations by early modern travelers.[3] These studies succeeded in pointing out the impact that experiences of foreignness or difference had on the travelers and showed how those perceptions were mirrored in the sources.

---

1   Cf. BRENNER, 1990; MACZAK/TEUTEBERG, 1982; MAURER, 1999.
2   BABEL/PARAVICINI, 2005; BAUSINGER, 1991; BERNS, 1988; BLACK, 1992; BRILLI, 1997; CSÁKY-LOEBENSTEIN (1971); LEIBETSEDER, 2004; MĄCZAK, 1995; MEAD, 1914; STOYE, 1982.
3   ALTGELD, 1984; BRILLI, 1998; GEYKEN, 2002; IBID., 2004; HEITMANN/SCAMARDI, 1993; NOLDE, 2006a; IBID., 2006b; OSWALD, 1985.

Yet, it is generally accepted that distinctiveness and foreignness are consequences of the perception of a known or familiar cultural system contrary to the experience of an unknown culture or country and its norms; hence, they are not objective phenomena but generated through the perception of the authors own cultural and normative set of values and knowledge which serves as a reference frame.[4] In travel accounts, foreignness often appears as a kind of unfamiliarity with those cultural and religious norms that are valid within a spatial relation. If and how travelers perceive foreignness strongly depends on their own subjective way of seeing the world, which is formed by the cultural and religious norms of their native countries. Hence, it was an important means for the travelers' self-reinsurance on the one hand, important for distinguishing themselves of what they perceived on their journeys. On the other hand, the spreading of narratives concerning foreignness and distinctiveness through the travel accounts had a wider influence. It was essential for the construction and evolution of an (national) identity, in particular if subjects of Religion were touched. Dorothea Nolde used the sociological concept of a "narrative identity" to show how authors did not only use travel records to relate themselves to existing constructions of identities, but to adjust those constructions dynamically.[5] They were a means to the "world making", as Jörg Rogge points out in his introduction to this volume.

Even though religion proves to be one of the most powerful marks of foreignness and difference in early modern travel accounts and although the tie between culture and religion is obvious, studies regarding the link between the Grand Tour and aspects of the *confessionalisation* and confessional differences in travel accounts are generally rare, as Michael Maurer stated recently.[6] That is surprising, because in 17th and 18th century, English or British, thus protestant, travelers published the majority of the printed travel books. As the hot spots of the classic Grand Tour were nearly always France and Italy, thus catholic countries, the perception of confessional differences usually occupied a

---

4   Cf. HARBSMEIER, 1982 for typologies of foreignness in travel accounts. For a definition of the terms *perception* and *distinctiveness* cf. STROHMEYER, 2007, pp. 8-10.
5   NOLDE, 2006a.
6   NOLDE, 2006b, p. 13; MAURER, 1999; MAURER, 2013; MACZAK, 1995; NEBGEN, 2014.

considerable part of the travelers' experiences; consequently, confessional differences are often mirrored in printed travel accounts. This paper shall link with studies concerning the experience of difference in early modern travel accounts and the perception of confessional differences in general. Its aim is to answer the question if and how the recounting of experiences of foreignness and difference in these sources was used to translate ordinary distinctions in culture and norms into accounts of deviant behavior and what narrative strategies were used to relabel experiences of foreignness and difference as forms of divergent behavior.

Early modern travel accounts as historical sources

To do so, some basic considerations concerning the underlying sources on one hand and – as this paper sets its focus exclusively on English or British travel accounts – the self-perception of 17th and 18th century British travelers in general on the other seem to be essential. As previously mentioned, travel accounts, in particular the literary kind, are highly subjective narratives. They show the authors' perceptions of what they found on their journeys, thus they have to be read and analyzed as any other self-referential genre. Those sources reveal more about their authors than about their primary subject. That is because through the description of what was foreign to a traveler, his own cultural and normative framework becomes visible.[7] On the other hand, travel accounts are characterized by their distinctive intertextuality. The vast number of particularly anglophone travel- and guidebooks published from 16th to 19th century shows the popularity of this literary genre on the British Islands. Travelling was one of the favorite pastimes for the English and British nobility and upper class. Those without the possibility or opportunity to travel became "armchair travelers": readers and consumers of travel accounts published on the island.[8] When – due

---

7   HARBSMEIER, 1982. For the frequent use of self-referential sources such as self-portrayals for the self-fashioning and self-reassurance see ARNOLD/SCHMOLINSKY/ZAHND, 1999, VON GREYERZ/MEDICK/VEIT, 2001 and JANCKE/ULBRICH, 2005.

8   GEYKEN, 2002, p. 322.

to its lack of exclusiveness – the Grand Tour lost its educational purpose, it was the entertainment value of the books that rendered it popular. Consequently, the authors of travel accounts were confronted with a
market demand created by readers who could not leave the Island but
yearned for the aforesaid confirmation of their national, protestant and
enlightened identity. Those readers expected an explicit distinction
from other, primarily Catholic countries and Catholics in general. The
close interweavement of a British national and religious identity, based
on the success of the Glorious Revolution 1688/89, was the foundation
of the self-perception as an elect nation, and leader into modernity that
faced the opposition of the papism. And it required constant confirmation.[9] Thus, British readers of travel accounts expected a boost of their
self-confidence as enlightened, modern people, distinguished from the
superstitious and underdeveloped Catholics. That became of major
importance, since English travelers who passed through the channel to
tour the continent left a space almost absolutely dominated by
protestant culture. Hence, it must be considered that the most important
characteristics distinguishing the Island from the continent were Protestantism and Catholicism.[10] As Anti-papism was the main antagonist to
the British self-perception, there was no tolerance toward Catholic
norms on the island. In contrast to that space where Protestantism
formed an unchallenged majority, a traveler who crossed the channel
onto the continent was confronted by a confessional pluralism he had
usually heard of, but had never before experienced. It is unquestionable
whether British travelers generally knew about Catholic norms and
traditions. But they often had no real experience with them. New and
unfamiliar was especially the homogeneity of Catholicism in the main
destinations of the Grand Tour, France and Italy. For this reason, I
consider the demand for narratives about the extent of confessional
differences to be an essential content of travel accounts and one of the
major causes for the intertextuality, in particular of literary texts in 17th
and 18th century. If an author wanted to not only satisfy his readers'
expectations regarding completeness but also their want for distinction,
he had to include topoi of foreignness and oddity just as any other information related to topographical or geographic facts that could be of

9   ASCH, 2000; GRABES, 1986.
10 GEYKEN, 2002, p. 186.

value for travelers. This leads to the subject of reliability in general: in many cases, the manuscripts for the printed travel accounts were completed years after the travel itself. Quite often, authors merged their own notes with other narratives and descriptions passed on in earlier, successful travel accounts.[11]

Approaching and defining deviance in travel accounts

Travelling meant a close interaction with local people and local social and religious norms. At first glance, this makes it rather difficult to identify deviance in its common form. Considering this, the main problem is that the labelling of behavioral forms that diverged from the normative background of a traveler did not necessarily diverge from the norms or the cultural settings the respective traveler had entered by travelling. What was deviant in England (or Great Britain after 1707) was not necessarily considered deviant in other countries. Thus, readers of travel accounts are rather confronted with a double translation of experiences made through traveling. On one hand, those experiences were converted into a textual genre by the authors; on the other hand, they were transferred into a different normative setting, characterized by an identity formed by religious and cultural norms of the readers. By this means, the travel records became a tool for the forward projection of the British's own identity as illustrated above. Regarding the expectations of the book market and the cultural delimitations between travelers and inhabitants of traveled countries, the sources may tell a lot about the strategies and targets authors followed in their recounting – especially concerning the violations of behavioral expectations.

This paper puts forward exemplary relations – mostly – made by British 18th century travelers concerning any kind of behavior which can be described as divergent or deviant in a broader sense. Using a labeling approach on deviant behavior, I understand the term deviance as a category of attribution toward individuals or groups that diverge in a negative sense of those rules and norms that are valid in a relational

---

11   STOYE, 1982, pp. 136-137, 139, 140-141.

space as well as inherent to the cited authors.[12] Those attributions or perceptions did not necessarily lead to expulsion or condemnation; the extent of reactions rather depended on the power of actors.[13] Hence, sanctions and expulsion understood as legal actions are not a necessity to label deviance. Divergent behavior could also have been marked through literary narrative strategies. Authors, clerks or writers in general were able to use a rash of narrative devices to label any behavior as divergent or deviant. Focusing on travel accounts as a textual genre the most common stylistic device is to make derisive remarks about countries, people or social systems in general. Attributions of ridiculousness, polemics and critics in general can be considered as a social sanction and therefor mark deviant behavior.[14] Hence, an expulsion of a community is not a necessity.

Out of the vast number of printed travel accounts this paper exemplifies the recounting of divergent or deviant behavior through an analysis of exemplary extracts of two travel-records. The first is "Miscellaneous Remarks" by Sacheverell Stevens, an English 18th century traveler who is particular known for his description of France and Italy and his harsh anti-Catholic views on the countries he had travelled.[15] His recounting of divergent or deviant behavior will be contrasted to some extracts from Gilbert Burnet's "Letters, containing an account of what seemed most remarkable in travelling thro' Switzerland, Italy and some parts of Germany" in 1685 and 1686, first published in 1687.[16] Burnet is well known as a Scottish theologian, historian and Bishop of Salisbury.[17] Both authors have in common that they recount different kinds of cultural and political differences, both are not holding themselves back in expressing their own perceptions of differences between the travelled countries and cultures and their native country, thus their British and protestant identity.

Before focusing on the few examples this paper can offer due to its limited extent, some general considerations on constellations regarding

---

12 CLINARD/MEIER, 2001, pp. 131-141; KÄSTNER/SCHWERHOFF, 2013, pp. 27-34.
13 KÄSTNER, SCHWERHOF, 2013, p. 32.
14 NEEF, 2014, p. 196; RADCLIFFE-BROWN, 1965, p. 206.
15 STEVENS, 1756.
16 BURNET, 1724.
17 GREIG, 2004.

the traveler and the travelled space and the labelling of behavior as deviant shall be highlighted. The analytical approach to deviance in travel requires to constantly remember that the authors translated their experiences not only into written texts but also into a different space, which is the country in which their works were published. Thus, it seems fruitful to specify four possible constellations of perceptions of divergence.

1. Travelers themselves could get expulsed by a community for not obeying norms common within the traveled space. This could be a consequence of ignorance or clumsiness due to not knowing the norms and regulations valid in the travelled country. It could also be a consequence of personal demarcation expressed through open mocking of the community's norms, regulations or rituals. The latter could happen if a traveler did not share or accept the rules valid within the travelled space. It can therefore be helpful to examine how and if travelers re-count their own behavior if it was obviously marked as deviant by their environment.

2. Travelers could move within a space where their native und therefore subjective norms were valid. In their accounts, they could report the violation of those norms by the inhabitants of the entered space.[18]

3. Travelers could enter a space where foreign norms were valid, apparently well known and nevertheless offended by the inhabitants of a country or a distinctive social group. Thus, they could report the divergent behavior against the norms and regulations of a foreign community of values. This constellation shows the difficulty of linking the attribution of deviance to modes of sanction or expulsion from a community. Obviously, a traveler who did not share the same values could not practice any sanctions other than decisive remarks.

4. Travelers could describe experiences or behavior that, without any doubt, would be labelled deviant in his own normative or cultural system, but were recounted as common and reputable in a traveled space. Thus, one might ask if and how deviant behavior could be

---

18 NOLDE, 2006b, pp. 21-23, speaks of "foreignness inside of the own" ["Das Fremde im Eigenen"].

relabeled to conform with local norms, e.g. the visit of prostitutes as one of the common topoi regarding visits of Venice.

Due to the extent of most literary travel accounts and because not all constellations can be found in a single travel account, not all of these considerations are taken into account in this paper. Moreover, only the named publications shall form the base for this analysis. Under this aspect, this paper is to be considered as a first try attempt to approach deviance in early modern travel accounts through identifying narrative or discursive constructions used by translating the travelers experience into re-counts of deviant behavior.

Deviant behavior by travelers

By entering Catholic countries, travelers could easily run the risk of being excluded for not obeying the cultural or religious norms valid in situ. This was well known, and if sufficiently prepared, foreigners were aware of this danger. This was thanks to the numerous travel-instructions that warned their readers of any dangers in foreign countries, Catholicism in particular. It was not only the fear for young men being threatened by "the infectious Ayre of other Countries".[19] At the same time, the danger of being identified as a Protestant, e.g. by means of behavior or clothing, was well known, particularly in the 16th century; not to attract attention through visual deviation, for instance, was a known etiquette in Renaissance already[20] and almost every travel record recounts experiences of its author being excluded for acting against prevailing norms, be it cultural or confessional or just due to the travelers foreign appearance. A well-known example is the German 16th century traveler Bartolomeo Sastrow, who was identified as a German and thus a Protestant in Venice due to his foreign and divergent clothing. Sastrow obviously felt the imminent danger and had his clothes

---

19 DAVIDSON, 1633, [unnumbered]. The dangerous influence of the Catholic church was a constant danger in particular for protestant Princes due to Catholic efforts regarding conversions. See RICHTER, 1992; SCHNETTGER, 2013.
20 DELLA CASA, 2003, pp. 16-17.

adapted to the Italian style.[21] Considering the expulsion Sastrow experienced, it is not inept to understand his anecdote as an example for recounting deviance.

In 18th century, Sacheverell Stevens made a similar experience at the very beginning of his tour through the continent, when he was identified as a Protestant not by his clothes, but by his deviant behavior. After his arrival at Montreuil in France, Stevens took a view of the town and found a "very fine" Catholic Church, which aroused his curiosity. Prompted by his "natural love of novelty", as he confirms, he entered the building where, at that very moment, a Catholic mass was held. By his conduct, he must have been immediately identified as a Protestant:

> "Being quite a stranger to it [the ceremonious office], I went very innocently up to the high altar, and stopped there some time to see the priest and his congregation act their respective parts, which to me seemed a meer farce, instead of a divine service. After the ceremony was finished, I was returning very quietly to the inn, but at the church-door found myself surrounded by a parcel of swarthy, dirty, ill-looking fellows, whose stern aspects and manner of expression seemed to threaten me much: though at the time I understood not their language, yet I could plainly perceive my behavior had given them great offence; I imagine it was my not kneeling, but standing like an irreligious heretic."[22]

What becomes obvious here is one of those perceptions of confessional differences that are common in travel accounts and that are often characterized by debasing Catholics in general or through mocking them for following "meer farce[s]". The implication of backwardness and underdevelopment in every sense is one of the major topoi used by protestant travelers to relate Catholic countries in general.[23] Nevertheless, this particular episode is more interesting because it allows approaching the deviant behavior of the traveler. Stevens introduces himself as a "very innocent" visitor, using this exact wording to express his intention to

---

21 SASTROW, 1912, p. 88.
22 STEVENS, 1756, p. 6.
23 Other topoi were topographical specifics of Catholic countries as wasteland, its physiognomy, the disapproval of veneration of saints, belief in miracles or Catholic pomp e.g.; cf. MAURER, 2013; NEBGEN, 2014.

not degrade what he saw. But, in fact, he does the contrary and admits to perceive his behavior as an offence and a violation of the valid religious norm. Hence, his account of his own behavior is somewhat dissociated. Focusing on the question whether deviance is produced by its translation into a textual relation, the account of Montreuil reveals the very reverse. Stevens admits that his own acting was perceived as deviant by the locals, but he does not recount it as divergent in any way. Thus, the text shows no sign of labeling himself as deviant. Of course there is no doubt that Stevens did have a contrary intention and I do not want to exaggerate this conclusion as a big surprise. But his action is quite the contrary. He labels the behavior of the said "rascals" as deviant while not broaching the issue of offending the Catholics' feelings. Obviously, narrative and discursive strategies make it possible to shroud deviance and to relabel it onto other people. That opens the question if and how at all a text produces the perception of any behavior as deviant by recounting a violation of norms.

However, authors such as Stevens did not always disguise their behavior as compliant to rules. After his arrival in Italy, he recounts a similar situation. On the first day of Lent, he and his acquaintances, a Catholic traveler, a priest and a Turkish convert set out from Viterbo. Because, as he emphasizes particularly, an Englishman who was traveling during Lent might expect to be "either starved or poisoned", he supplied himself with some meat and concealed it cautiously in his chaise where he then had an obviously nutritive meal. This action definitely violated a prevailing norm in Catholic countries.

> "My companion was a Roman Catholic, whose pulse I first felt, and, finding hunger had made him forget his religion, I discovered my lamb, with which he seemed highly pleased, and soon came into my way of thinking; that it was no sin for a person to eat what he could get, when he was hungry: the Turk and his governor, who were in the first chaise, frequently stopped, and got some eggs fried in oil, and civilly asked me to eat some with them, which I refused; so that the priest took me to be a saint of a Protestant, to fast all day; little suspecting how heretically I was provided for; but his good opinion did not continue long, for inadvertently we left bones in the chaise, which the postilion seeing, discovered them to the priest; he excused me, as an Englishman, but threatened the other with the

inquisition, which would certainly have been his doom, had I not brought him off, by declaring, that tho' often desired by me, he still refused to eat."[24]

This time, Stevens expulsed against the catholic obligation to participate in the Lenting fast and was avenged immediately by the postilion. Beside the mockery, the account remains distant, because due to being excused a Protestant, it does not show any form of expulsion. The anecdote thus might have worked very well to satisfy his reader's aforesaid expectations on how two-faced and underdeveloped Italian Catholics were. Anyway, it is again an adjective, "inadvertently", that shows his awareness of the offence he had committed. Once more, Stevens does not use any stylistic devices, which would label his own behavior as deviant, and that is, as I said above, no surprise. On the contrary, it is Stevens' acquaintance whose divergent behavior is blamed through blaming him for "forgetting his religion".[25] Other authors of travel accounts describe similar constellations. The Roman Catholic rule to participate in Lent is, e.g., also focused on in Tobias Smoletts' "Travells", but it is always connoted as non-compulsory for travelers and as a form of confessional divergence.[26]

The two episodes show the violation of cultural and religious norms by the traveler followed by expulsion or denunciation. What an expulsion could mean for personal security becomes evident through one of Stevens' accounts of his visit of Rome, where he had met fellow travelers. Being at the French coffeehouse in Piazza di Spagna, the group was "on a sudden alarmed by a most terrible noise" and ran outside where they found themselves in the middle of the procession of St. Anthony. Almost immediately, they started mocking and laughing about the Catholic rituals and the Catholics "extreme folly".

"This so much incensed them [the Romans], that instantly they bawled out, see these English hereticks [!], who make a game of this great miracle of St. Anthony; they then rushed upon us with so much fury and resentment, that

---

24 STEVENS, 1756, pp. 163-164.
25 IBID.
26 SMOLLETT, 2010, pp. 220-221.

had not a gentleman of humanity in a friendly manner opened his house-door, and let us in, we had infallibly been tore to pieces."[27]

Again, there is no sign that the author scrutinizes his or his group's behavior as deviant. Instead, by using stylistic devices, he erects a border between the Catholics and himself as the "English heretic". As every protestant traveler, Stevens obviously moved within a space delimited by his very own cultural and religious norms; the borders of that space were further fortified the more he wanted to delimit himself from the inhabitants of the Catholic countries he had traveled. However, this delimitation was an essential feature of travel reports in general and it formed the background for labeling what he saw as deviant. Hence, the translation of the experiences of difference or foreignness into a travel report does not constrain its representation as deviant behavior. Travelers very well could and did shroud their own deviant behavior. Ex negativo it suggests itself that authors were aware that foreignness might very well be translated into accounts of deviant behavior through narrative and stylistic devices.

Recounting the deviance of the inhabitants of France and Italy

Similar, but still different in a certain way are the descriptions of the inhabitants of France and Italy made by the protestant Bishop Gilbert Burnet. Through his accounts, he pictures himself as more sophisticated then Sacheverell Stevens had obviously been. That could also be due to the fact that Burnet, as a theologian, was much better acquainted with religious norms, even with those of the Catholics. However, this did not stop him from generalizing his criticism of Catholic practice, for instance when he condemns the Italians' idolatry to be damaging the Christian faith in whole.[28] Yet, the Catholics' idolatry is a common and general topos of travel reports and does therefor not fit very well to approach the recounting of deviant behavior.

---

27 STEVENS, 1756, pp. 221-222.
28 MAURER, 2013, p. 257.

It may be more promising to focus on reports of interactions with or descriptions of local groups, people, officeholders or clerics that violated their own rules, thus the rules and norms that were valid in the visited and traveled country or spatial constellation. The fact that this could also concern those spaces where travelers shared or at least thought to share the same principles or norms as the inhabitants becomes evident through Gilbert Burnet's account of a Lutheran Church in the imperial town of Frankfurt:

> "The *Lutherans* have here built a new Church, called *St. Katherin's*, in which there is as much Painting as ever I saw in a *Popish* Church; and over the high Altar there is a huge carved Crucifix, as there are painted ones in other Places of their Church."[29]

Obviously, the decorations of St. Katherin's were not suitable for the Protestant Bishop, who expected convergence with the norms valid in his native country. Anyway, one may discuss whether deviance is the right concept to approach those divergences from protestant church decorations as it was known or considered appropriate by Burnet. As anyone is expulsed or offended personally, a clear classification is hard to be made. But we can consider comparison to popish churches as an evident sign of an emotion caused by divergence of afore assumed uniformity in Protestant faith. Still remarkable is the self-positioning of the author, who talks about "the Lutherans", leaving no doubt about the delimitation between the Protestant faiths in Germany and Scotland. Nevertheless, unlike Stevens, Burnet does not use any mocking or degrading adjectives. As the following extracts will show, this is not at all a particularity of his language. I suppose, his opinion about St. Katherin's is skeptical but nonetheless respectful due to the kindred ship between the Lutheran and the Presbyterian Church in general.

His accounts of the Catholic clergy that, in his eyes, violated the alleged Catholic religious norms, especially priests and nuns, are much more distinct; one might even say harder. Burnet often claims the duplicity of Catholic priests in his report, especially their sinfulness. In this respect, his relation about the elections of priests by their prospective Parish in Venice (he, the protestant Bishop, does not omit

---

29   BURNET, 1724, pp. 302-303.

to emphasize the uncommon independence from the Bishop) puts this forward:

> "those [...] was the most scandalous thing possible; for the several Candidates appear on the Day of Election, and set out their own Merits, and defame the other Pretenders in the foulest Language, and in the most scurrilous manner imaginable; the Secretes of all their Lives are publish'd [!] in most reproachful Terms; and nothing is so abject and ridiculous, that is not put in Practice [...]."[30]

Burnet judges this misconduct as result of the "great Libertinage that is so undecently [!] practiced by most sorts of People at Venice" and therefor spread to all spheres of live. In Venice this would even affect the core of the families. As the Bishop proceeds, those were characterized by the rule that for the common preservation of the house only one of the sons should marry. He then does not finish his comments without referring that it would be "generally believed, that [this] Wive is common to the whole Family"[31]. It is self-evident that he does not only imply the wives' representative and organizational function in the household. The implicit blame of the Venetians to violate the commandment of marital fidelity is unquestionably a form of recounting a type of deviant behavior, even if in this context it is described as hearsay. Insinuations such as the latter are forms of labeling a whole group as deviant. They do not differ very much from the use of adjectives and possessive pronouns ("their own Merits", their Lives") serving as delimitations, as they are used in the account of the priests' elections. Both are forms of discursive strategies that make groups appear in the worst light possible and therefor serve to feed the readers expectations. This is an obvious similarity to Steven's description of the people at Montreuil. The increased use of – mostly degrading – adjectives, the self-delimitation through the use of possessive pronouns and insinuations were modes of translating the authors (self-)perception and his perceptions of foreignness and difference into a textual genre not only but to a considerable part designed to validate the British protestant identity and culture. As the existence of norms does not provide any

---

30 IBID., p. 153.
31 IBID., p. 158.

information regarding their enforcement, stories of deviance should not be read as clear signs of the appearance of deviance – but it is a form of constructing a narration of deviant behavior by people that belong to or form a part of a different cultural system.

The attribution of deviance through the narrative of difference is mostly used in the context of confessional difference and the degrading of Catholicism and its double standards in general. Besides the male clerics, he involves the female clerics, too. In this regard, the condemnation of the Venetian nuns through Burnet's account worked in the same way as the above mentioned. Chiefly those of St. Zachary and St. Laurence, open exclusively for Venetian nobles, were focused upon by the Bishop and criticized for not observing their very own Catholic norms and customs. Burnet judges as follows:

"They are not vailed; their Neck and Breast are bare, and they receive much Company; but that which I saw was in a publick Room, in which there were many Grills for several parlours, so that the conversation is very confused, for there being a different Company at every Grill, [...] the Noise of so many loud Talkers is very disagreeable. The Nuns talk much, and very ungracefully, and allow themselves a Liberty in rallying, that other Places could not bear".[32]

Similar is the anecdote of two nuns near Rome who "perceived a very strange Change in Nature, and that their Sex was altered", is demasked to what it "offereth itself is, that these two had been always what they then appeard to be; but that had gone into a Nunnery in a Disguise, to gratify a brutal Appetite".[33] We might consider this and the relation about two special vaults at a Nunnery at Brescia – one for the men entering, the other for the pregnant nuns leaving –, as an intertextual link to Boccaccios *Decamerone*. But, as stated above, in the end it describes the clergies' violation of catholic norms. This is clearly recounted with the objective of stressing the deviant and superficial behavior of the Catholic clergy and therefor feeding the widely spread stereotypes in Protestant countries and communities with what the armchair travelers wanted to read. Closing his account of the Venetian customs by

---

32 IBID., p. 154.
33 IBID., p. 263.

labeling the inhabitants of the Republic as "generally ignorant of the Matters of Religion to a Scandal; and [...] as unconcerned in them, as they are Strangers to them"[34], he expands this judgement to the complete Catholic community. But those accusations were not only directed to Religion as a primary topic. The Bishop blamed the entire Venetian nobility to be of "most supine Ignorance of all sorts of Knowledge, that a man cannot easily imagine to what Height this is grown"[35]. Be it the cowardice by the Venetians who hire strangers to fight their wars, be it the "downright Lewdness" of the Venetian women, who were "perhaps as vicious as in other Places"[36], the general superiority of the English, Scottish and later the British was highlighted by labeling an entire foreign society as deviant in morals, manners and acknowledged norms. However, a specification of vices or misdeeds remains vague. Burnet's accusations of either the clergy or the Venetians in general mainly pertain to the area of confession and *confessionalisation* pictured through religious norms and standards. Comparing the specification of vices as they are normally in the focus of scholars using concepts of deviance, a broader look on the recounting of deviance in travel accounts seems rather difficult.

In this regard Sacheverell Stevens' "Miscellaneous remarks" seem to be, at least partially, more distinct. Although the anti-Catholic Stevens also pays special attention to the description and the ridiculing of religious rituals in his account, there are at least few relations of deviant and divergent behavior in the narrower sense. The two examples I shall mention have one thing in common, which is why they give a hint as to the precondition required for labeling an action or behavior as deviant in travel records: a canon of values that is common and thus valid across national boundaries, e.g. the Christian commandment to charity with its premise of "honest poverty". In this context, Stevens' account of the beggars at Paris shows a violation of a norm valid as well in his own cultural system as in the Catholic cultural system.

"[They] are the most insolent, I believe, that can be met with in all Christendom, I observed them, with all the assurance imaginable, go into several

---

34 IBID., p. 156.
35 IBID.
36 IBID., p. 159.

shops to demand rather than to crave alm: tho' they appeared to me to be objects no way deserving the least pity or compassion, but, on the contrary, a shameful crew of indolent, healthful vagrants; yet they were relieved at several places at least with a farthing, or what they term a leard; and in case the donor had none in his pocket, these beggars, with the greatest impudence and composure, would pull out their purses, and offer change, and afterwards move off, without thinking themselves under any obligation, and frequently without so much as returning thanks to the benefactor."[37]

To take up the issue if deviance was merely produced by translation of an action into a narrative text, it seems useful to compare Stevens' account of Paris to that put forward in the beginning of this paper. As in the description of the incident in the Catholic Church at Montreuil, especially the extensive use of depreciating adjectives is outstanding. The beggars' attitude is put forward not only as a form of bad behavior, but also as a practice of exploiting a fundamental Christian value and duty. Due to the strong part generally taken by the description of foreignness in travel-reports, the question whether the extract shows signs of an expulsion from "community" is not as easy to answer. I tend to read the authors self-positioning through using the personal pronouns "they", "these", "their", "themselves" etc. not only as a means to construct a borderline between the author and the inhabitants of the travelled countries. They work as a demarcation between a majority who respects Christian values and those who boldly exploit them.

Similar narrative and/or discursive translations are found in the description of the warning of knavery that travelers should avoid. In the case of Naples, Stevens warns about dealing "with the lower class of people, who have the art of deceiving in a superlative degree", so that it was "impossible for a stranger to deal with them without being overreached" and nearly sure to be "cheated into bargain". As he explains – "the Neapolitans of this class exceed their fraternity in all other places in knavery, and are the most cheating, imposing rascals in the whole world". [38] In – more or less – the same way he describes the so called "antiquarians" at Rome who offered themselves to English travelers as connoisseurs in antiquity and city guides. Mainly such travelers who

---

37 STEVENS, 1756, p. 16.
38 IBID., p. 282.

were "not competent judges" in arts were made to believe a copy "to be an original of Raphael, Angelo, Titian or any other great painter, which they purchase at an extravagant price, and procure an handsome premium from both buyer and seller" which was indeed a popular ploy toward travelers.[39] In his account, Stevens uses again mostly personal pronouns to describe those swindlers and closes by labeling them as "these knavish, ignorant antiquarians"[40].

A further specification of any kind of divergence or foreignness seems to have the same function: "nationality" as a pre-modern attribute that has an expulsion already inherent. Due to the rareness of this attribute in the underlying sources only one example, Stevens' relation of him visiting St. Peter's at Rome, has to suffice here. Examining the cathedral's decors, he rested by some valuable statues of marble beside Bernini's Cathedra Petri (Chair of St. Peter) at the main choir. There he refers to "especially one on the left [...] of a beautiful woman, naked, so curiously and inimitably done, that it excited the passion of a Spaniard to commit a very indecent action before it, upon which the part that so much gained the esteem of the Spaniard was ordered to be covered, as it was when I saw it".[41] In this case, we do have the recounting of a behavior that can unquestionably be described as deviant. However, an excessive use of degrading adjectives attributed to the stranger cannot be identified here.

Therefore, it seems rather difficult to answer to the question whether the translation of perceptions of foreignness into the literal genre of travel accounts generally formed the basis for re-counting deviance. It strongly depends on the self-positioning of the authors and their very own decision to use specific stylistic devices to delimitate themselves of a community of values and to ascribe an action or a fact as deviant. In any case, the carrying capacity of this assumption should be limited due to the exemplary basis of sources upon which this paper focused. There are still many travel records to be analyzed before one should pass a final sentence. The assumptions presented here should therefore be considered as a trial balloon still worthy of discussion.

---

39 IBID., p. 180; DÖNIKE, 2011.
40 STEVENS, 1756, p. 181.
41 IBID., p. 170.

Recounting confessional difference as deviant behavior?

To conclude this paper it seems helpful to broaden the focus to a field which is definitely not considered as an example of deviant behavior by cultural history: the description and perception of confessional difference expressed through the travelers contacts to religious rituals and practicing religion. Since the before mentioned expressions of foreignness were mostly a consequence of different cultural or religious norms, the perception of a religious ritual went far beyond that. By reading early-modern travel accounts it becomes obvious that it was not the subjects of faith followed by confessional families, but the exercised religious practices that produced the perceptions of foreignness the travelers accounted for in their reports. Considering the ritual aspect of early modern religiousness and Clifford Geertz saying that religious rituals had a double function to represent and shape the social and symbolic order of the world, it is no wonder that travelers mainly described the practices of religion.[42] Moreover, although most English travelers were at least partly familiar with the Catholic faith and Catholic exercise of religion, the participation or observation of rituals and practices nonetheless rouse the travelers' curiosity and was, on the other hand, one of the most interesting subjects for the reader at home: what was more convenient to confirm the English or British self-perception as the leading enlightened Nation than to catch the superstitious Catholics in the act? It has therefor to be assumed that the readers' demands influenced the authors considerably when choosing their contents. Thus, it is no surprise that it is Sacheverell Stevens who dedicates several entries at different stations of this travel to the "ridiculous" and "superstitious" rituals of the Roman Catholics.[43] Based on the aforesaid conclusions regarding the recounting of deviant behavior it remains to be asked, whether the same discursive and narrative strategies are used to describe catholic rituals. To put it simply: Do travel accounts recount the travelers' perception of confessional difference in the context of Catholic rituals as a perception of deviant behavior?

---

42   NOLDE, 2006b, pp. 14-15; GEERTZ, 1993, pp. 112-114.
43   Cf. e.g. STEVENS, 1756, pp. 48-49; 123-126; 272-273; 286-289.

Many derogatory accounts of processions, such as that for St. John including an extra acting as the saint himself at Florence ("by their ridiculous behavior appeared so ignorant, that I believe they took him for the real saint; so far has superstition blinded the understandings of the inferior sort of people in the country")[44], to the procession to St. Peter's at Rom in the Holy Week or to St. Mary's ("I shall describe only one more of their ridiculous ceremonies, which I flatter myself will be diverting to the reader [...].")[45] by Stevens seem to confirm this assumption. As a single example can serve his description of the miracle of the liquefying of St. Januarius' blood in Naples, the Catholic ritual most often recounted by English travelers in their travel-reports:

"This miracle is generally twice a year, or oftener, on the approach of expectation of any public calamity, such as war, plague [...] and the like, which infinitely pleases the ignorant, bigoted inhabitants of this metropolis, the most so I believe in the world. [...] I got as near the altar as possible, not only the living attended, but the images of dead, for about thirty silver statues very large, were carried by thirty persons thro' the streets in grand procession, and placed in the church near the altar; I suppose that they might be *eye-witnesses* of the miracle, one being as probable as the other; after a great many useless, unmeaning ceremonies exhibited by the priests, which to outward appearance seemed hard and congealed; they also brought forth the silver head, in which they pretend is the real one of St. Januarius [...]. The operation used to be over in four minutes, but five being expired, and no miracle, a panic seized the multitude, who concluded the saint was angry, and that some great calamity would soon befall them; then might you have seen them all upon their knees, some with their very faces to the ground, others humping their breasts, and some so horribly ignorant, as to beg of the virgin Mari to desire her son to intercede with the saint to perform the miracle."[46]

When Stevens perceives the blood to liquefy he judges the whole thing as "one of the most bungling tricks" he ever saw, and adjoins that

44 STEVENS, 1756, p. 125.
45 IBID., p. 273.
46 IBID., pp. 297-299.

"however dexterous they have been in many other particulars, yet in this sham miracle, these priestly jugglers are infinitely outdone by your ordinary fellows, who ramble about from place to place, and get their bread by their dexterity and flight of hand; however, as soon as it was known amongst the mob, they began one and all to bawl out, a miracle!"[47]

In his description of the ritual Stevens uses largely the same discursive and narrative strategies that already showed up in other contexts. The distinguishing of a crowd of bigot and naive people of Naples, the extensive use of degrading adjectives and the mocking got visible before by his and Burnet's judgment of the Italian clergy or the beggars at Paris. Even stronger seems the comparison of the priests with thimble riggers.

However, I do refuse giving the verdict that travelers in general looked at religious rituals as kind of a deviant behavior, most notably because they were very aware of the differences between confessions or religions. But on the other hand accounts like that on the miracle of St. Januarius were a powerful means to force the own and the protestant readers' distinction of the enlightened and progressive Protestants from the superstitious and underdeveloped Catholics. On one hand, that was the primary aim of every respected Protestant. On the other, the descriptions of Catholic rituals were a stereotype, but, as already mentioned, they formed a considerable part of the demand on the book marked. From this point of view, it seems very well possible to identify a form of sanction or expulsion. In the eyes of the protestant readers, the Catholic community was expulsed due to its backwardness compared to the enlightened protestant community on the British Islands. Therefor I tend to answer in the affirmative the question, whether deviance and divergence were produced in the underlying travel-reports through a narrative and discursive strategy used primarily for the re-counting of the experience of any kind of differences, be it cultural, confessional or religious.

---

47 IBID., p. 299.

Conclusion

To stress their self-delimitation and their own identity, the authors of the cited travel accounts used particular narrative and discursive strategies to exaggerate cultural, normative and confessional differences and thereupon recounted perceptions of difference as forms of deviant behavior. This was due to their inherent need of reinsurance about their own (protestant) identity as well as the demand of the book market, which expected the verification of the British self-perception as an enlightened and thus leading nation of the world. Generally, there are four different settings that lead to perceptions of foreignness and difference and thereby to the recounting of the travelers' experiences as forms of deviant behavior. These are the deviance of the traveler himself within a foreign system of norms, the divergence of such norms a traveler is familiar with, the violation of norms that are foreign to the traveler but recognized as valid in a spatial relation and the recounting of such behavior that was considered as deviant in the travelers' native country but not sanctioned on the road. The former three categories have been exemplified here. These typologies of divergence were inherent to the authors. At the same time, the translation of those experiences into a textual genre and simultaneously into another norm setting, i.e. the transfer to the British book market, has to be kept in mind. The individual self-reinsurance authors experienced through the perception of foreignness, distinctiveness and thus deviance was transferred into a wider frame as the travel accounts had the same impact on the book market. Its messages were widely spread. The relabeling of distinctiveness into deviance was a means for the dynamic construction of the British identity. The highlighted accounts of different kinds of deviance are therefore purposive constructions.

Literature

Sources

BURNET, GILBERT, Some Letters, containing an account of what seem'd most remarkable in travelling thro' Switzerland, Italy, some Parts of Germany etc. in the Years 1685 and 1686, London 1724.

DAVIDSON, WILLAM, Profitable instructions: describing what speciall observations are to be taken by trauellers in all nations, states and countries; pleasant and profitable. By the three much admired, Robert, late Earle of Essex, Sir Philip Sidney, and Secretary Davison, London 1633.

DELLA CASA, GIOVANNI, Galateo. Introduzione e note di Saverio Orlando, Milano, 6th ed., 2003.

SASTROW, BARTHOLOMÄUS, Ein deutscher Bürger des sechzehnten Jahrhunderts: Selbstschilderung des Stralsunder Bürgermeisters Bartholomäus Sastrow, ed. by Horst Kohl, Leipzig 1912.

SMOLLETT, TOBIAS, Travels through France and Italy, London 2010.

STEVENS, SACHEVERELL, Miscellaneous remarks made on the spot, in a late seven years tour through France, Italy, Germany and Holland. Containing observations on every Thing Remarkable in the aforesaid Countries, viz. The Disposition of the Inhabitants; their Religion, Annual Processions, Policy, Public Edifices, Water-Works, Paintings, Sculptures, and Antient Ruins; many of which have not hitherto been taken Notice of by former Writers: With an authentic Account of the Coronation of the present Pope, and the Ceremonies observed at the late Jubilee. Interspersed with Several particular and pleasing Incidents, which occurred to the Author, during the above Period, London 1756.

Secondary Literature

ALTGELD, WOLFGANG, Das politische Italienbild der Deutschen zwischen Aufklärung und europäischer Revolution von 1848, (Bibliothek des Deutschen Historischen Instituts in Rom, 59), Tübingen 1984.

ARNOLD, KLAUS/SCHMOLINSKY, SABINE/ZAHND, URS MARTIN (eds.), Das dargestellte Ich. Studien zu Selbstzeugnissen des späteren Mittelalters und der frühen Neuzeit (Selbstzeugnisse des Mittelalters und der beginnenden Neuzeit, 1), Bochum 1999.

ASCH, RONALD G., An elect nation? Protestantismus, nationales Selbstbewußtsein und nationale Feindbilder in England und Irland von zirka 1560 bis 1660, in: "Gottes auserwählte Völker". Erwählungsvorstellungen und kollektive Selbstfindung in der Geschichte, ed. by ALOIS MOSER, Frankfurt am Main 2000, pp. 117-141.

BABEL, RAINER/PARAVICINI, WERNER (Eds.), Grand Tour. Adeliges Reisen und europäische Kultur vom 14. bis zum 18. Jahrhundert (Beihefte der Francia, 60), Ostfildern 2005.

BAUSINGER, HERMANN (Ed.), Reisekultur. Von der Pilgerfahrt zum modernen Tourismus. München 1991.

BERNS, JÖRG-JOCHEN, Peregrenatio academica und Kavalierstour. Bildungsreisen junger Deutscher in der Frühen Neuzeit, in: Rom – Paris – London. Erfahrung und Selbsterfahrung deutscher Schriftsteller und Künstler in den fremden Metropolen, ed. by CONRAD WIEDEMANN, Stuttgart 1988, pp. 155-181.

BLACK, JEREMY, The British Abroad. The Grand Tour in Eighteenth Century, Sproud/New York 1992.

BRENNER, PETER J., Der Reisebericht in der deutschen Literatur. Ein Forschungsüberblick als Vorstudie zu einer Gattungsgeschichte (Internationales Archiv für Sozialgeschichte der deutschen Literatur. Sonderheft 2), Tübingen 1990.

BRILLI, ATTILIO, Reisen in Italien. Die Kulturgeschichte der klassischen Italienreise vom 16. bis 19. Jahrhundert, Köln 1989.

ID., Als Reisen eine Kunst war. Vom Beginn des modernen Tourismus. Die Grand Tour, Berlin 1997.

CLINARD, MARSHALL B./MEIER, ROBERT F. (Eds.), Sociology of deviant behavior, 11th ed., Fort Worth (u.a.) 2001.

CSÁKY-LOEBENSTEIN, Eva-Maria, Studien zur Kavalierstour österreichischer Adliger im 17. Jahrhundert, in: Mitteilungen des Instituts für Österreichische Geschichtsforschung 79 (1971), pp. 408-434.

DÖNIKE, MARTIN, "From Russia with love": Agents and their victims, in: Double Agents. Cultural and Political Brokerage in Early Modern Europe, ed. by. MARIKA KEBULSEK/BEDELOCH VERA NOLDUS, Leiden 2011, pp. 234-246.

GEERTZ, CLIFFORD, Religion as a cultural system, in: The Interpretation of cultures. Selected essays, ed. by CLIFFORD GEERTZ, London 1993, pp. 87-125.

GEYKEN, FRAUKE, Gentlemen auf Reisen. Das britische Deutschlandbild im 18. Jahrhundert, Frankfurt am Main 2002.

ID., A Legal Government, and a Religion free of Superstition. Die Wahrnehmung deutscher katholischer Territorien durch britische Reisende im 18. Jahrhundert, in: Die Welt erfahren. Reisen als kulturelle Begegnung von 1780 bis heute, ed. by ARND BAUERNKÄMPER/HANS-ERICH BÖDEKER/BERNHARD STRUCK, Frankfurt am Main 2004, pp. 321-336.

GRABES, HERBERT, Elect Nation. Der Fundierungsmythos englischer Identität in der Frühen Neuzeit, in: Mythos und Nation, ed. by HELMUT BERDING, Frankfurt am Main 1996, pp. 84-103.

GREIG, MARTIN, Burnet, Gilbert (1643–1715), in: Oxford Dictionary of National Biography, Oxford 2004; online edition, Sept 2013, http://www.oxforddnb.com/view/article/4061, 17.07.2015.

GREYERZ, KASPAR VON/MEDICK, HANS/VEIT, PATRIS (eds.), Von der dargestellten Person zum erinnerten Ich. Europäische Selbstzeugnisse als historische Quelle (1500-1800) (Selbstzeugnisse der Neuzeit, 9), Köln 2001.

HARBSMEIER, MICHAEL, Reisebeschreibungen als mentalitätsgeschichtliche Quellen: Überlegungen zu einer historisch-anthropologischen Untersuchung frühneuzeitlicher deutscher Reisebeschreibungen, in: Reiseberichte als Quellen europäischer Kulturgeschichte, ed. by ANTONI MĄCZAK/HANS JÜRGEN TEUTEBERG, Wolfenbüttel 1982, pp. 1-32.

HEITMANN, KLAUS/SCAMARDI, TEODORO (Eds.), Deutsches Italienbild und italienisches Deutschlandbild im 18. Jahrhundert (Reihe der Villa Vigoni, 9), Tübingen 1993.

JANCKE, GABRIELE/ULBRICH, CLAUDIA (eds.), Vom Individuum zur Person. Neue Konzepte im Spannungsfeld von Autobiographietheorie und Selbstzeugnisforschung (Querelles. Jahrbuch für Frauen- und Geschlechterforschung, 10), Göttingen 2005.

KÄSTNER, ALEXANDER/SCHWERHOFF, GERD, Religiöse Devianz in alteuropäischen Stadtgesellschaften. Eine Einführung in systematischer Absicht, in: Göttlicher Zorn und menschliches Maß. Religiöse Abweichung in frühneuzeitlichen Stadtgesellschaften, ed. by ALEXANDER KÄSTNER/GERD SCHWERHOFF, Konstanz/München 2003, pp. 9-43.

LEIBETSEDER, MATHIS, Die Kavalierstour. Adlige Erziehungsreisen im 17. und 18. Jahrhundert (Beihefte zum Archiv für Kulturgeschichte, 56), Köln/Weimar/Wien 2004.

MAURER, MICHAEL, Reisen interdisziplinär – ein Forschungsbericht in kulturgeschichtlicher Perspektive, in: Neue Impulse der Reiseforschung (Aufklärung und Europa), ed. by MICHAEL MAURER, Berlin 1999, pp. 287-410.

ID., Neue Impulse der Reiseforschung (Aufklärung und Europa. Beiträge zum 18. Jahrhundert), Berlin 1999.

ID., Reisende Protestanten auf der Grand Tour in Italien, in: Protestanten zwischen Venedig und Rom in der Frühen Neuzeit, ed. by UWE ISRAEL/MICHAEL MATTHEUS, Berlin 2013, pp. 251-268.

MĄCZAK, ANTONI/TEUTEBERG, HANS JÜRGEN (Eds.), Reiseberichte als Quellen europäischer Kulturgeschichte. Aufgaben und Möglichkeiten der historischen Reiseforschung (Wolfenbütteler Forschungen, 21), Wolfenbüttel 1982.

MĄCZAK, ANTONI, Travel in Early Modern Europe, Cambridge 1995.

MEAD, WILLIAM E., The Grand Tour in Eighteenth Century, Boston/New York 1914.

NEBGEN, CHRISTOPH, Konfessionelle Differenzerfahrungen. Reiseberichte vom Rhein (1648-1815) (Ancien Régime. Aufklärung und Revolution, 40), München 2014.

NEEF, KATHARINA, Multiple Devianz. Zu Fassbarkeit und Struktur eines alternativ-kulturellen Phänomens, in: Devianz und Dynamik. Festschrift für Hubert Seiwert zum 65. Geburtstag, ed. by CHRISTOPH KLEINE/ HEINZ MÜRMEL/EDITH FRANKE, Göttingen 2014, pp. 185-203.

NOLDE, DOROTHEA, Religion und narrative Identität in Reiseberichten der Frühen Neuzeit, in: Historische Diskursanalysen. Genealogie, Theorie, Anwendungen, ed. by FRANZ X. EDER, Wiesbaden 2006a, pp. 271-289.

ID., Andächtiges Staunen – Ungläubige Verwunderung. Religiöse Differenzerfahrun-gen in französischen und deutschen Reiseberichten der Frühen Neuzeit, in: Francia. Forschungen zur westeuropäischen Geschichte 33,2 (2006b), pp. 13-34.

OSWALD, STEFAN, Italienbilder. Beiträge zur Wandlung der deutschen Italienauffassung 1770-1840 (Germanisch-romanische Monatsschrift. Beiheft 6), Heidelberg 1985.

RADCLIFFE-BROWN, ALFRED R., Structure and function in primitive society: essays and addresses, London 1965.

RICHTER, Dieter, Die Angst des Reisenden, die Gefahren der Reise, in: Reisekultur. Von der Pilgerfahrt zum modernen Tourismus, ed. by HERMANN BAUSINGER München 1991, pp. 100-108.

SCHNETTGER, MATTHIAS, Die römische Kurie und die Fürstenkonversionen – Wahrnehmung und Handlungsstrategien, in: Barocke Bekehrungen. Konversionsszenarien im Rom der Frühen Neuzeit, ed. by RICARDA MATHEUS/ELISABETH OY-MARRA/KLAUS PIETSCHMANN, Bielefeld 2013, pp. 117-148.

STROHMEYER, ARNO, Wahrnehmungen des Fremden: Differenzerfahrungen von Diplomaten im 16. und 17. Jahrhundert: Forschungsstand – Erträge – Perspektiven, in: Wahrnehmungen des Fremden. Differenzerfahrungen von Diplomaten im 16. und 17. Jahrhundert, ed. by MICHAEL ROHRSCHNEIDER/ARNO STROHMEYER, Münster 2007, pp. 1-50.

STOYE, JOHN, Reisende Engländer im Europa des 17. Jahrhunderts und ihre Reisemotive, in: Reiseberichte als Quellen europäischer Kulturgeschichte. Aufgaben und Möglichkeiten der historischen Reiseforschung (Wolfenbütteler Forschungen, 21), ed. by ANTONI MĄCZAK/HANS JÜRGEN TEUTEBERG, Wolfenbüttel 1982, pp. 131-152.

CONTRIBUTORS

Barbierato, Federico is assistant professor of Early Modern History and of Historical Anthropology at the University of Verona, Italy. He studied, in particular, religious dissent, unbelief censorship and the circulation of forbidden books in Venice between 16th and 18th century.

Becker, Sebastian is a research assistant in the Department of Early Modern History at the University of Mainz. His research interests cover the Holy Roman Empire, the small principalities of Italy, cultural history of the Italian peninsula and the papacy as well as transfer processes of technological knowledge and industrial espionage in early modern Europe.

Frohnapfel-Leis, Monika obtained her PhD in Early Modern History in 2015 at the University of Mainz, Germany for her thesis on the perception of sorcery and false saintliness in Early Modern Spain. Her current research interests are spatial practices, religious deviances and forms of future prediction, especially prophecies.

Mengler, Judith is PhD student and research associate at the Research Unit Historical Cultural Sciences, Mainz. She works at the project "Fighting Bodies – Bodies of Fighting. Studies on the representation of bellicose bodies in references of the 14th to the early 16th century". Her research interests are the history of the body, medieval military history, the interdependence of warfare and medical knowledge, and the history of logistics and nutrition.

Morosini, Giulia is a Masters graduate in the Historical Sciences at the University of Padua, Italy. Her main research interests are Emotional History, Military History of the Italian Renaissance and Early Modern Cultural History.

Rogge, Jörg is Professor of History, Middle Ages, at the University of Mainz, Germany. He is also Spokesperson of the Research Unit Historical Cultural Sciences, Mainz. His main research interests are methods and theory of historical cultural sciences, politics, and culture in Late Medieval Europe.

Schäfer, Regina studied History, Literature, Sociology and Journalism at the Universities of Mainz (Germany) and Dijon (France). She is Research Associate at the Department of Medieval History and Comparative Regional Studies at the Johannes Gutenberg University Mainz. Her research interests focus on nobility, social mobility and rural life in the late middle ages. She is currently working on the edition and translation of the court records of the village Ingelheim ("Die Ingelheimer Haderbücher").

Vettore, Luca is a master student of the Department of Historical, Geographical and Antique Sciences (DISSGeA) at the University of Padua, Italy. He is due to present a thesis over the use and regulation of blasphemous acts and speeches in late 17th century Venice. His main interests concern forms of non-canonical religious and intellectual believes, history of dissent in modern Europe, history of Venice, social and cultural anthropology of late modern Italy.